Letters from Happy Valley

Also by Dan L. Walker

SECONDHAND SUMMER

Letters from Happy Valley

Memories of an Alaska Homesteader's Son

Dan L. Walker

EMBER PRESS
PALMER, ALASKA

Text © 2018 Dan L. Walker
Photo and letter collection © 2018 Dan L. Walker

All rights reserved. No part of this book may be reproduced or transmitted in any form or by any means, electronic or mechanical, including photocopying, recording, or by an information storage and retrieval system without written permission of the publisher.

Library of Congress Number: 2018956942
ISBN 978-0-9986883-2-9

Editors: Deb Vanesse, Joeth Zucco
Proofreader: Melissa Alger, Joeth Zucco
Cover and text design: Nanette Stevenson
Maps: Marge Mueller, Gray Mouse Graphics

Printed in the United States of America

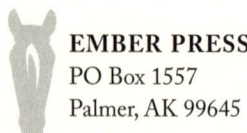

EMBER PRESS
PO Box 1557
Palmer, AK 99645

Facing page photo: *Chet and Briar Walker.* Title page photo: *The Goggins' cabin, where the Walkers spent their first months in Alaska.*

Acknowledgments

No project of this dimension can be completed without the support and contribution of many people. My coauthors, Chet and Briar Walker, wrote these incredible letters that brought to life some of the most pivotal months of my life. Viola Walker, my Grandma Walker, saved those letters, caching them for me to find almost sixty years later. My sister-in-law Dona and cousins Martha and Esther shepherded the letters and rounded up photos to help tell our story. Early on, James Engelhardt, Nick Jans, and Sherry Simpson saw promise in the story and pushed me to go deeper and write stronger. My sisters, Amy Garroutte and Peggy Walker, encouraged, critiqued, and teased as I tried to write about something I couldn't remember. Kaylene Johnson-Sullivan, Nanette Stevenson, and Joeth Zucco at Ember Press were tough critics and powerful cheerleaders for the book. Finally, my wife, Madelyn, who holds the endurance record for writer support, picked me up when I stumbled and made me write my best or do it over.

To my nieces, nephews, and grandchildren,

who need to know the story as my parents lived it,

and as I remembered it.

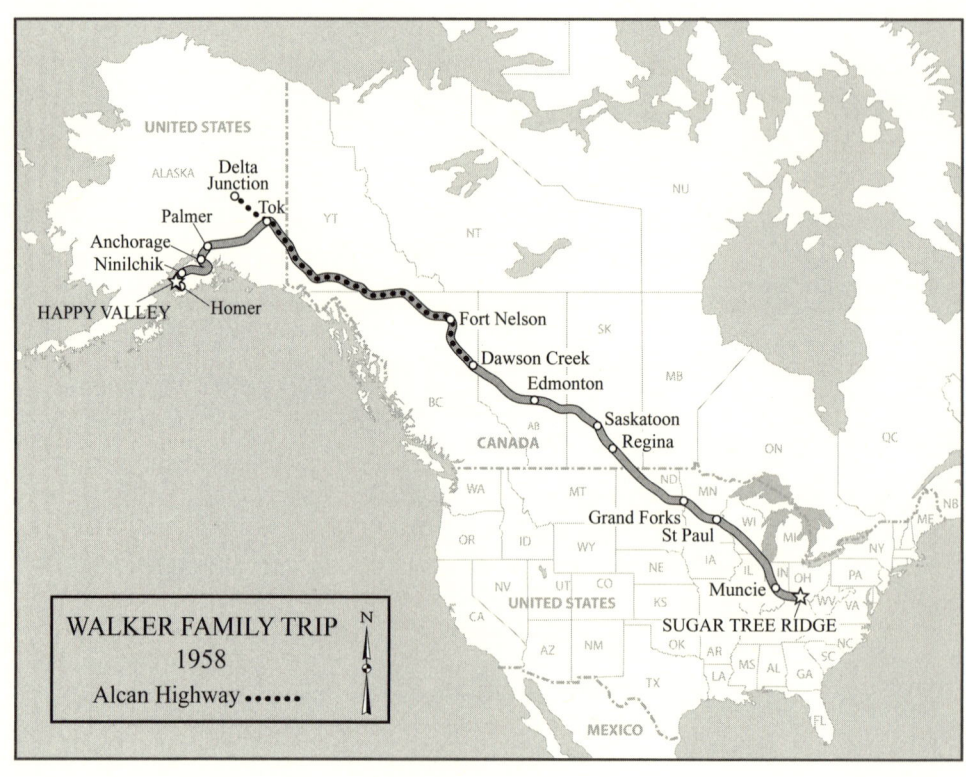

Preface

A few years ago when I was already much too old to be the hero of an adventure story, a packet of letters started me on a quest. A quest not for gold or lost cities but for answers, for lost years, and for stories. These letters were more than fifty years old and for me represented a wormhole back to 1958 when I was five years old. I was being offered a chance few people get—to relive a time in my life that I barely remembered, for these were not just "Hi, The weather is fine. I miss you" kind of letters. These were journal-like narratives penned by my mother and father during our family's move from Ohio to Alaska, where we filed on thirty-five acres of homestead land.

What a treasure trove for me! These letters offered a chance to know my dad, who died when I was young, and our life in the woods was still a possibility. The letters were also a calling, a treasure map from a boy's adventure story. As I read, my parents' distinct writing style came through, and I strained to hear their voices rise from the page. Once more I was a five-year-old with a toothache and too many questions on the highway to Alaska.

I read the packet of letters in one sitting, stretching my night far into the morning as I followed the story I had once lived. Tucked in my parents' letters were letters from my brothers and sisters and even one from me transcribed by an older brother. As the months of 1958 passed, I found where I had written "DANNY" in the margin of a letter and then later, a letter in my own hand.

When I read the last of the letters, I knew I would return to that time and tell a story of a family from Ohio who crossed the continent and started a new life in a wild new land. A memoir began to take shape in my mind, a shared writing between my parents and me created nearly sixty years apart. In this process the letters opened memories, and memories led to conversations, and conversations led to introspection. I looked with different eyes at the topography and ecology of the land we settled in, at the homesteaders who came and stayed as well as the ones who came and left.

Finally, I wrote. I wrote what I remembered. I wrote what I discovered in the letters and of the people who penned them. I wrote the shared stories of our family folklore as I searched for my father. I wrote about the homesteaders and frontier and realized that from the First Americans to the immigrants of the twenty-first century, we are a country made of people who packed up and left some other place to come here. This is the story of one such family, in so many ways the ideal pioneers.

The letters included here are as written, complete and unedited.

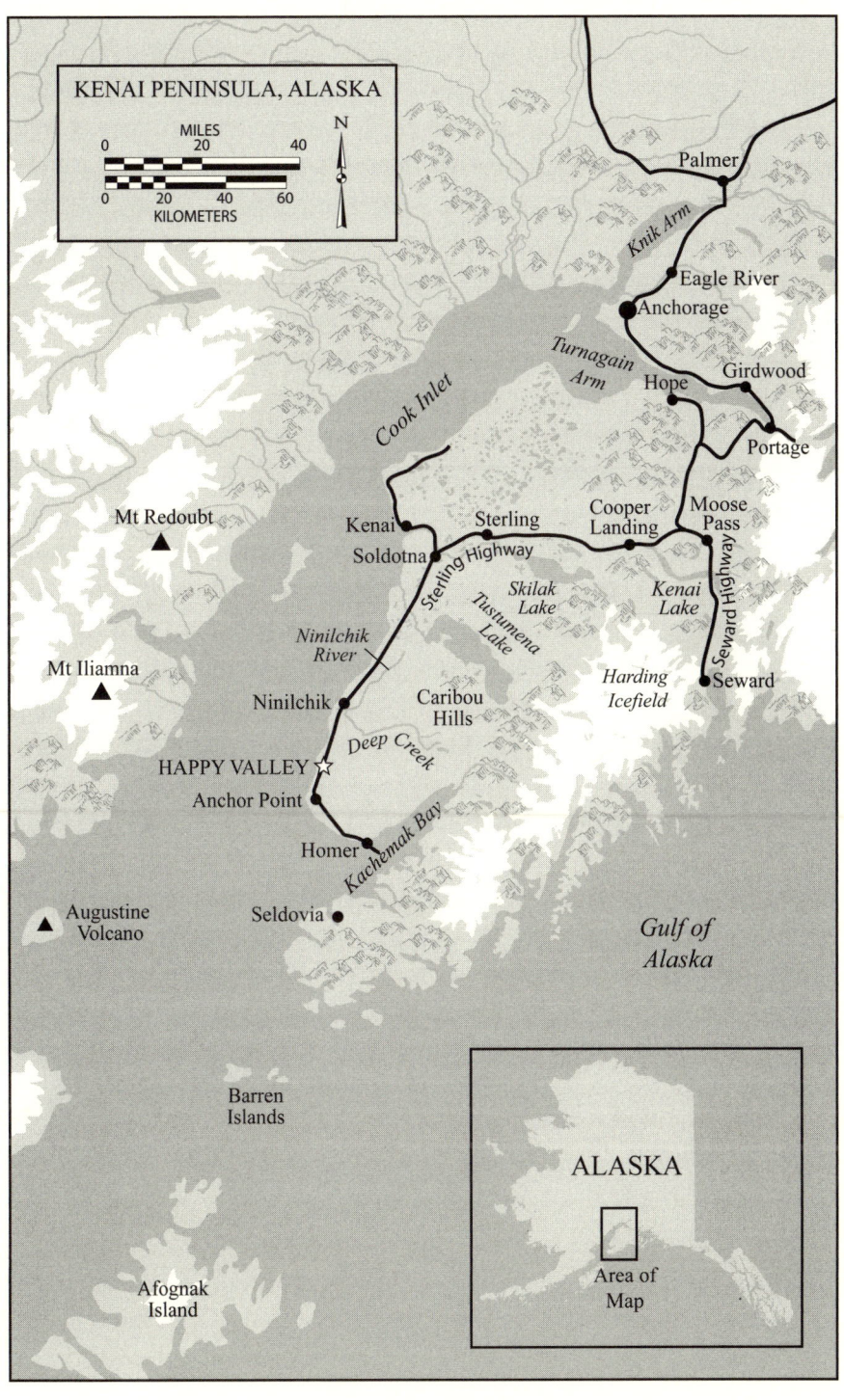

Letters from Happy Valley

The house at Sugar Tree Ridge, Ohio, still standing in 2007.

One

Homestead: The house and adjoining farmland where a family lives; a piece of government land that a person could acquire by living on it and farming it when the western part of the United States was being settled; the holy grail of American pioneers.

On New Year's Day, 1959, Chet Walker awoke early and crossed the cold floor to build a fire in the kitchen range and add wood to the coals left in the box stove. For the third day in a row the temperature had dropped below zero, so he slipped on some wool socks and slippers and then stepped out the backdoor to pee. A sound drew his attention to the willows along the skid road he'd opened when cutting trees for the cabin. In the dim light of early dawn, he could see a moose feeding. He didn't dawdle on the back step but left the moose to its browsing and went back to the stove where he found the firebox crackling and the heat coming to him. He set the percolator on the cooktop, grabbed a wool shirt, and stepped back to the door to look for the moose.

The back of the cabin looked out on a virgin forest of spruce trees that pushed their Christmas tree tops into the horizon of a growing dawn. He'd cut more than a hundred trees to build the cabin. And today, with winter building snowbanks and cold spells all around them, the Walkers had turned over the New Year in their new cabin in the Alaska woods. This was the home Chet and Briar had dreamed of and planned for during seventeen years of marriage. True, no one was bringing in a paycheck and kids had to be fed and clothed, but that could all be solved.

When the coffee started perking, Chet moved it to the back of the stove and lit a cigarette then retrieved the can of Carnation evaporated milk from the cold windowsill and set it beside the sugar bowl and spoon as he waited for the coffee. Even from inside the cabin, he could hear the moose tearing at the willows. Along with the crackling fires and perking coffee, it was all he could hear that winter morning. Soon it would be light enough to shoot, but not yet. He lit another cigarette and looked out the window at the shadowed forest where the moose waited.

Chet was a month from turning forty-two and was the father of six with another on the way. If he turned his head, he could hear them all breathing in their sleep and their mother with them. One of the kids stirred, and he listened for a moment then went to the coffeepot, poured a cup, and added two sugars and a splash of milk. He sat at the kitchen table he'd built and blew smoke rings into the aroma the coffee. Above his head, one of the two boys in the loft rolled, and he imagined one of them tossing back the covers as the two woodstoves chased the cold from the attic. The two older boys were bunking in the second bedroom and the girls were on a pallet in his and Briar's room where she was starting to stir, probably smelling the coffee.

He checked the window again for the moose and found that the morning light had grown so he could see its silhouette even through the double layers of plastic. Windows in the cabin were without glass, but glass would come along, as would electricity, cupboards, and kitchen linoleum. In the spring, he would build another bedroom and a bath. For now, though, this was enough: his family sleeping around him and a fire to warm them all.

The clock had swept well past eight o'clock when he finished his second cup of coffee, and the first true light of day streamed through the windows. He stepped out the backdoor again, but this time he took down the ought-six. The moose had turned sideways, and when it started moving, Chet quickly squeezed the trigger. The moose kept moving, and he fired again. This time it went down, and he could go into the warm cabin to get a coat and boots. By then, Briar was up and big eyed, "What in the world, Peabody?"

He just laughed, "Put some breakfast on, woman. We got a moose to butcher. And get them kids up to help!"

Briar smiled. "You aren't wasting your morning, are you?" Then, as if they weren't already roused by the shooting, "Come on kids! You're wasting the day! Your Dad's got a moose down!"

Tom and Mike busted out of the bedroom, and Amy pushed into the middle of whatever was going on. Bill and I scampered down the ladder and rushed out in our pajamas to ogle the wonder that our father had wrought at dawn's breaking. Only Peggy had to be pulled out of bed, angry at giving up the warmth of the morning blankets.

Mom made more coffee and started a batch of biscuits while Tom and Mike dressed to go outside. In the morning twilight they each grabbed a long hairy leg and helped their father gut and skin his first moose. Dad was a homestead hunter without license or season, so he and the boys hauled the skin, guts, and head of the animal to the site of the last bonfire, heaped slash on it, and started a fire to cover the evidence. The carcass was cut into quarters and stashed in the snowbanks, and clean snow was shoveled over the bloodstains—all before breakfast. Then they sat down to biscuits and moose steaks sliced thin, fried, and covered in gravy, the first meal of the New Year in their new home. Tomorrow Chet would go to Homer and look for work.

I was the youngest in that cabin, so my bed was in the rafters with my brother Bill. We climbed a ladder and crawled under army blankets and old quilts close beneath the sloping rough-cut rafters. Warmed by the stoves, the green rafters and roof boards oozed pitch that dripped onto our blankets, adding the scent of evergreen to the smell of sawdust and last evening's supper. Until the fire died late at night we would be hot—probably too hot some nights—and then the cold would eventually creep in beneath the wood and tarpaper, making us huddle together under our blankets. Bill told stories of the forts we would build next summer, and I felt so grown up there with my eleven-year-old brother in the loft of our cabin in the woods as we planned great adventures.

Dear Papaw,
We moved in our house. I like it fine.
Danny

We had been in the new cabin for a week when I wrote my own words of contentment in a letter to Grandpa Walker. Grandma saved this first letter, and six decades later I hold it my hand once more. I can look at the letter and know this is where the writing started. Yet the story itself started long before.

I was a hatchling then, my sisters too, and that cabin was a warm and nurturing nest that shaped us into who we are, just as the farm in Ohio had shaped our older brothers. That cabin in its clearing and the surrounding woods sheltered us for the years of our young lives, and we couldn't imagine that we would ever leave.

*Chet and Briar with infant Tom during World War II.
Chet served in the U.S. Army Air Corps.*

Two

Pioneer: One of the first to settle in a territory or start a new thing; one who makes a home in the unknown or unclaimed land. (Verb) to prepare an area or open a way.

On June 4, 1958, Chet and Briar Walker loaded six kids and all their belongings into a Ford sedan and a two-ton truck and left Sugar Tree Ridge, Ohio, bound for Alaska. I was five years old and beginning a journey that would make me an Alaska homesteader on the Last Frontier rather than an Ohio farm boy in the Midwest.

The Ohio that I remember was a place of farmhouses and white churches set among rolling hills and fields of corn and soybeans, a place where one could count on grandparents for Sunday dinner, usually fried chicken, served after church by women in flowered aprons to sun-browned men in starched white shirts. Of my short time there, I can still see the house at Sugar Tree Ridge with its musty smell and boldly flowered wallpaper. In that house, I was put down for naps under a painting of Jesus standing among a herd of sheep. For some reason, I found that scene unsettling and scary. I was not comforted to lie down in green pastures.

Today, you can "drive" through Sugar Tree Ridge via Google Maps. From that vantage the place has changed little since I left this farm hamlet with its storybook name. The road is still lined with shade trees and frame houses with deep porches, a place where one feels the steady pulse of the American heartland. A memory rises of a blind man who lived next door and made brooms by hand and a pasture that sloped away from the backyard where a white horse that wasn't ours grazed and mesmerized me as a young boy.

My parents married just before the war, and Dad was shipped out to Panama when Tom and Mike were toddlers. There he maintained P-38 fighter planes and complained of the boredom and the heat. After World War II he returned to farming, first as a tenant farmer and then on his own land. It wasn't long before luck, hogs, and soybeans all let him down, and he and Mom sold the farm and moved us to Sugar Tree Ridge. Dad had to take on a regular job, but even then, his eyes were looking north to Alaska.

I have one bold memory of my father from that time. He was a delivery driver for the farm co-op in Highland County, and one day he lifted me up to sit with him in the cab of that big delivery truck, and I got to ride along as he made deliveries of feed and salt blocks. At one of our stops, he bought a bag of cookies. The images are clear but brief, just a short film clip of my dad and me on the seat of that big truck eating store-bought cookies with icing. For some reason, I can pull that piece of my life out like a photo from my wallet and, for a brief sliver of time, taste those cookies I ate the day that I had my father all to myself.

Another early recollection is watching my sister Peggy being hit by a car as she ran across the street during a church picnic. When I "drove" through Sugar Tree Ridge on Google Maps, I followed the street where this happened. She must have been five or six at the time, and although scary and messy and with no lasting ill effects on my sister, it is strong and clear in my memory, like a short clip of movie footage of a little girl in the street overhung by trees, running in her summer dress and a fender coming into view.

I can also recall sitting in our kitchen on another day while my mother put ice cubes on my bleeding head. Peggy and I had been playing in an ash pile behind the shed, and for some reason she was chopping them with an old rusty ax. As she swung the ax I bent over to play in the ashes and took a blow to the back of the head. As if I was someone else watching the scene unfold, I see myself screaming toward the house and my mother carrying me inside, setting me down, and laying ice on the open wound. I see the white kitchen and the blood running out over the white. I don't remember the pain. The reality might be different from the memory, but I was hit with an ax and my sister struck by a car. How each is remembered is a very personal thing for me and for everyone else recalling such an event.

As for our road trip to Alaska, my memories are sparse and have faded with age. I can't tell if they are misplaced like the odd sock lost between my foot and the dryer or truly gone like the glove I left on top of the car. What few memories I do have, I don't trust for not only is memory selective but it is shaped by time. What we call "the past" is really just what we remember, and the true past is often lost, buried in our own private revisionist history. Our family recollections were shared between seven brothers and sisters until the images and experiences were structured into a rich fiction of what actual transpired. No family diaries record this experience, and only a few foggy photos captured us during that time. Our few charming anecdotes were all we had.

Before she died, Mom wrote a notebook full of stories about her young life, but she didn't get to our Alaska story with the homestead at the end. Tom, the oldest, was the best one for having the whole story, but he was a victim of Alzheimer's, and that terrible destruction of his mind meant that he and his memories left us even before he died.

Now, in this time when my life has slowed, I own the burden of preserving what's left of the Walker family story. My memories seem to start with homestead days, and there the lamps are brighter and details emerge while the childhood journey to Alaska left me just a small handful of postcard-sized recollections.

Then, a few years ago, an aged shoebox arrived in the mail like an unexpected gift when no one had a birthday coming. The shoebox, stuffed with bundles of letters that my parents wrote over fifty years ago, was a time capsule waiting for my opening. No memory needed. These words are what was.

Back in Ohio, just miles from the birthplace of my father, his sister Catherine had died, and while going through her things, the cousins discovered a cache of family letters written to Dad's parents from 1958 through 1960. Grandma had packed most of the letters in their original envelopes with the date of arrival written in her careful hand. The letters waited for twenty years on her closet shelf and then another thirty in Aunt Catherine's. More than fifty years later they are back in our hands, returned to sender.

Starting from the first day of the trip, these letters narrate the living story of our separation from Ohio to start fresh in a place new and starkly different. Nearly every night by the light of a Coleman lantern or in the quiet of the morning camp—and later in an unfinished cabin—my mom and dad had penned letters home. My own first writings, "Danny," in the crude penmanship of a five-year-old, appeared at the bottom of several letters, and salted in the box were letters from my brothers and sisters. Now these letters create a family journal, an unabashed memoir of the time that affords me the chance to relive this migration north and rediscover a piece of my childhood.

In my father's letters I found the language of this man we lost when I was still young. The letters, in their carefully addressed par avion envelopes, create a tableful of faded paper that once passed through my father's hands, under his pen, and before his critical eye. In the readings, I find that sometimes the hand and eye were tired and lonely, sometimes hopeful and confident. Other times there is pride in the words and a sense of achievement. Dad's letters are full of humor, news, family updates, and always weather reports. It is perhaps most poignant to me that his letters were to his father, a man who ended up outliving both of his sons, and that makes me wonder what our relationship would have been if he had lived to see me grow into a teenager, an adult.

I hold memories of my father but not the three-dimensional Kodachrome color images of the man in all his flavors. What memories I have preserved came from our family's mythology, the collected tales of Chet Walker, a mythology of the builder, mechanic, farmer, and father who could work all day and half the night, day after day. He had a legendary temper celebrated in tales of tools and tractor parts thrown so far they could not be recovered. His humor is lauded in quotes and pranks of a man who loved to laugh. This Chet Walker was a man who people liked to be around—competent, considerate, and positive.

As an adult looking back, I know there was more to the man than these stories, and these letters might be my second chance to know my father—the man, not the legend. I already know my dad's life was a list of failures and near misses. He sold the farm because it went broke; it was blamed on an epidemic of hog cholera. In 1958 he was in his forties and working a minimum wage job with his family living in poverty. In Alaska he tried to start an auto shop and then a Texaco station but couldn't make them pay. He selected thirty-five acres of land to homestead, only half of which was dry enough to build on or cultivate; the rest was soggy muskeg, a mossy peat bog. What was missing from his repertoire? Why was he not able to share the wealth of the post–World War II boom? Could it be that there was a Chet Walker that I didn't understand? Perhaps I would find answers in his letters.

About half of the letters are in my mother's graceful script. The day we left Ohio, she wrote the earliest letter in the box. This short opening chapter of our Alaska adventure is written in first person.

June 4, 1958

> *Hi folks,*
> *Guess you know by now we didn't get off until Wednesday morning. Then yesterday we had a tire go bad. That took an hour. Then a fuel pump went out. That took two hours. So we spent the night here in Muncie. Found a dandy park to camp in. Tom has a brother here and he came and visited and all his kids and grandkids. Tried to call Tom and Liz but no answer. They are only about fifteen miles away. Will write again tonight. They are ready to roll now.*
> *Love,*
> *Briar*

Mom—whom Dad nicknamed Briar because she was a "briar-hopper," or hillbilly, from Kentucky—wrote with a graceful, scholarly cursive, the kind you see in penmanship books, the kind that never seems hurried, as if great care is given to each word and its place on the page. Briar Walker always valued language and words, from the classic writings of Dickens and Cooper, to the artfully crafted adages from her eastern Kentucky upbringing. She might say of a promising child, "He'll be a sweet nut come crackin' time," and when she first saw Alaska's largest city, she wrote, "Anchorage is a sloppy riotous place." She loved words and used vocabulary lavishly every day like other women used makeup.

June 5, 1958

>*Dear Mom and Pop —*
>*Second night out. Camped at a trailer camp outside Muncie. Made 300 mi. today no trouble except we got separated outside of Chicago but got together again, only bad drive about nine miles out of the way to get a campground. It is a large state park by a lake. Supper over and dishes washed. Kids all in bed. Bill in one truck cab. Tom one. The other three above the big truck. The girls all in one tent. Tom and Mary in one and us'ns and Danny in the other. We put the table in the big tent. It can slide over and make room to sleep in there with plenty of room. Everyone is feeling fine and enjoying the trip. The country we came through around Chicago is much like Dayton or Cincinnati. We are just over in the edge of Wisconsin at Lake Geneva. We head towards Minneapolis. Had lots of wind and dust today but only a little bit of rain ... Ate dinner at a roadside park, sandwiches and coffee. Had fried chicken, potatoes, gravy, corn, and cake for supper.*
>*All told, we had a very good day. We got off to a bad start all the way around but guess no harm done. This is sure a nice campground. Trees and picnic tables but no picnicking only camping. We got in about sunset; it sure was pretty. Got pretty near set up before dark. All us writing letters then to bed. Indiana sure isn't anything as far as scenery goes, but the part of Illinois we just came through is really pretty. They are plowing corn and putting grass in silos here now. We saw acre after acre of tomatoes most are about 8 inches high. Corn seems all up here and some soybeans are up and plowed. Think I'll roll out a mattress and go to bed.*
>*Bye for now,*
>*Chet and Family*

A photo, taken probably only days before we left, shows a lean and tan family stretched across a living room couch. The faces are full of hope and optimism, perhaps even then looking forward to that day when we would break the bonds of family and community to take the road north.

The Walkers in their Sugar Tree Ridge home. (Standing) *Bill, Tom, and Mike;* (seated) *Briar, Chet, Dan, Peggy, and Amy.*

There were eight of us Walkers. Chester James and Jeanette (Briar) were married December 28, 1941, and ten months later the babies started arriving. First came Thomas Chester, the oldest, biggest, and as the firstborn he held all the cards. Then Michael James, with poor eyesight out in front of a brilliant, rebellious mind. William Franklin, was next, in the tough position of being third behind two brothers who would always be bigger and faster and first. Bill was to become the lover boy of the family, the dude.

Finally, along came a girl, Amy Sue, and like most girls at that time in that part of the country, she wasn't just Amy, she was Amy Sue. She was the oldest of the younger half of the family, for it seems our family was actually two units, "the boys" and "the young'uns" with Amy in the lead and Peggy Ann just two years after Amy. They were close from day one, a mismatched set of salt and pepper shakers. Amy, small and raven-haired, was playfully serious, and Peggy, tall and blonde, was seriously playful. I remember them always together and usually with me in hand.

I was the last of the Walkers born in Ohio. I arrived weighing over ten pounds in a mid-April snowstorm as if even then I was meant for the north country.

I try to imagine what that day was like when we loaded up and left Sugar Tree Ridge. Was it windy or rainy? Had the heat and humidity of summer come by then? Did family and friends turn out to wave goodbye, or did we rise early and drive quietly north? Were we all looking back out the rear windows and rearview mirrors for a last look at the tiny hamlet with the storybook name? I can only think it was an early day with people too excited to sleep, ready for the road, but finding it oh so hard to leave. With a little research, I discovered that it was a hot day and, in fact, June 5, 1958, was a record-setting eighty-eight degrees.

Traveling with us was the Butler family, a couple with two children who were friends of ours. Tom and Dad had gone in as partners to buy the two-ton truck and generator, and Tom's oldest son, Dennis, was a friend of my brother Tom. Like us, they were breaking the bonds with Ohio and turning their dream north to the great unknown.

What feelings must have arisen in the silence of those first nights on the road with home not far behind, but so far away, and a road out front, long and unknown. But there was still the comfort of fried chicken and all the fixins at the end of a long day of driving, for these were people harvested from the deep soil of the heartland, and their traditions and perceptions traveled with them. They were farmers who saw the world through the eyes of planters and sowers, breeders and husbanders, tillers of the soil.

Both of my parents had ancestors who pioneered the legendary Ohio Valley when it was home to the Shawnee and Miami people. Back then it was known as the western frontier. The progenitors of the Walkers came through the Cumberland Gap with Daniel Boone and helped build the Wilderness Road. Generations lived and died in Highland and Clinton Counties, filling whole cemeteries, some of them so full of dead Walkers that they carry that surname. On my mother's side, across the Ohio River in eastern Kentucky, roots were just as deep. In the decades after the Revolutionary War, the Barger, Bowling, and Eversole roots of the family tree made the journey from Virginia and North Carolina to build towns and traditions in the wild land of "Kaintukee."

Through the last centuries, the American frontier had continuously moved west and north. When the country was young, the Ohio Valley was the frontier, then it moved west of the Mississippi, then to the Rockies, California, and Oregon. What lay beyond was the northern border of the United States, and beyond that was the next frontier, shrouded in mystery and shadow.

And now, for the first time in more than a century, a branch of the family was leaving the heartland to pioneer the new frontier, a place so distant that until World War II, it was completely off the mental map of most Americans. For our caravan of would-be homesteaders and the people we were leaving behind, even Minnesota and Wisconsin were considered distant lands. Alaska must have seemed to be at the end of the earth, a place out on the edge of the known world and far beyond the familiar, an exotic place like Timbuktu or Shangri-la; it was the far frontier, and the Walkers were going to find it.

Three

Mountie: (informal) A constable of the Royal Canadian Mounted Police; a national police force organized in Canada in 1873 and formerly known as the Northwest Canadian Mounted Police; also known for scarlet jackets, campaign hats, and Dudley Do-Right.

One thing I never found in my family's letters is a listing of complaints and miseries experienced along the way. Even though the distances of geography and culture would make this a most permanent and painful separation for the Walkers, we never aired dirty laundry, and whining about anything by anyone was frowned upon. Mom's letters never complained about her kids nor would Dad recount family arguments or bemoan the defiant child or disappointing spouse. All that mess stayed within what my wife calls "the Walker family vault" where all such pain is stored.

I don't need letters to tell me that a mix of dread, loss, and eagerness must have hung in the air on those first days on the road. Tom and Mike, both teenagers at the time, were not happy to leave their rich social lives and go traipsing over the horizon with no company but their younger brothers and sisters. Who would? Mike was madly in love with a preacher's daughter at the time, and Tom was deep into baseball. Surely they were sulking and resentful with their broken hearts aching as we drove away from Sugar Tree Ridge.

Bill, Amy, and Peggy would also have friends to whom they were saying a last farewell. They were all leaving an Ohio full of pals, cousins, and church groups, ball teams, and girlfriends, and I'm sure they swore that love affairs and friendships would carry on by mail. Who could believe that people we treasured would eventually fade in our memories, and down the road we would find new friends long before the ones we left behind did the same.

I imagine my father and I were eager and excited. He was pursuing a dream, and I was leaving a different Ohio than my brothers and sisters. For them, leaving meant going away from everything to a place that had nothing, but for five-year-old me—in the center of a circle formed by Mom, Dad, brothers, and sisters—everything that was important was going with us.

June 8, 1958

Dear Mom and Pop,
We are camped at a state park in northwest Minnesota right on the shore of a lake about like "Rocky Fork." It was raining most awful hard when we pulled in here yesterday evening but quit in a little while. We have traveled about 950 miles already, had two flat tires on the pickup and fuel pump went out on it. That's all the trouble we have had. Wisconsin is a mess of resorts and not very pretty for the most part but we spent the night in "Big Foot" Forest State Park at Black River Falls, Thursday night at Lake Geneva, Wisconsin. We figure to make Grand Forks, North Dakota tomorrow (Monday) night at Turtle State Park. The campgrounds are real nice the people are very nice too. The fishing here must be pretty good but you have to use a boat to really get them. Two fellows caught 200 crappies yesterday.
Minnesota is sure a wet and boggy place. The corn is almost as big as the weeds and grass in it. Crops are behind down there. They do lots of strip farming. Corn, oats, and hay all in the same field; seen lots of Holstein cattle all the way up. They still have one-room schoolhouses up here. Traffic has been awful heavy up till yesterday but after we got around St Paul and Minneapolis it slowed down so driving was pretty good. The kids are doing very well and seem to be enjoying every bit of it. Well I hope this finds you all as usual and about to go fishing, so long for now.
Will write again soon,
Chet

With the vault closed to juicy family drama, I must become a placer miner among these letters, sifting through the gravel for nuggets. Yet the pay dirt I find comes in gold dust, not nuggets. I found a man who could turn a phrase like, "The corn is almost as big as the weeds and grass in it" and layer his writing with humor and optimism. He called two flat tires and a failed fuel pump in less than a thousand miles of driving "all the trouble we have had," like they were no more hassle than a dirty windshield. In fact, Dad spent World War II keeping a finicky P-38 Lightning airworthy, so rebuilding and repairing equipment was just part of everyday living. He expected breakdowns and was ready for them. Beneath that confidence I also felt an energetic lust for the adventure at hand and the opportunities ahead. If it was too easy, it might not be worth going there.

This is a man with the courage to pursue a dream that would take him far from comfortable and safe, far from Sunday church full of faces he knew, and far from the Ohio that made him who he was. My dad must have been the roamer in the Ohio litter of Walkers. Other relatives who were more concerned with staying than going were happy to spend their lives in a community packed with the familiar and predictable. Dad was about leaving and risk-taking, and in 1958 he couldn't stay put any longer.

By the time we made camp at a lake three states away from home, we were clearly committed and perhaps separated from Ohio enough that "home" was no longer spelled with a capital *H*. Out in front stretched a highway of the unknown with just enough threat to be exciting.

On Google Maps, the Walkers' route traces a blue path across North America from Sugar Tree Ridge, Ohio, across five states before crossing into Canada and through Regina, Saskatchewan. The driving route itself hasn't changed much in fifty years, although I am sure that the scenery has. This was long before the interstate highways made the transit of towns and states smooth, fast, and predictable.

By the time we passed by Edmonton, we had covered 2,227 miles (about 225 miles a day) since the journey had started on June 4. It would have been slow travel for the twenty-first century, but in 1958 the roadmap was guiding them over a route of state highways that wended across the heartland. They drove through, not around, every city, village, and town in a way that would burn miles too slowly for a modern driver. Without the express lanes of the interstate, there was no avoiding small towns. The rich economic blood flowing through these crossroads and county seats would have made these communities more lively and vibrant than the shriveling ghost towns created by President Eisenhower's interstate highway system.

In my own twenty-first century perspective, it's a scary prospect to drive away from the hometown with six kids and all you own in the back of a truck. No relatives to fall in on, no health insurance, no guarantee or even promise of work in Alaska, and no community of friends waiting at the end of the dusty road. What wonderful self-confidence did Dad draw from as they camped by a lake in Minnesota and considered the journey ahead and the prospects waiting at its end?

June 12, 1958

> *7:30am*
> *Dear folks,*
> *I was going to write this last night but it was so cold that by the time I got ready for bed I just went to sleep. We are in Saskatchewan Province in Canada. We are about 300 miles north of the border nearing Saskatoon, you can probably find it on Pop's Atlas. We camped last night on the prairie by the side of the road. No water (we sent Tom and Dennis back to town with a 10 gallon milk can for some), no toilet, not a tree for miles in any direction.*
> *This is flat as a dining room table and has been for 500 miles or so. This morning we are beginning to see a few hills. Also saw our first coyotes this morning. Tom B. is driving the big truck, Dennis the pickup, Mary Lois their Chevy and Chet and I took off in hunt of white gasoline. It can only be bought in Imperial Bulk Plants. I am writing this while Chet drives so it is not too neat. It gets hot as blazes here during the day and real cold at night. This prairie wind blows constantly and evening is icy cold. When I got up this morning there was ice in the wash pan and water bucket. Out in the open. Chet and Danny and I sleep together and no cover at all except the sleeping bag. We crawl inside in just our underwear and zip it up and we slept good and warm even last night.*
> *Danny had been feeling pretty bad and was cross. We had a jaw tooth pulled for him the day before we left and had to stop in Rugby, North Dakota the day*

before yesterday and have another one pulled. But the dentist said he figured that would be the end of it. And I could tell he feels better today. He ate two of Papaw's eggs for breakfast. Peggy did too. They all eat good.

We stopped in Regina yesterday for a couple hours and went out to the Mounted Police barracks and we saw the Mounties drilling on foot and horseback. The kids really liked that. Also went through their museum. It was really interesting. This country is really barren. Miles and miles between houses and a lot of them just grub shacks used only in summer. They raise square mile fields of wheat and oats and once in awhile we see herds of cattle. Most of the cowboys are just kids, boys and girls on horseback. It is real daylight here at 10 or 10:30 pm and it's always light when I wake up, the earliest so far is 4:15. Hard to get used to going to bed in the middle of afternoon. Also sometimes we drive for 20 miles and see no cars or anything.

The people are very nice though. Anytime we stop and ask where to camp. They say, "anywhere you want." There's plenty of room and no one cares. The first night over the border we stayed right in town, a filling station owner said just pull around back. I've plenty of room and you're welcome to all of it and no one charges a cent. We had to pay 50 cents to a dollar a tent to sleep in state parks in the states. Chet said to tell you there are thousands of dollars worth of machinery and it just sets out in the open all year. No sheds at all. Huge combines and disc 20 feet wide. And you'd love this endless wind. Well must close. Have to write to Mother.

Love,
Jeanette and all.

It is in Regina that I find my first memory of the trip, although in my mind I had somehow moved it to Fort Nelson. But here it is in ink on fifty-year-old paper. The Royal Canadian Mounted Police have their heritage center in Regina, and even today one can have that same experience of watching Mounties in scarlet tunics and campaign hats stirring up a dust storm astride their highly trained horses in a reconstructed nineteenth-century log fort.

Somewhere in the scrapbooks of family pictures is a photograph of me with a Sergeant Preston of the Yukon comic clutched proudly in a posed family moment. Perhaps that photograph has helped me forget having two teeth pulled, but I still remember vividly the Sergeant Preston parade. It does reinforce the argument by psychologists that humans have the ability to forget unpleasant experiences. Discoveries like this feed my distrust of childhood memories. Am I clinging to lies? Is a twisted and flawed past stuffed reckless into the unsecured storage locker of my mind? Although the pages are as old as my memories, unlike the recollections of a five-year-old boy, the words are fixed and unedited by fifty years in the box.

June 13, 1958

Dear Folks,
Just a few lines tonight because we are going into Edmonton, Alberta, tomorrow and after that the ALCAN Highway and the post office won't be so close.
We saw so many pretty horses today, two or more on every farm and they are really slick and pretty. Other than that there is not much different. The ground is more fertile I think, judging from the looks of grass. Lilacs are just now blooming and they are pink instead of purple. Also some are just now plowing. They use a disc plow. All behind one big, and I mean big, tractor. About 8–10 or 12 bottom plow and disc on behind. Then they plant it. Also the houses in Alberta are nice. I'll close now and write again when we hit a post office. Bye now and be good.
Love,
Chet and Jeanette

Towns like Regina didn't draw much attention from Dad and Mom. As farmers are inclined to do, they were looking at the land. They had entered the great expanses of the Canadian plains, where the vast empty distance wears one down with mile after mile of sprawling carpet that evokes a sense of the infinite.

If one isn't accustomed to it, the Great Plains of southern Canada looks best in a rearview mirror. In 1975 I drove alone across the girth of the plains on a more southern route from Chicago to Idaho, my first experience in a place without mountains to mark the horizon or trees to obscure it. West of Chicago, I faced a great undulating eternity, reaching off into the inestimable distance, broken only by changing tones of green in the carpet before me. Some have called it a sea of grass, and indeed, as I looked across the humps of rolling land, the plains seemed to sweep away like the mountainous swells of the open ocean, receding in such a rush that it sucked at my will, leaving a lost, desolate feeling such as comes from looking helplessly into a broad bottomless hole and finding no end to it. With no barrier for the eye to set the contrast of distance and contour, the endless swells of land wore me down, burdening my spirit with such a malaise that I stopped at an interstate rest area to pull myself together. Too wretched with anxiety to continue, I wandered about for an hour on this tiny island of asphalt, trying to clear my head of the vacant drain of it all.

I was crossing this interminable expanse at sixty-five miles an hour. But 150 years ago, people left places like southern Ohio and crossed the continent to make their new home in the famous Oregon Territory. Imagine how brutally the plains would have eroded their resolve, their dreams, their equipment as they crossed the hundreds of miles of such emptiness, plodding along in or behind slow-moving wagons and carts at the glacial pace of fifteen miles a day. They too were answering the call to the far frontiers.

On such a vast endless plain, one's eyes reach for a focal point, a place for the vision to stop, that point where the light bounces back to the retina and a horizon is found and held. But the horizon is only the subtle curve of the land falling away from you. Instead of approaching and rising as foothills or forests might, this horizon recedes forever without being achieved. No mountains mark your progress, no change in terrain, and no meandering roadways to make some break in rhythm or gait, just one foot forward then another, one swell of land after another until sundown, day after day. Thank goodness, on the way to Alaska, I was in the backseat of a '51 Ford, anticipating the mountains and rivers that lay ahead and not bumping along in a Conestoga wagon.

This rumpled, endless green terrain did not daunt Chet and Briar Walker, two people of the earth watching each great swell of land running out over an endless horizon to another field, another crop, another harvest. All through southern Canada they passed the miles by cataloging farming techniques, identifying equipment, and grading the soil by looking at what was growing.

My reading of these letters threatens to have the same effect as if I was traveling on the Great Plains. I opened them eagerly, anticipating a great ascent of understanding, a well-defined horizon of recognition of the father I sought with the answers to all my questions coming along as regularly as mile markers. But the horizon falls away from me and the terrain—though rich in family history—feels like the undulation of ocean waves lifting me just a little on their crest and then lowering me into the trough as the wave passes and the next one comes on.

The miles of highway are just more gravel and forest. I am learning about the journey, but Dad is still a shadow, a legend told fondly by others, a mysterious product of a memory that has proven flawed. When I have finish reading the letters, will I be disappointed? Dismayed that what little I do remember isn't true? Am I going to learn a new truth or none at all? Can I trust any of my recollections? Or will these letters be their disproval?

June 15, 1958

> *Sunday afternoon we are camped in a park by the river in a little town about 75 miles northwest of Edmonton, Alberta, Canada. 2227 mi from "Take off" we had a nice week. Since last Sunday we have come through Minnesota, N Dakota, Saskatchewan and about through Alberta. We got your first two letters from Edmonton yesterday also one from aunt Daisy. Hope this finds you all well. We are very fine and having a very good trip, no bad trouble this week a blow out on the pick-up is all that amounted to anything. Last Monday night we stayed at Turtle River State Park ND. Tuesday night at a parking lot back of a service station in Canada, next night on the prairie at a roadside table. Thursday night at a Service Station Park lot. Friday at Elk Island National Forest in Alberta. All the places had one thing in common – WIND. The women had a place to do laundry Thursday night and an old wood range to cook on today. Groceries are not any higher here than there; the brands are some different. The water is alkali here and the stuff sure makes sorry coffee.*

Wisconsin is all motels and sign boards. Minnesota is lakes and bogs. We passed the path of a hurricane Monday and I mean it sure laid things low. The farmland there is good and lays nice but is most awful wet. N Dakota is prairie with not much of anything you can see along the highway except tumbleweeds and a few cattle and barbwire. I couldn't want any of it. We went through north portal to Canada, went thru customs slick as a whistle, no trouble at all. Then we hit Saskatchewan and its wheat land and elevators; every 10 miles on an average you find an elevator and a small town. These raise wheat, oats, barley and rye oats and flax. Not many nice buildings nor big towns. They just raise wheat etc.

The country is very level, you can see for miles, no trees except those planted for windbreak around houses and towns. The biggest job driving up here is staying awake. Alberta Canada is much nicer than Saskatchewan. They have trees up here, cows, horses, hogs. Small farms 160 acres mostly but there is a tendency for big ones to take over. The small towns here have no paved streets and remind you of small towns in the cowboy movies. They sell radio batteries here and the hardware stores look like 1925 or 30 back there, only they have cars and trucks. There is very little traffic on the weekdays except big trucks.

The people are very friendly and will let you stay anywhere you want to. Right here they are mostly French or Ukrainian. Haven't hit any good fishing yet but will soon I hope. I think it's trying to blow up a storm. Guess I'll have to tighten up the tents. Tell anyone you see where we are and we are all well and sure love the life of a gypsy. Wouldn't do anything else if I could afford it. Tell all we will write more when we get up there now we hardly have time. Take care of everything and be careful. Bye for now, Chet and family

PS—seen lots of log houses and barns yesterday.

Mom, we bought vanilla yesterday and it was in one of those old-fashioned baby bottles like you put a little nipple on. We had one for Tom, remember. It had an old fashioned cork for a stopper. They sell 25 lb. sacks of flour in striped and checked dishtowel bags real fine material. Flour and sugar in 10 lb. sack, plain white, real nice. Bread is about 8 cents a loaf cheaper but plain soda crackers are 39 cents a pound. Jeannette

Before these letters, I'd always thought that our great adventure started with the homestead in Alaska. In my mind, we dashed up the highway and went to work building our wilderness home. Somehow, my memory skipped over the trek that crossed most of the continent to the Last Frontier, crossing the plains, surmounting the Rockies, and driving nearly to the Arctic Circle before turning south to cross Alaska to the Kenai Peninsula. It turns out those weeks on the road were a period of great freedom, time suspended between leaving and arriving, and if Dad and Mom spent their evening fretting about the future and questioning their choices, none of that comes through in their correspondence home. They were moving loosely through the days and miles of this great experience.

Chet and Briar were embracing life on the road. They had pulled up their long roots from the soil of the Ohio Valley, and they were in no hurry to plant them again too soon. At least for a time, there was no pressure to get there or anywhere. The road was enough of a place to be, and they demonstrated a willingness to drift awhile before setting their roots down. On one page they make it seem like they have done no more than take a drive in the country, a casual highway tour of North America that they will eventually finish and then drive home. On other pages, they are wandering in a foreign land where each day is filled with mystery and wonder. With Edmonton behind them, there was a real sense that the adventure was just beginning.

I have made this trip north from Edmonton several times. Always, I was driving to Alaska through Canada from the west via Washington, Idaho, or Montana instead of from the east as we did in 1958. At Edmonton the endless plains fold into hills cut with river valleys and filled with pines trees and birches. Farther on, these hills become mountains that raise their rocky noses high above tree line. These mountains, the jagged Canadian Rockies, form the backbone of Canada, and the meandering Alaska Canada Highway is a labyrinth through which we must pass to reach our destination, the Last Frontier.

I first drove the highway myself in 1975 when Mom was moving back to Alaska in one of the many transitions in her life. Her homesteader's dream had died ten years earlier when the love of her life died and left her alone with seven kids to raise. The transfiguration of Briar Walker after Chet's death is a classic tale of frontier resolve and determination. With only a high school education, my mother moved herself from a hand-to-mouth homestead wife to a hostess in the restaurant of the swankiest hotel in Anchorage, on to the front desk, then the reservations office until she was head of housekeeping. A decade later, she was moving from one hotel opening to the next to set up housekeeping service for the latest property of the Westin Hotel chain. In 1975 work brought her home again to Alaska.

I flew to Chicago, and we packed her furniture and household goods from an urban high-rise into a U-Haul trailer and hooked it to her Mercury two-door hardtop. Once I escaped the canyons of downtown Chicago, I drove to Idaho and gathered my wife, Madelyn, and we made the sojourn across Canada to Alaska while Mom hopped ahead by plane.

The Alcan Highway was still a winding gravel road back then, so we elected to put the loaded trailer on a barge out of Seattle. Ironically, the barge was lost in a storm, and the only possessions of Mom's that made it back to Alaska were an ugly table lamp too delicate for the trailer and a box of family photos that I had packed in the car to show Madelyn. Gone was the cast iron skillet with the broken handle and paper-thin bottom that had traveled to Ohio through the Cumberland Gap in a covered wagon. Gone were the heirloom photos and Mom's treasured china teacups. Even then, when the Alcan was a gravel and pothole hell, it wasn't as destructive as the Gulf of Alaska. Although the loss was not of my doing, I felt small and insufficient. Dad led two families and all their belongings up the highway to Alaska. I couldn't get one U-Haul trailer there. Something in me is hoping things weren't as easy for him as his letters would lead us to believe.

Four

Alcan: The original name for the 1,700-mile military road constructed during World War II from Dawson Creek, British Columbia, to Delta Junction, Alaska. Optimistically renamed the Alaska Highway it now follows only 20 percent of the original grades and routes.

June 19, 1958

Hi Folks,

We are stopped now at a service station so I'll start this now and finish it sometime. We had some trouble since we wrote last. The oil pump went bad on the big truck and we lost past 24 hours exactly fixing a rod that went out because of it. We were at Milepost 136 which means 136 miles from Dawson Creek. That is 136 miles of the worst road in the world. No kidding it is. From here on, the road is about like the best gravel roads at home.

Well, it's noon now and we are at mile 171 at another station where we stopped to eat. The roads have been very good so far but the truck has a main bearing out, also caused by the oil pump. They are not decided whether to limp along on it or camp here and fix it now. The closest repairs are at Fort Nelson 130 miles north. Chet had to drive back to Fort St John yesterday for a rod. That was about 90 miles one way. There are mileposts at every mile so you know where you are for there are no farms, no houses, no crossroads. Only trees. About every 40 miles or so there is a gas station and once in awhile a little store, but everything is almost two times what it was before, so we stocked up good in Edmonton.

(Briar)

In 1978 I followed my father's footsteps again when my pregnant wife and I were moving back to Alaska after college, and our Ford truck broke down in Fort Nelson. Fort Nelson was bigger than it was in 1958, but we were still hunkered down for a couple of days to wait for truck parts.

We were moving to Alaska ostensibly for graduate school. For me, it was homecoming; for Madelyn, it was fulfilling a promise made when she married me. We would make our home in Alaska. I had spent six years living outside of Alaska, roaming as far south as the mountains of southern Mexico. Every place that I saw, every road that I drove, and every natural wonder that I gawked at made me more sure that I was not only from Alaska but needed to be in Alaska.

I had left for college with a duffle bag and footlocker. Coming home, I had to figure out if a one-ton truck was big enough. When Madelyn and I were married four years earlier, we had decided not to burden the world with children. Biology trumped logic, however, and on the road, we already knew one more heartbeat was heading north with us to be born in Alaska. Like Dad and Mom, we set forth with a sense of great adventure.

We thought we were putting it on the line when we left a job with health insurance coverage with Madelyn three months pregnant. We financed our move with a massive yard sale, where we sold everything that wouldn't fit in the truck. My parents did the same with a farm auction. We were heading for the University of Alaska, Fairbanks, and graduate school, but we were doing so with no place to live when we got there, no real plan, no contacts in Fairbanks beyond a university acceptance letter. We felt like rugged pioneers, perhaps trying to grasp the little that I remembered of the Walkers' first journey north.

I am still awed by the level of risk my parents took when they struck out for Alaska. There was no safety net for a family of eight, no one at the end of the road to catch them if they fell. Madelyn and I were going home to a place I knew, a place populated with family, friends, and opportunity. We were driving a different road in a different time with support at either end of the highway only a phone call away.

The road one takes across Canada to reach Alaska is a wondrous drive through scenic country, from the expanses of the Great Plains to the soaring Rockies, but the size and distance has a person driving through the same postcard for an entire day. In such imposing but monotonous landscapes, even the hardiest traveler might find time for wallowing in self-doubt and trepidation of the road forward and the land beyond. As I recall, however, I only fretted about the truck holding together, not about the future or whether I was heading in the right direction at the right time. Perhaps, as found in Mom and Dad's letters, we were all too excited about bringing our family to Alaska to be fearful of what lay ahead. Just as it was in 1958, the unknown was part of the attraction.

In 1978 I was a forward-looking man, unsure of the future but confident that I was moving in the right direction. In 1958 Chet Walker showed us the same tendency in his words—or a lack of them. There was no remorse in his writing, not one sentence given to second guesses, and no looks of regret over the shoulder. The regrets were all mine, regrets of a man who would grow past his prime before getting to know his father. In my time with him, I wasn't studying him or caching memories. I wasn't trying to save anything for later or analyzing the inner man as he stalked a moose in his underwear or hand dug a homestead well. He was just Dad, and that's not much to remember of a man, a man whose footsteps I followed.

I have not completely forgotten him. I remember the man who found a secondhand bike and made it sparkle with fresh paint and shiny chrome so his boy's eleventh birthday wish would come true. I see him at the table with his coffee and cigarettes and still feel the broad swat of his hand on my ass when I offered backtalk or was slow to move toward my chores. I remember the tobacco smell in his shirt. But his voice is mute, and I can't read his eyes in the photos. The trail fades with time, but now in these letters it is fresh again.

June 20, 1958

> *Dear Pop and Mom,*
> *We are camped along the Muskwa River, 3.5 miles out of town. The main bearings are all out of the truck. We tore it down Friday and had to order parts out of Edmonton, Alberta, flown in by plane. They were supposed to come in last night. We'll put them in Monday. This is a little oil boom town. Shacks and log*

cabins. Some are real nice, others are real shacks. Throwed up out of anything. The town sits in the middle of a forest of cottonwood trees. The stores are like storybook places you read of during the gold rush. The people are very nice and the country beautiful.

Tuesday night after we had went thru Dawson Creek and started up the "Alaska Highway" we stopped at a Service Station and camped at mi 74. Next morning we went 61 mi and a connecting rod went out on the truck at mile 135. We pulled off in a gravel pit and stayed over and fixed it. Next day we drove 165 mi with main bearings pounding to Fort Nelson. That's about it I guess. We drove through mountains Thurs all day. The road was better than the level country we just came through. It is built out of dirt and gravel. Reminds me of Mt Olive end of the panhandle when they first built it. Traffic is trucks and travelers and salesmen.

There is an oil boom in Canada or business would be very poor. There is a little cleared land up here but not much. The land is too swampy to do anything with. They can only drill for oil in the freeze up during the winter. There is a shortage of drinking water here. They haul it in in trucks all the time. There is a bank, post office, "credit union," "a loan co," several stores and filling stations and a big new school house here. Population 900. Tell everyone we said hello, all well for the most part, having a wonderful time (discount flat tires and bearings). They all go with it though. Will write again soon as we get rolling. This won't go out till Monday. They don't get mail every day. Bread comes once a week. We unloaded the generator and the women washed Friday – 38 pairs of overalls – we sure had some real dirty clothes. The road and every place here is real dusty. They have had very little rain. Take care of everything and yourselves. Will write again soon.

Bye for now,
Chet and family.

For some reason I recall a layover at Watson Lake in the Yukon Territory where a great mountain of laundry was washed, and I can see a bridge, the same bridge I crossed and recognized in 1975 and 1978. Apparently all this actually happened 300 miles before Watson Lake.

Here it is, one bold clear recollection of my own from 1958: We were camped beside a river near the bridge with my five-year-old legs covered in mosquito bites. I surely suffered loudly and made a pain of myself, for mosquito bites will itch and burn until one is sure that no relief is possible. The bites would redden and swell, and I would dig and itch until my legs were covered from ankle to hip with welts. Since that June long past, I have proved to be a magnet for mosquitoes and other biting pests. Many an outing is made miserably memorable by swarming mosquitoes, all of this to the son of a woman who has never been bitten. My mother could sit undisturbed in the same berry patch as the rest of us while we swatted bugs and swabbed on all manner of repellent. She was one of those for whom the mosquito is of no concern for she was never bitten to any of our memories. I can only think that Mom and others have an odor or secretion that serves as a natural repellent. That would have been nice to inherit instead of my natural mosquito magnetism.

Dad and Tom had unloaded and fired up the power plant and hooked up the wringer washing machine. The women started laundry by boiling water on the Coleman stove then they filled the washer and added soap and dirty clothes. The wringer washer was a big tub on legs with an agitator in the middle, much like a modern washer, but rather than a spin cycle, the old-style washer had an arm above the tub with rollers that squeezed the water out. The wet clothes were lifted from the hot water with a "warsh stick" and fed through the wringer by hand.

Lois Jean Butler, the older girl of the other family in our troop, was feeding clothes into the wringer when suddenly she started screaming. Her hand had been drawn in with some clothes and squeezed between the rollers of the wringer. For a small boy it was a terrifying scene as the frantic, screaming teenager lunged against the white dispassionate machine until adult hands killed the power plant and cleared her hand from the ringer. Then the only sounds were the rushing river and a sobbing girl.

I think now, confronted with the letters, this drama is from another place. Perhaps it was Fort Nelson where the thirty-eight overalls were laundered. Dad said the drive was pretty much straight through from there. Perhaps the hand in the wringer was not the big deal that I made of it, for it is neither mentioned in the letters nor held in the memories of my sisters, the only others left to make testament about the events of that time. The imagination of a five-year-old must have made much of what was really a minor incident. My sister Amy was, and is, a busy, energetic person who could always be found in the middle of any work being done. She would have surely been elbow deep in this laundry undertaking and therefore would have witnessed and been upset by a screaming teenager with her hand caught in piece of machinery. I told her this story and she just shook her head, "No, Dan, I don't remember anything like that."

Memory experts tell us that some of our clearest memories are incorrect, that we can distort our telling of the past and make memories fit our personal model of the world and of its history. An interesting occurrence of confused memory was exposed when Amy and I were sharing these recollections of the trip, and she told about losing her sweatshirt when we picnicked outside of Anchorage. She even remembered the campground where we stopped. Her memory so strong that she could probably recount what we ate that day nearly sixty years ago.

I have an almost identical memory of that day except I was the one who lost the sweatshirt. Of course, I was too embarrassed to admit that I owned a memory identical to hers because maybe I had hijacked it. In fact, the picnic in Turnagain Pass is my first clear, personal memory of Alaska. A postcard of that scene is filed in my mind. We kids, wearing the new hooded sweatshirts the folks had bought us in Anchorage, are all sitting in the sun on mountain tundra in Turnagain Pass, just an hour from Anchorage. I remember that I took mine off and lost it that day; it was left behind when we packed up and drove on to Happy Valley. I doubt that Amy and I both lost our sweatshirts at the same time and place. I was unwilling to challenge her on it because one of us is surely wrong, and does it really matter who?

Some recollections are as sharp and bright as a *Life* magazine cover, and they insist on being accepted even when uncorroborated by others. Like the day on the Alcan when Mom patched a hole in the gas tank on the Ford sedan with the collected chewing gum of everyone riding with her. That patch lasted the life of the car; the memory even longer. Another day our little troupe drove through the rain and camped in an unfinished frame building where my parents and I slept on loose boards laid out on the floor joist. This memory is a treasure that I keep close, and I will rue the day that it won't be fresh in my mind. We bedded down listening to the rain on the roof of an unfinished barn. I lay adrift in the darkness, blanketed in the mysteries beyond the halo of the kerosene lantern humming in the night. I remember waking to the cold music of the rain and the warm aroma of oatmeal cooking in a great pot on the green Coleman camp stove. Looking out into the misty rain of a northern forest somewhere in Canada, I was eating brown sugar oatmeal with raisins like I was where I belonged.

I have to think that Dad and Mom might not have slept as well as I did that night. They were well into the journey now and their route had carried us far out into the unknown like a ship gone from the sight of land. Experience tells us what our letter writers will not. We know that rain and rough roads would have made the time and distance seem indefinite and volatile, and carloads of bored, squabbling kids would make the mountains steeper and the roads narrower. The miles must have been wearing on them, and there are breakdowns and delays too, enough to cripple the élan of even an optimistic traveler. The rest of the Alcan lay ahead, hundreds of miles of gravel, mud, and mountains.

Five

Frontier: The untamed limits of civilization; that region beyond the farthest limits of civilization; the edge of the unknown; aka home.

At Fort Nelson, the Walkers had reached a place so wild that the road had only been open for ten years, and the soft edges of modern civilization were far behind. We were driving the notorious Alcan Highway, a world away from southern Ohio. The road was built during World War II and opened to the public in 1948, but it was more like a logging road than a public thoroughfare. Although each year more corners were straightened, more gravel was spread, and more wooden bridges were replaced by steel ones, money was as short as the construction season, and the highway was a long, nasty snake of road across the wilderness of Canada.

For most of history, Alaska was the land left to Native hunters-gatherers and then came the gold stampeders, wild trappers, and intrepid whalers. Until World War II, it was as magical and distant as Australia or Shangri-la, and any story of Alaska was an adventure story. Explorers got lost looking for the Northwest Passage, surveyors disappeared putting unknown places on the map, and engineers died building trails and railroads. This was the land at the end of the earth, the land of snow, ice, fur, gold, and fish. Alaska was like a woman of ill repute that Americans would visit and use then leave behind.

When Japan and the United States fought for mastery of the Pacific in World War II, suddenly the Alaska coast became critical to both countries. Japan wanted a foothold in North America and chose the Aleutian Islands as steppingstones to the mainland. Seward's Icebox became a hot spot in the war, which meant thousands of Americans got a firsthand look at the rich diversity of land and opportunity that Alaska had to offer. The U.S. military built forts and naval bases, inviting many GIs to spend their war years protecting the coast in towns like Seward, Dutch Harbor, and Whittier. They fought the Japanese on the rugged chain of Aleutian Islands. Other soldiers perched on rocky lookouts on storm-swept islands all along Alaska's coast, waiting for an invasion. The Lend-Lease Act of 1941 was a means for providing U.S. military aid to foreign nations. From bases in interior Alaska, airmen and -women shuttled planes and war supplies to Russia to help fight the eastern front of World War II.

At the start of the war, Alaska was only accessible by air or sea, unless you considered the trails and wagon roads used by Alaska Natives, miners, and explorers. No land route existed for moving convoys of troops and equipment into Alaska except the Alaska railroad, which ran from Seward to Fairbanks. In 1942 U.S. Army engineers, including three regiments of black soldiers—many of them from the South, poorly clothed, and unaccustomed to northern winters—were put to work building a highway through northern Canada to connect Alaska to the continental United States. They fought mosquitoes, frostbite, and bitter cold to slash a road through the last of the wildest land on the continent filled with bedrock, muskegs, and permafrost. The bedrock resisted all but the jackhammer and explosives, muskeg made the road a bottomless mud pit, and permafrost was no longer permanent when exposed. The result was a road with a lot of mudholes and many stretches with rolling crests and troughs called frost heaves that ran on mile after mile. The builders fought for every mile of right-of-way in a war against terrain, weather, and geography. The Alaska Canada Highway, surveyed and constructed in just a few months, was heralded as one of the most incredible accomplishments of its time.

By 1943 Alaska was connected to the Lower 48 via a maze of Canadian Highways plus a brutal, meandering, wilderness road 1,700 miles long known as the Alcan. Originally only accessible by the U.S. and Canadian military, the Alcan was a silver lining in the cloud of World War II.

It was a rough road, but it was a road, and the first direct land route to the territory of Alaska. By the time it opened to civilian traffic in 1948, there were restless veterans like my dad waiting to travel it to get to available homesteading land up north.

I'm not sure what took my dad so long to scratch his itch to go north. I was always told that he had talked about Alaska as soon as he came home from World War II, but in letters from his time overseas in 1945, he was talking about getting a job and putting together money to buy a farm. I think that is exactly what he did, for a time. Like many men just off the farm, Dad got a taste of the big wide world during the war and the wandering spirit of his ancestors awakened in him. But in 1945 he was no footloose GI ready to head over the horizon. He was almost thirty years old and had a wife and three kids. Add to that the death of his only brother during the war—ironically killed by a drunk driver while home on leave—and I see the man with a dream held back by his obligations. Family came first and the itch went unscratched for thirteen years.

Instead, Dad became a successful sharecropper, renting farmland or working it in exchange for a share of the profit. He made a living this way and soon had more kids and enough money to buy his own farm near Sugar Tree Ridge. Usually a farmer is grounded to the earth, especially when he owns it, but I have to think there were times when Dad would be plowing soybean or driving the corn picker in the heat of the summer sun and his eyes would lift to the horizon and his gaze would hold on the open sky to the north. Mom once said that Dad was a hell of a sharecropper, but when he bought his own place, his luck went sour. When a bad year for soybeans backed up against a hog cholera epidemic, he had to put the farm up for auction. It wasn't long before his gaze lifted to the horizon and didn't turn away.

Originally, a house full of kids may have been part of what held Dad in Ohio those years, but in the end those kids embraced his dream and shared his great adventure to the Last Frontier. It may well be that a man like Dad is stronger with family, that he is at once buoyed and anchored by these farm children who would become homestead kids.

June 28, 1958

Dear Grandma Walker,
How are you? I played with Eunice and we played train and Eunice was the leader. We walked on one bench then we walked on another bench then Danny fell off but he never cried, he got back on and we had fun all the rest of the time. After that we went to the swings and swung. We had truck trouble. We went on a walk and saw deer tracks and Bear tracks. We are now crossing the Rocky Mountains. We saw a pretty malamute at Pink Mountain. We saw where a forest fire had been. I saw lots of horses. We saw lots of pretty flowers. We crossed the Peace River on a railroad track. We saw lots of pretty hills and trees. We saw two kittens and we saw a baby that was asleep. Now we are on the Alaska Highway. I saw a big white dog and I saw a black and white dog. I quit sucking my thumb and mommy is going to buy me a purse and a comb and mirror and a hankie. Be sure to answer my letter.
I love you,
Peggy Ann

Eighteen months older than me, Peggy was a pretty blonde with a stubborn streak. She loved her comforts, such as sleep, playing with her dolls, and sucking her thumb. Amy remembers the bribe Mom offered. She told Peggy she would buy her a purse if she quit sucking her thumb by the time we reached Alaska. Of course, this was a time when such childhood habits were frowned upon, and it didn't reflect well on my parents that a seven-year-old girl was sucking her thumb. Such a sign of weakness was not something to be tolerated. All the standard cures made Peggy dig her feet in harder so that the chapped, red patch on her lip grew more and more obvious, broadcasting the family shame.

My mother must have been at her wits' end because she was not one to use rewards. Given a choice, the stick came before the carrot. According to Amy, Peggy met the challenge and quit sucking her thumb. When we arrived in Anchorage, Mom kept her promise and bought Peggy a new purse. Amy was indignant. She knew her sister well enough to know this was a ploy. Sure enough, in no time at all, Peg was right back sucking her thumb. Maybe Mom was worn down by a passel of kids that she had to keep contained, if not entertained, in the back seat of the 1951 Ford sedan as they drove down the meanest of highways.

June 29, 1958

> *Dear Pop and Mom —*
> *We arrived here Sat night around 6pm. Slept Friday night in Alaska. Was no use to write sooner as mail only leaves Northern Canada once a week. We put the truck together Monday and started from Fort Nelson (Mile 300) Tuesday morning. We then drove steady the next five days and did very well. That road is without a doubt the roughest road I ever in my life seen so much of. The scenery is wonderful mountains, rivers, hills, valleys, glaciers, it is beyond imagination. There was hundreds of miles you never see anything except a gas station now and then. Once in awhile a place for hunters to get outfits to go into the mountains.*
> *It has rained a little nearly every day since we left. Never too bad though. We all stood the trip fine and no one has been sick. To get back to the road it was stone to more stone where it wasn't full of holes it was full of washboards. We are on the blacktop again and it sure looks good. Today we went into Palmer to church then afternoon we went out to Wasilla and hunted a fellow up I had written once or twice. Seen his place and some others. Not too bad but we can I believe find nicer locations farther south and farther from "Anchorage" the largest city.*
> *Tomorrow, Monday, we head south, first Anchorage then down to the Kenai Peninsula. To see the Trents. I want to see about them fish he told me about. There is several large farms near here and not too much different from those around there, lots of log buildings going up and about all the outbuildings are log or slabs off logs. Barbwire fences but mostly none. All back the highway. There is sections marked where horses run on open range. We seen several horses today, some cattle. Acres of potatoes and oats.*
> *The man we talked to today sure gave us inside dope on the homestead situation and he has lived here 6 years. We are not the least bit discouraged and it looks like a real wild beautiful frontier country. Will write again soon,*
>   *Chet and family.*

We crossed the border to Alaska on June 27, 1958, and I don't remember any of it—no recollection, no images. I am an empty vessel, and I hunger for much more than I read in these letters. I'm sure we stopped at the border and whooped and howled for we have never been a quiet bunch, and someone must have taken a picture though none survive. Dad's dream of moving to Alaska had been realized. The goal was reached and now it had to be held, for such dreams are enduring but fragile. We made the drive, now it was time to make a new life. The old life was history.

We entered a land as foreign as any place most of us had ever been. We held more questions than answers, and the comforts of neighbors and family were now far in the past. Dad and Mom were working with information gathered from government pamphlets and letters from people like the Trents, who lived on the Kenai Peninsula and shared their experiences with us during the months of planning that must have preceded all of this.

Palmer and Wasilla are familiar territory for me, so when I read my dad's skepticism about the area, I wondered what was the issue? This was and is the prime farming region in the territory of Alaska. I reach for deeper meaning in the words. Is it too close to Anchorage? Too settled? Too many people crowded into this one community? Palmer and Wasilla are in the Matanuska River Valley, where farmers from the upper Midwest settled during the Great Depression as part of a government relocation project. The region had rich, relatively flat, and well-drained land that folks thought, and proved, could be turned to farmland. Drive through the Matanuska River Valley today, and you will be transported to America's heartland, complete with flat expanses of farmland, lofty barns, and fence lines cutting the country into rectangles. Even in 1958 this was farm country, and maybe it looked just familiar enough to make the Butlers homesick and the Walkers want more. Chet and Briar Walker didn't travel all this way to end up in their old backyard. "The Last Frontier" is Alaska's nickname and the defining element of the Alaskan character. I figure Chet Walker was looking for that frontier and the Matanuska Valley wasn't it.

Frontier has always been that locale farthest from cities and civilization, where the land dominates the people instead of the other way around. The word *frontier* is from the same Latin root as *front*, and those who are there are in the "front" of the movement into a new land and "at the edge." Frontier offers both opportunity and openness, and those who enter it must decide how remote they are willing to be.

By 1958 most of the quality farmland in this part of the "frontier" was gone, and I have to imagine that Dad was still thinking about something more remote but still farmable. This would soon change.

There can be little doubt that the Alaska homesteading boom of the fifties was a consequence of restless World War II veterans. Some soldiers come home from war wounded or crippled, and others find the bonds that once held them in place are broken and they feel a longing to move on. Maybe the travel to foreign lands is a stimulus, maybe the trauma or the long separation, but somehow coming home isn't enough. In the late forties and early fifties many of those restless veterans headed for the frontier, the Last Frontier. One has to wonder what we will do when such places are gone.

The Walkers and Butlers were pushing close to the edge, and Palmer and Wasilla didn't offer enough of either opportunity or openness for a party that had traveled four thousand miles to find them. That's the picture I get from Dad and Mom's letters, but Tom and Lois Butler are silent voices in this telling. I can guess that they were following Dad's lead, and the party would journey deeper into Alaska, nearer the frontier and farther from the land once called home. I can hear Dad's unwritten words, "We can do better."

July 7, 1959

Dear folks —
Well here we are, we made it. We got here to the Trents' Monday evening last week and have really been in a whirl since. They were delighted to see us. Everybody up here greets you like a long lost brother. The first thing Tuesday morning they took us clam digging. Not one of us had ever seen a clam before. You see, Ninilchik is right on Cook Inlet, which is an arm of the ocean. The water is salt and they fish for salmon, tuna, crabs etc. just like the ocean. It wasn't long before we were all digging clams like old hands. They look about like a mussel only a little larger. We had two washtubs full by the time the tide came in. Of course it covered the beach and then we had to quit.

You can all write us here now. Happy Valley Route Ninilchik Alaska. Sent airmail they get to Ninilchik in about three days. This is pronounced Ni-nil' –chik. The accent on nil. We are "squatted" here in a cabin no one is using but has filed on. They don't care though. The man who filed on it told us we could stay there all winter if we wanted to. We are looking around a lot before we file. There is plenty of land in all sorts of places. None of it is as hard to get to as we had imagined. This cabin is on a private road about like our lane used to be but is about 3 mi long in all. There are five cabins (no one calls them houses) on it. It comes out on a gravel road just like any gravel road.

There are moose everywhere. We see them on the road right in front of the house. They don't come around where people are if they can help it tho. Moose are open season in August. They look a lot like a horse in a way and they are big. There are bear droppings around but we've seen no bear yet. Lots of "spruce hens." They look about like a bantam chicken. The young ones will be ready to kill in a few weeks. Mrs Veater down the road gave us three jars of canned moose and it's just like canned beef. We like it. Mrs. Trent gave us a quart of home canned red salmon. I'm going to use it today. We canned eight quarts and four pints of those clams we dug besides two full meals for Walkers, Butlers and Trents.

We went to Church of Christ at Anchor Point, twelve miles south yesterday morning and at the Methodist at Ninilchik seven miles north last night. It was nice both places. All the people are so friendly and helpful.

I guess Mary Lois and Tom are not going to stay here. They are going to take the pickup and go back down the ALCAN highway to Dawson Creek and then down the Hart Highway to Oregon and I don't know where from there. Don't publish this around. I don't know when they'll tell people back there they don't like it here but they can tell it themselves. It's just like we thought we'd find. Just like everything we read said it would be. We like it fine and the kids are wild about it. Well guess I better fix breakfast.

Love Jeanette.

The Walkers drove over 4,000 miles of highway, about 1,500 of it the gravel misery of the Alcan, including what Dad and Mom called "136 miles of the worst road in the world." We made it to the great land, deep into Alaska. After driving northwest from Ohio for 3,600 miles, the route turned south at Tok, Alaska, for another 600 miles to Ninilchik. While most of this route was paved, the last 40 miles, from Soldotna to Ninilchik, was back on gravel. Another few miles and we would have driven as far west as one can drive on the North American continent. We traveled until we about ran out of road. No, we had not crossed the Rockies by wagon train or climbed Chilkoot Pass to the Klondike on foot, but we had traveled with the same spirit. From this day forward, the Walkers would never, individually or as a family, be the same.

To remain in Ohio would have meant years and generations of uniform, predictable Middle American life. The neighbors would be the people we grew up with and who looked and acted much like us. We would likely be baptized, married, and buried in the same church and surrounded by familiar faces. We would celebrate these milestones with meals of fried chicken, mashed potatoes and gravy, corn on the cob, and coleslaw shared with cousins, aunts, and uncles who formed a fence of conformity around our life. Maybe the Butlers suddenly realized they didn't want to do without that. It does take some courage to go to a distant place and make a home. But there is courage too for someone to admit a mistake and turn away rather than make a bigger one. The Butlers, as it turned out, found that moving to Alaska had been a mistake for them, but wouldn't staying make it worse?

We Walkers had broken the grip of habit, exposing ourselves to new possibilities, possibilities that could only be predicted to be new and different. We would attend different churches, hear new languages, and eat wild and exotic foods. Our choices and opportunities would expand, and with that our view of the world would grow and change because when we leave the comfort of our community, we encounter the possibility of the rest of the world. And there anything was possible.

Such a bold arrival was cause for celebration, and we made a feast of razor clams on the Cook Inlet beach. What a feast that must have been, to eat the razor clams we dug ourselves, our first clams I'm sure. There is a saying on the Kenai Peninsula, "When the tide is out, the table is set." The second highest tides in the world, as much as thirty feet, are found in Cook Inlet. This means that every month, a period of radical tidal change leaves the beaches bare during low tide and exposes the area where the razor clams live. Razor clams are harvested by spotting subtle dimples in the sand and then digging, sometimes shoulder deep, to pull them out before the clams burrow deeper. What a sight it must have been, a bunch of hayseeds out on the beach, most of us for the first time, learning the fine art of clam digging.

We probably dined without recognition or grandiose speechifying about our traverse of a continent to find this new home on the shores of Cook Inlet. For our part, harvesting razor clams from a Cook Inlet beach was just another first among many, and two washtubs full of clams were an impressive beginning. There is tradition and ritual here that my sister Amy carries forward. Even today, her children, their cousins, and friends—two generations down the line from that first clam digging expedition—change their work schedules every summer to gather on the Ninilchik beach when the big minus tides leave the clam beds open to diggers. The setting alone is breathtaking with a distant horizon marked by three snow-covered volcanoes, the rolling surf of Cook Inlet, and the ubiquitous bald eagle soaring above.

The tide sets the time schedule. We want to be at the beach digging at least thirty minutes before low tide; one hour is even better. Buckets and shovels and gloves are staged in the back of the beach rig, a four-by-four truck with as many beach miles on the odometer as highway miles. Some of us will pile in this rig while others ride ATVs or other trucks. North and south of Ninilchik, the clam beds are exposed and clam diggers swarm the beaches for miles. Rigs park in a ragged line below the bluff, and diggers walk out to the mudflats in raingear and rubber boots.

Razor clam digging is an inglorious affair with too much mud, sand, wind, and cold to allow for fashion or glamour. Perhaps that is part of the appeal. It is hard, dirty work digging a twelve- to twenty-four-inch-deep hole for each clam, digging first with the shovel and then with just the hands to end in a tug-of-war with a marine bivalve the size of a cellphone. We look for dimples and then dig and kneel and dig and tug. Then another dimple, another hole, another tug until the legal limit is reached or the tide chases us off the beach. We slog back up across the sand to the mud and across that to the gravel to the truck with our buckets of clams soaking in the seawater and our boots and raingear caked in sand and mud.

We sit on the tailgate and drink a beer as we watch the other diggers, some walking up, some still digging, and some driving back up the beach as if they're on a schedule. All that awaits us is lunch and then an afternoon of cleaning clams while we talk clam digging and share family stories and miss those who are gone. By the time the clams are cleaned, the raingear has been hosed off and hung to dry, the buckets and shovels rinsed and stowed in the storeroom behind the greenhouse, and the gurry and shells thrown back into the woods, someone is working on dinner. Even if we're serving steak, ribs, or salmon off the grill, there will be fried clams too. If the sun is shining on that day, then so much the better.

When it comes to food, need and want are a long way apart. We modern hunter-gatherers dig clams mostly for fun. That's also true of the salmon fishing and moose hunting. We can get through the winter without living off the land. Not one of us is living a subsistence lifestyle, but some fifty years ago we were. What we do for fun now helps us remember a time when living off the land was not an option; it was a necessity.

In that first Happy Valley summer, our two families, the Walkers and the Butlers, saw different Alaskas. I imagine that the Butlers saw a wild forest uncut by the plow as a dense and dark place so sinister that it pressed in against their dreams until they were crushed. The trepidation and discomfort ran deeper than what a roof and a meal could allay, so they left. The Walkers found this place full of comfort and hope that calmed any fears they carried.

So the Butlers moved on, failing to experience that sense of place, of belonging, which was so strong in my family. Happy Valley was new and wild, but already it was home, even though for most of us, this was the first sight of the ocean, the first taste of seafood, and the first trip to the beach. We were settled in a cabin not knowing if it was permanent or just a stopover, but from this day on, we marked our family origin from Happy Valley. This land, this beach, and this arm of the ocean were in us and could not be removed. Our family had come to rest.

Six

Sourdough: A leavening agent consisting of live yeast; any bread using such a live leavening agent; a veteran of the north who has spent at least one winter in the north country.

Imagine driving into the woods on a dirt road you have never traveled, looking for a boarded-up cabin, and hoping that it might be a shelter for your family after six weeks on the road. The grass and fireweed is head high, and only the roof is visible from the dirt trace someone called a road. You pull off the dirt and wade through the greenery and the mosquitoes, surveying as you go. Is the cabin sturdy and dry? Is there room for all of us? How much garbage has to be cleared away? Where is the outhouse? What about water? Such great hope and anxiety must have been in the air that day. Even standing on the land isn't enough for until the grass and alders are hacked down to ground level and the yard reclaimed, it would be hard to see anything. But if you walk out past the cabin a few yards, the land falls away to a view of the shallow creek bottom with a rivulet running through the muskeg and disappearing into the spruce forest on its way to the inlet. This was Happy Valley.

After eight years of neglect, this cabin was ready for some fixing up. Mice, voles, squirrels, and even, perhaps, a porcupine had set up camp. As Amy reports in her letter, the windows would need new Visqueen. Often two layers of plastic were installed with an air space between them to provide more insulation. Most cabins started with plastic windows, and Visqueen was the most common brand, so it became the common name. If Dad didn't have this with him, he would find it in Homer. The rolled clear plastic was cheap, durable, and portable, while glass was none of those. Visqueen worked well as a window material, and still does, but it is fragile in the cold, which we had plenty of, and it slowly deteriorates in the sun, becoming brittle and crumbly.

I'm sure this cabin needed more than new windows, but after weeks on the road Dad must have been glad to take tools in his hands. He was handy, and he liked to put things "in apple pie order," as my mother liked to say. They cleaned the inside of the cabin and made it livable and set the boys to hacking weeds before unloading the truck. It was time for the Walkers to set up housekeeping.

Mom must have had her washer and cookstove running full bore, and we kids had acres of woods in which to play with that one great luxury of childhood—to live today without worry about tomorrow. While we played, Dad and Mom were well aware that they had a place to live for the time being, but they were three months from winter and crowded into a cabin so small that two boys lived in a tent.

July 9, 1958

Dear Pop and Mom —
I think I told you we are "Squatters." This cabin actually belongs to the government. A man has contested the title to it so he can file on it but that is a long drawn out process and no one knows how it will come out. Meanwhile we are here, possession is 9 points you know, ha ha.

We have looked at a lot of land but have not decided definitely but think we will file on 80 acres that lays within a half mile of the highway on a gravel road. It lays on a ridge and part of it slopes down and runs out into a bog. That is worthless except for moose pasture. There is half or better dry with nice timber, it lays like this.

We could then file on 80 more anytime anyplace we wanted. Right now the road situation is too tough to file back too far. But roads are coming in so it will pay to wait.

I intend to go to Anchorage soon as we get clear of the Butlers and by then will know what I aim to file on. Then I think I can get construction work till fall. Even tho it takes all I make to live, it will beat not making anything. It may take three months before we know for sure we can build a cabin on the land we file on. It all takes time and government works slow.

Briar and the kids all just love it here. The temperature here don't get above 65 or 70 during the day and goes down towards 50 at night. Its daylight 'til 11 o'clock pm and gets daylight about 1 am. I have hammered around here patching up and built a table 36 inches x 68 in long out of boards we had in the big truck, ripped 2x4 for legs.

This is the log cabin There is two bunks in the back. The girls sleep on one. Bill and Danny on one. We are real cozy. Tom and Mike sleep in the tent. Pop,

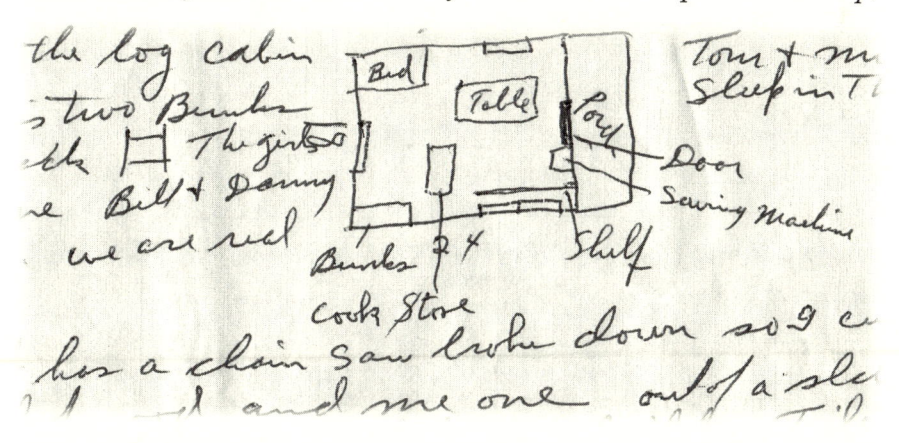

[handwritten sketch of cabin floor plan with labels: the log cabin, two Bunks, The girls, Bill + Danny, we are real, Bed, Table, Bunks, Shelf, Cook Stove, Tom + M sleep in T, Door, Sewing Machine; followed by handwritten text: "has a chain saw broke down so I ... and me one out of a sl..."]

that cabin never seen a cyclone till we moved in. That's about the worst thing that could happen to it.

Trent has a chainsaw broke down so I cut him a load of wood and me one out of a slab pile. He gave me enough slabs to build a toilet. I only put three sides, a seat, and a roof, cost me work and nails. I picked up a piece of tarpaulin for a roof this morning. I'll put a door on it maybe. We don't know just how long we will stay here. I know our letters have been few and far between but up to this week mail only went out once a week and we had lots of complications.

The trip up was far from a picnic only because of the Butlers' attitude. They sure froze up and got miserable to be around. Otherwise if we had come alone we would have had a grand trip. We dissolved partnership last Thursday night except for the truck and light plant. The truck is in my name and he can't haul the light plant so he will just have to wait till such a time as I can afford to pay him off or sell them and divide the money. He is pulling out, not me. Enough of that, it tastes bad. Soon as they leave we will get our bearings and be able to think straight and get organized.

To tell the end first, Butlers are loading up to come back to the states. They "chickened" out real quick. It all started back down the line when the truck broke down and the mosquitoes got big and brave. The missus just couldn't take it. Then no one jumped up and offered him a fine job and a nice house with all the comforts of city life, sooooo. They are going back down the highway and down through the west now. I'll bet by September 1 they will be back in Sugar Tree Ridge.

But they will settle somewhere else. It's hard to say just what they will do. The main cause lies with her, she really didn't want to come to begin with and I somehow wonder about him. They were disappointed in the country after they got here but I can't say as much. We found everything just exactly the way every one we wrote told us they found things. This is new country, wild but civilized. Jobs are seasonal and you have to hunt for them or make your own. The people are fine, generous to a fault. But they more or less lay low and watch you and figure out whether you are on the level or a stinker. Then if they like you they will go all out to help you.

Yesterday evening, a man named Denny Bell came in here, I had met him last Saturday, he gave us a box of fresh trout at least 15 of them 12–18 inches long. The people in the next cabin gave us three jars of moose meat. Mrs. Trent gave us a can (qt) of salmon. All sure good eating and it helps on the groceries. We like the country fine and the people better. The first year will be hard and we knew it but one won't starve. There is plenty of food for the taking and wood for the cutting so one can be sure of being warm and belly full of grub.

Oh yes. This is funny. We all talked about living off the land up here before we came. Well, Tuesday we went down to Clam Gulch up the road a piece with Trents. Dug two tubs full, we ate fried clams for dinner and clam chowder for supper. They haven't eaten with us since. They got cured quick. They are camped across the trail from us now. They did take some the fish and ate them, but I am surprised they did.

It sure seems strange to be in Alaska when everyone back there thinks of this place all snow and ice and here seashore right along the road for miles, seafoods in abundance, crabs, clams, salmon. Then trout and moose and bear, spruce

chickens (grouse) on the other side of the road. Moose is the meat supply of the homesteader. I guess that this gives you a pretty good picture of things at present and we will keep you informed as we go along. Oh yes. There is no bad feelings between us if any, it's theirs towards us and they don't say anything about it.
   Bye for now,
   Chet and Family

   PS. Tell Maude she'd never guess what a sensation this stove has caused up here. They all think it is really wonderful. You see all kinds of old wood-burning stoves up here. I am really upper crust with this one.

With the Butlers leaving, we were severing one more connection with Ohio, and all about was a sense of new things happening each day that the Walkers would have to face alone. Luckily, there were other families on the same road in their own stages of making a go of it. We were making new friends with the Trents and Veators, and later we would find support from the Bell family. They homesteaded a full 160 acres and had three kids. One can tell from the letters that they were one of the biggest helps we had in getting settled at Happy Valley. Denny Bell's tractor hauled the logs from the woods when Dad had felled and limbed them, and his sawmill shaped the logs and ripped the lumber from trees.

Clearly, the Butlers left a sour taste in Dad's mouth, and it would be easy to call them quitters for turning back from their homestead dream. With the clarity that a rearview mirror affords us, we can look back and play down such changes of fortune, but we must remember, "Objects in this mirror are closer than they appear." Maybe the Butler fiasco was bigger than it appears from Dad's limited confession. Maybe having the partnership breakup made things just a little more unsteady. Maybe Dad was looking over his shoulder a bit now as he moved his family into a squatter's cabin a long way from Sugar Tree Ridge.

The idea of two families traveling in tandem must have offered a sense of strength and resource when we all set out for Alaska. It would be like bringing your old neighbor with you, but now that link, that extra hand, was gone. Dad seemed unswayed by the Butlers' choice and his plans moved forward. How much better for everyone that the Butlers didn't put themselves and everyone else through a year of misery before calling it quits. It sounds as though Dad had already had enough of them, and perhaps suddenly the road and his head were clear.

The cabin that Mr. Goggins built and that we moved into was put together with unpeeled spruce logs and hunkered against the ground, low and gray on a ridge across a muskeg from the land where we would eventually settle. The clearing was surrounded by forest that overlooked Happy Valley and the creek running through it. We were only squatters—people living on land they didn't own or rent—but we were in frontier Alaska. Squatting was not a thing to be ashamed of; we were just borrowing the cabin and the land because no one else was using it at the time.

There was no well, so we had to haul water from a spring half a mile farther up the road. Every day one of my brothers made the hike toting an old-fashioned yoke across his shoulders that held a bucket on each end. The buckets were five-gallon metal Blazo—a common brand of white gas—cans with the tops cut out and a bail added. I often went along on these water-hauling trips to provide entertainment. I remember my brothers cursing "Killer Hill" that had to be climbed with full buckets, and they also cursed me for being too small to help. I was frequently reminded that I wasn't much help with chores.

Happy Valley is located fifteen miles north of the hamlet of Anchor Point and about seven miles south of Ninilchik. Both communities are located among gently rolling hills and muskegs along the road to Homer. Much of the land is covered in mossy tussocks and is too wet for trees to grow well, so there are broad, treeless flats between the expanses of dense forest. The forest is primarily white spruce, with sprinklings of birch and cottonwood, and it makes a home for moose, brown and black bear, wolverine, wolf, and coyote. During this homesteading time, the forest along the Sterling Highway was dense and thick with stands of old-growth spruce. Today, after the bark beetle blight a few decades ago, the land is open and the eyes can find the horizon along the Caribou Hills, miles off to the east. The spruce trees have been slow to return, and the land may never look the same again.

Long before the World War II veterans started homesteading here, the Kenai Peninsula was home to the Dena'ina until the Russians overran them during their quest for furs. Although Capt. James Cook explored the area and named many landmarks, including Anchor Point where he lost an anchor, the impact of the Russian occupation is more significant and apparent in the traditional communities. Generally, the Native residents of Ninilchik village referred to themselves as Russians until the seventies when Alaska Native Claims Settlement Act (ANCSA) and indigenous pride gave some of them a reason to call themselves Alaska Natives. They were probably right both times, for Ninilchik has an interesting and complex history with several versions of its founding.

There are, in a sense, two Ninilchiks: the "village" below the bluff at the mouth of the Ninilchik River and the newer Ninilchik that developed along the highway. The village was made up of intermarried Dena'ina (Alaskan Natives), Russians, and other early immigrants. A picturesque century-old Russian Orthodox Church overlooks the village and the inlet beyond.

Local and official history can't confirm the origin of the village. Some say Russian fur traders and laborers chose to retire here with their Native wives rather than return to Russia. One version suggests that this was a Dena'ina village when the Russians arrived, and it slowly became more Russian and less Dena'ina. Whatever the origin, explorers in the region documented good farmland, fresh water, and salmon, all of which would make the area good homesteading ground, just as it made good homes for prehistoric families, whose ancient pit homes tell us that the area has been occupied for thousands of years.

Until the highway was built, immigrants consisted of gold seekers, fisherman, and a few homesteaders in search of truly remote parcels "off the grid." Then in 1950 the Sterling Highway was built to open the southern Kenai Peninsula to homesteading and provide access to Homer from Anchorage. This started a rush for land along the highway corridor between Soldotna and Homer, and this is still the farthest west one can go on the road system in North America. Alaskans are driving around on more westerly roads in places like Bethel and Kodiak, but they aren't connected to the national road system and require a traveler to ferry, barge, or fly a car to get to them.

This gravel road, the Sterling Highway, is the reason that we found lean pickins for land to claim. There is nothing like a road to get people moving into an area, and this road opened the western and southern Kenai Peninsula. For seven years, families with the same dream as ours had been filing homestead claims along this new thoroughfare. As pleased as Chet and Briar Walker were with this place called Happy Valley, they were taking potluck on finding open land. By the time we arrived, there was really nothing available but leftovers. The Goggins' cabin must have looked pretty good about now.

July 18, 1958

Dear Folks —
We have had three rainy days in a row, don't rain real hard, neither does the wind blow to speak of. No thunder or lightning. Just a slow steady rain. The kids all just love it here even "Tom." He was not very much interested, but he has sure changed. I hate to see the roof leak so I put all of 34 cents worth of cement on it and a good hours work the other day. The worse place is about 3x4 around the "jack" the stove pipe goes up through. The tar paper is about shot.

We have not definitely decided where we will homestead. This place is tied up, it will take quite a while to get the title straightened out. There is 80 acres that corners on a gravel road that we are more interested in than any others we have seen. I have about decided to build a frame instead of log but I could change my mind. We are just in the planning stage. We have settled on 20x24 with two 10x10 bedrooms and that would leave 14x20 for kitchen, living room and our bed like so. We find out you can get by with lots less room when you don't have it piled full of furniture.

We cut some wood today, cooked on the range. Tell Maude that her old Home Comfort sure makes these women up here set up and take notice. Most of them don't have any way nicer that good a stove. They sure do drool. It hardly got a scratch on the way and sure does bake good bread. She bakes 12 loaves at a time about 3 times a week. The boys have slowed down on it a little but not much. Glad you are catching some fish. We haven't went yet. Just haven't got round to it. The Butler family is long gone I guess. They sent us some mail down from Palmer but we haven't heard anything from Thursday.

Well guess that's about all for now, not much news but we are all well and happy. Soon as we know anything new we will let you know.

As always, Chet and Family

Like good pioneers, the Walkers were modernizing the frontier. When we came to the end of the road, we did not come to hunker down in a hovel and cook in a pot over an open fire. We brought what we needed from Ohio to make ourselves comfortable. The back of the truck contained a gasoline wringer washer, an electric power plant, and a Home Comfort range. Dad refers to acquiring the stove from Maude, but none of us still alive knows who that was. The cast iron range with its white porcelain facade and an oven big enough to cook for the eight of us was to become the center of our home at Happy Valley. Probably a product of the late nineteenth century, this stove was a mass of iron with a cooktop the size of a kitchen table. Above the cook surface were two warming ovens that seemed to always have bread or rolls rising. On one end of the stove a reservoir offered hot water all the time the stove was hot. The wood fuel had to be split thin and fed often into the narrow firebox. This was the Cadillac of cookstoves and probably our most valuable possession.

One would think that every homestead family would make a good cookstove a priority, but apparently we were the exception, not the rule. Most people were getting by with cheap sheet metal cookstoves or no oven at all. For a baker like Briar Walker, a good stove was a necessity, not a luxury.

Mom was a good cook, but she cooked because she had to. What she really enjoyed was baking, and bread was her pride and joy, so that range was busy from breakfast coffee until the sourdough was set to proof in the warming oven at bedtime. On winter mornings, the stove was roaring by the time we rushed from our warm cocoons to stand in front of an open oven to change from our pajamas into clothes. While the stovetop was turning out pots of coffee and oatmeal, sourdough pancakes, and bacon and eggs, the oven was producing a steady flow of bread, biscuits, cornbread, rolls, pies, and cookies. I only remember eating store-bought bread when we visited Anchorage where Mom would buy a couple loaves of Wonder bread and some sliced bologna for sandwiches. At home it was all homemade, and the best was the hot heel of a loaf smeared with butter and eaten in a kitchen toasted by the smell of baking.

Maybe it is nostalgia for this time that finds me with a woodstove in my own house fifty years later. I can well afford to use my boiler and forgo the finding, felling, hauling, splitting, and storing of firewood; but where is the fun in that? None of my brothers or sisters has my same aesthetic for wood-burning stoves. They claim I was too young and spoiled when we homesteaded to learn to hate it, and by the time I was old enough, the wood cookstove had been replaced with a modern propane range that lit at the twist of a knob, another victim of the homesteaders' move to modernization.

Seven

Sad iron: A clothes iron, also called a flatiron, made of solid iron and heated on a stove; often with a removable wooden handle. *Sad* is an Old English term for *solid*. A necessity for families wanting to look their best.

When I read about the Home Comfort range and the other details I find in these letters, memories are retrieved, and I find that as much as I learn, I remember. Lost files are found in the deep recesses of the mind, so that I can remember scrambling out of bed, grabbing my clothes, and rushing to the cookstove to warm them on the open oven door before dressing. My tongue remembers biscuits and cobblers and cornbread from that oven, and I hear the clink of a spoon on glass as Dad and I ate cornbread and milk after supper. I can see him now, seated at the table, his plate pushed back and replaced with a coffee mug. I watch as my mother scolds him when he runs his hand under her dress as she pours his coffee. He laughs and adds sugar and milk from a can of Carnation evaporated milk before he crosses one leg over the other, takes a Camel cigarette from the pack in his front shirt pocket, and lights it with his brass Zippo lighter.

Such images draw me to the few photographs from that time, and I study the face of the man I want so much to know. One photograph from the summer of 1954 shows the whole family except me. They are crowded on a farmhouse porch swing wearing their Sunday best and Hollywood tans. Dad is lean and wholesome in a white shirt with a boldly patterned tie loosened to open the neck of his shirt. He is thirty-seven years old, fit, and handsome.

The second photo shows the whole crew assembled around a couch probably just before we left Ohio in 1958, and Dad is a different man. He is just past forty, but there is a strain in his eyes, and he seems less comfortable seated there on the edge of adventure. I can be lost for a moment or more looking into that face, and then I realize that my four-year-old self, smiling into the camera eagerly, is perched between his legs, my big head beginning to obscure his face. Is there a story in his eyes, or do I read my own message there, written by what I now know?

My brothers are lined up behind the couch and show their true spirits. Tom is tall and gawky, towering over his brothers behind Dad, while Bill is caught mid-laugh, and that's what he was remembered for, his sense of humor. Tom is stern and serious, wearing the burden of the elder sibling like a judge's robe, while Mike stares off in the distance, uneasy in this formal station, ready even then to be away from us. He would always be stepping away uneasy, restless, and seeking.

My sisters sit elbow to elbow. Amy close and buttoned; Peggy is open and reaching out, leaning into the camera, into the next thing. Amy is eight years old, and already she has a certain oversight of the family. Tidy, organized, and energetic, she wanted to be in the middle of everything. She would be the leader of the younger children, and she still plays that role nearly fifty years later. In this photo, she sits erect with each hair in place and looks straight into the camera, the proper photographic subject.

July 23, 1958

> *Dear grandma and grandpa,*
> *We are staying in a log cabin back off the road 1 mi. and everybody likes it. Every time you talk about changing the house Danny gets mad and balls for an hour. Daddy put windows in. And you can really tell the difference from windows and boards. The windows are only plastic but who cares, they let in light and keep rain and snow out (I hope).*
> *Mommy mixed up bread today and she wrote a letter to you and the bread got so big it fell over the side of the pan and it was a mess.*
> *We are 7 miles from Ninilchik and up on the hill there is part of it and down over the hill and there is a little fishing village by the ocean. I baked 1 cake, 1 cookie batch, and Mommy made 3 or 4 cakes and 3 or 4 cookies. Tom is cleaning his guns and one didn't need it. I have to go to bed now so I will say good-bye.*
> *Love always, Amy*

July 23, 1958

> *Dear Grandma and Grampa*
> *How are you? I am fine. Well we made it safe and sound. We're in Alaska having fun. We live in a big cabin. Dad's been to Anchorage twice. We live on a homestead. We all like it up here and the only thing is it rains a lot. Saw a bear track twice as big as a softball and lots of moose and spruce hens. Dad is moose hunting and has been all day. The only thing we don't like is going to Anchorage. Mom bakes a lot and Danny is getting fat on sourdough pancakes. I've met several girls my age. Their names are Marcy Provast, Donna Bell, Bonnie Williams and others. Donna plays the mandolin and so does her mother. The muskeg are full of moose late at night. It is real sport rabbit hunting up here, snowshoe rabbits are white in the wintertime. Well I guess that's about all for now.*
> *With love,*
> *Bill*

When my brother Bill was eleven years old, he was already talking about girls, and well on the road to becoming a ladies' man. In his teenage years, he was always chasing a girl, in love with a girl, or fighting over a girl. Being a Don Juan and the dandy of the family meant that he was as nattily dressed and finely groomed as was possible on a Kenai Peninsula homestead. The girls, it seemed, loved him as much as he loved them. One day Mom was ironing starched white shirts (yes, a homesteader's boy wore starched white button-downs to school) and complaining about the extra effort to a friend over for coffee. Her friend's optimistic reply stuck with us forever, "Well, Briar, it's a poor family that can't afford one dude." Bill was definitely our dude.

Bill was the third brother, always racing to catch Tom and Mike—to be as tough as them and to be their equal. He was often caught in the trap of middle child between the two older and the three, eventually four, younger ones. In those first months and years at Happy Valley, though, he was my protector and companion. More than my other brothers, Bill would play with me, make me toys, and let me tag along on his big boy adventures. It is his hand that had transcribed my first letter to Grandpa and Grandma, his scrawl beginning to develop, even then the pen fighting to control the wandering flourishes of cursive letters as they meandered across the page, making his writing a challenge to read. When David came along, it was Bill among all of us kids that was the special caretaker of little brother. I see the same trait in my own son as he plays with his nephew, and I honor strong families with males who care about children and what that does for confidence and character.

After Dad died, Bill gave himself to the marines, and they fed him to the monster that was the Vietnam War, and we all learned that some wounds never heal.

As the youngest I was the smallest and slowest and the least help when chores came along. I remember being teased for being a crybaby, and apparently I had a taste for sourdough pancakes—I still do. I know I was already learning to read at this time, and this adventure suited me just fine. Our new Alaska life was perfect for five-year-old Danny Walker.

July 23, 1958

Dear folks —
Chet went to Anchorage yesterday and filed on a 40 tract. I'll let him tell you about it. One big reason for taking this is that it is in a very good location for the kids to go to school. Then after we prove up on this we can file on 120 more anywhere we want to. It's pretty wet now but I imagine as soon as it dries enough we will start cutting trees. There are other families here to build who will help on a share the work basis. Also some who are settled offered to help. Nearly everyone has a chainsaw.

Chet did think he'd try to get work in Anchorage and we'd spend the winter there in order to get a little more money ahead to put toward clearing the land and so on. He was supposed to have called in about one today but we talked it over and decided against it. It guaranteed him $550 per month. He didn't know just what it was but was only for 3 mos. Anchorage is a sloppy riotous place. Has lots more liquor stores than groceries. Also the kids would have to walk to school no matter where we lived there. There are no buses or streetcars. Out here we can pick berries to can and for jam. Also we can hunt for our meat and live rent free. And we can begin to build right away. On top of all this the kids nearly had a fit at the thought of going to Anchorage, so Chet decided we'd stay out here and I'm surely glad he did.

I'm baking again today. I have to bake bread every other day but takes a little less than it did. Eight loaves every other day does very well. We've been having sourdough hotcakes for breakfast twice a week. I'm not crazy about them but the rest are. Danny said, "Boy them's good, you'd better send that recipe to Papaw." So I will copy it off and you can try it if you like. Also, today I'm making one of Catherine's raisin nut cakes. I'm making it with no nuts but it is still good. This is the third one in about a week. We have been having a lot of rainy days and Amy and I bake cookies to pass the time away. They eat them though. We have been having several people dropping in evenings and up here they drink coffee all the time. Just like the Purdys. So we keep cookies for the kids. People are surely friendly and all want to help tell us where and how to buy to save.

You asked about the food prices. Most things are just a little higher, some cheaper and some sky high. Fish is given away here, and they say easy to catch but Chet hasn't got a license yet and they patrol too close to go without. We have been buying piece bacon for .59 a pound. Crisco .40 and margarine .29 cents. But people here send to Seattle once or twice a year and buy wholesale. They save about 20% this way. We aim to get an order to come in on the boat last of October. Should have our cabin ready by then or maybe sooner. Hard to guess really. Meanwhile you can get a flat 10% off any groceries by buying case lots. Since you drive 80 miles to get them this is better. Flour is 11.50/100, sugar 12.00, potatoes 5.00 per 100, powdered milk 21.50 per 100. In boxes of three pounds it is forty cents a pound. Coffee, tea, preserves, jelly, spices, Spam etc. are all about the same as Ohio.

About their language. They speak just like we do only use _much_ better grammar and diction than people in Ohio do. In the village (Ninilchik) the old people speak Russian, and all of the people there have an accent a foot thick. I haven't talked to any Indians but they are here. I've seen them and they dress very nicely. Better than the Villagers. I imagine they, too, speak English. There is one Eskimo woman and her son in the community. They are civilized and belong to the Baptist church.

I found one thing I should have brought and didn't. Sad irons. You can't buy them new even from Sears anymore and there are none not in use. One neighbor loaned me two and Mr. Sanborne (an old bachelor) is going to try to *find some but said don't get your hopes up. Too many people looking for them. There is electric in the highway and it will be available to us when we build but the minimum is $7.50 per month and I don't know if we'll get it or not. Won't be before next year anyway. I may be able to get a gasoline iron though. Have a line on one. Well, I'll sign off for now and let Chet write what I forgot. Be sure to keep them coming. Tell everyone hello for us.*

Love,
Briar

The Home Comfort range is long gone, probably sold to someone starting a homestead farther back into the Caribou Hills than we wanted to go, but I still have Mom's sad irons. I found them in the attic of the homestead years later. They are undramatic blocks of cast iron, made with a removable handle so it stays cool while the iron is heating on the stove. All these years I thought they were family heirlooms that had made the journey with us from Ohio. Although I can't imagine Mom traveling far from home without one, it turns out she forgot to pack them.

I guess she tracked irons down somewhere, and someday I will pass them on to my kids. For now they are simply pieces of history without particular beauty or artistic merit, just rusty chunks of iron with an interesting story behind them. And they are some of the few family possessions still around from that time.

I can just imagine Mom's consternation when she found she left Ohio ironless. "For heaven's sake!" she probably exclaimed. "What on earth was I thinking, traveling all this way without an iron? Gracious me!" It would be easy for most people to get by without ironing clothes on a homestead, but Briar Walker and her brood weren't "most people." Our tradition of neatly ironed clothes would not be turned aside simply because we were living in a squatter's cabin without electricity or indoor plumbing. And knowing Mom as I do, even in the squatter's cabin where we had to haul water, we went off to church on Sunday in starched white shirts and blouses pressed as smooth as window glass. She wouldn't have it any other way.

Jeans were hung out on pants stretchers so they dried smooth and creased without ironing. Pillowcases and sheets were pressed before folding, the napkins and kitchen towels too, as well as doilies and curtains. And yes, even the handkerchiefs were ironed. A glass bottle with a sprinkler cap was part of the ironing toolbox, and a basket of ironing would be sprinkled with water and each piece rolled and stacked in the basket while the irons heated. Often shirts and blouses were starched as well, not with a modern spray bottle but by dipping in starch-saturated water before drying.

I know I wasn't even in school yet when Mom stood me on a stool so I could reach the ironing board and learn how to take that big hot iron and run it over the dampened cloth until it was magically smooth and warm. I started ironing handkerchiefs and napkins, then pants and shirts when I was older. By then, the novelty had worn off and ironing was no longer fun, but someone had to do it, and if it wasn't that chore, it would be another.

Much of this manuscript was composed at a writing desk, or secretary, which had been Mom's before we left Ohio. It's a true family heirloom that I didn't know existed until about five years ago. A small, rickety desk of cheap pine, stained a coffee brown, it must have had hundreds of letters written on it over the years. The folks left it with Grandma and Papaw in 1958, and it finally made it to Alaska shortly after these letters arrived in 2010. Back in 1958 when the truck was loaded for Alaska there wasn't much room for furniture, and the little desk got left behind, but Grandma never got rid of it.

I wasn't aware that any of our furniture from Ohio had stayed in the family, but one of my cousins thought we ought to have this piece and sent it on. Imagine getting a piece of furniture back after fifty-some years. I wish I knew its story, but that's how family history is for most of us, a bunch of shoeboxes and scrapbooks in the hall closet, and a few pieces of wobbly legged furniture standing around in our lives so long that we forget when they weren't there. Heirlooms are rarely labeled or cataloged; they just share space in the house and trust us to remember their stories. Unfortunately, there is so much to remember in family history that without records, objects get lost and information is twisted or eroded until it is part of family myth not family history.

I look around at the collected objects from my life, only one generation's worth, that I hope my descendants will treasure. Will they remember that I kept that ragged, ixle shoulder bag because I carried it when I lived in the mountains of Oaxaca for two summers with the Zapotecs, where I also collected the terra cotta pottery? Will they remember that the shoe pot is from the Mixes and not the Zapotecs? Will someone remember that the black pottery piece is Zapotec, but from the valley of Oaxaca not the mountains, and that we actually bought it at garage sale in Colorado not in Mexico?

In my office, crowded on a shelf with other memorabilia and books, is a rustic toy wishing well made of wood scraps and a coffee can. Who will remember that Papaw Walker made this little treasure and that it is the only remnant of that man's life that I own except photos. Will my children remember that this desk was my mother's and that it arrived in Alaska a long time after the rest of our things?

It might well ruin the wonder of family treasures to archive and document the collection like museum pieces, but I think I do need to write some notes to preserve the stories about them. It is ironic that the least important parts of our lives, the mere objects, are what will abide when we're all gone. In fact, that is mostly what museums are, peoples' things left from the past, and some of them have a story. With so many of the pieces that made the trip to Alaska now lost to time—and the Gulf of Alaska—what few we have are special. Even before the U-Haul trailer on the barge fiasco, the Walker inventory of memorabilia was pretty limited.

We didn't come to Alaska with much, and we certainly didn't leave much behind. That two-ton truck was carrying it all, from the gas-powered washing machine and that massive cookstove to biscuit cutters and hair clippers, everything the Walkers would need except sad irons and luck.

When I came home to Alaska from college I had a truck nearly that big for just two peoples' lives, not eight. I guess that when it comes down to it, we were poor folk heading north for a new beginning. Mom and Dad didn't act poor and probably didn't see themselves that way, but Dad wasn't in Alaska long before he was looking for work, even to the point of trying to make a go at a mechanic's shop right in Ninilchik. "Livin' off the land," as he calls it, may not be just some romantic notion after all because we didn't have a choice.

Eight

Moose (*Alces americanus*): The largest member of the deer family, a ruminant found in the northern boreal forests and wetlands. Known for a bulbous nose, long legs, and palmate antlers; aka Eurasian elk (*Alces alces*) or Alaskan beef.

By the last week of July, the Walkers had selected a piece of ground and started clearing land for a cabin of our own. The property lay about a half mile off the highway on a dirt road that we would call "the lane." Trees were felled, stumps pulled—probably with the neighbor's tractor—and a house site selected. As attractive as the Goggins' property was, it must have looked like too much of a long shot since we could have worked all year fixing the place and not be able to claim it in the end.

As I was reading my parents' letters, I found myself for the first time wondering why here? Why this patch of land that's half muskeg and all of it a bit wet. I have always been so emotionally bound to the place that I hadn't looked at it from a practical perspective. It has no spectacular view, the ground is flat but doesn't drain water well, and only about half of it has trees. Without the family memories it's a just a patch of land on a dirt road with a muskeg out back.

In 2016, for the first time in decades, I visited the site of the Goggins' cabin and walked the clearing where the cabin once stood. The land is on a ridge looking down on Happy Creek, and the view offers a chance for the eyes to look beyond the trees to the mountains in the distance. The ground is firm and the clearing is dry with a covering of tall grass and fireweed. I could see why we all liked the place, and I feel guilty when I wish that we had stayed there instead of building a place across the valley for I am as smitten by this place today as I was all those decades ago. I wanted to write a letter and mail it back in time to argue with my father and try to convince him to wait and file on this place. I'd try to talk him into adding a lean-to onto the cabin for more space, and we could just tough it out for the winter. Maybe by next summer the title would be clear. But this is all advice from someone with the luxury of hindsight, and as Dad was known to say, "Hindsight is better than foresight by a damn sight." And now, some sixty years later, that fine building site overlooking Happy Valley is still vacant and no evidence is left that anyone ever loved any part of it.

I can feel Dad and Mom's impatience. I can hear them talking in the evening with us kids put to bed, balancing their options against their dreams and finally settling some big decisions. They weren't going to move to Anchorage for the winter. They would select some land and build a cabin. Now, two months into these letters, I know Dad was decisive and not one to look back at what might have been. He was making decisions based on what was best for his family. I read a certain calm when he was committed, or I want to, for if he is like me, once a decision is made—right, wrong, or indifferent—the pressure is eased for a time, just a little.

July 30, 1958

Hello folks —
Can't guess what I'm doing while I write – watching a pressure cooker full of meat. A neighbor "butchered" and I helped him for half, must have been 200 pounds dressed. Anyway, there will be fifty-four quarts of it, first cooker came off at 15 til nine this am. The last will come off about midnight. I had it all cut up and Briar had it all in cans by noon. We had some of the best steak I ever ate in my life, also we used the old sausage grinder and ground some "hamburger" for dinner, it sure was good, couldn't tell it from Ohio beef.

Butchered yesterday morning, was done and cleaned up by nine o'clock, let it cool in the shade all day all night. Sure did cool out nice. No need to publish this. One never knows.

Briar said to tell you she made soap the other day. Found a jar or two of old grease in the trash and took a half can of lye made a 9x10 cake bar of soap. It don't take much soap here. The spring water is soft as rain water.

You asked about groceries here. Meat, milk and eggs are the items out of this world. Other things not so bad. Flour $11.50 a hundred pounds, sugar

$13.95 a hundred. Beans $9.20 a fifty pound, canned stuff about the same as there maybe two or three cents a can higher. Oh yes, clams taste sort of like fried oysters only not so much so. We bought potatoes $5.00 a hundred. That seems to be the year round price up here.

 I guess the rainy weather has been really rough back there. It, according to the old timers, has been extremely wet here. In fact it has rained about 3 days a week ever since we got here. Don't rain hard but keeps at it.

 Hold your hat! I made a little money last Saturday. Hauled a load of wood for Trent up to Clam Gulch made $10.00, my first in Alaska. It's a start at least. Haven't caught a fish yet but have had several messes to eat. Just got my license Saturday then it rained.

 Well Tom and I about have a well dug. We are down twelve feet and water comes up three feet overnight. Need to square the bottom up a little; may go down a little farther later on. The well will be in the cellar (root cellar they call them here). We don't aim to carry water very far. This cabin here is ½ mile from a spring. That is no good. We got a start on the cellar it will be about 6x8 just for canned stuff and potatoes. They keep up here from one crop to another.

 We did get used to going to bed in daylight but now it's dark around 9:30 and daylight before we get up. The kids are all happy as larks, don't even complain about no TV. We play cards some and read a lot and they play all kinds of kid games outside. There are other kids in the neighborhood but we don't visit too much. Where we are building there is three children, one Tom's age and two younger. Oh yes, moose season officially opens August 20 but they say that they all head for the hills. Oh well.

 As ever,
 Chet and Family

Part of what family stories should do is explain not only what happened but why. This letter tells a story, but sometimes the why is evading me. My father, upright church-going Christian, is reputed to be honest as the day is long, yet we find him bragging of being a part of moose poaching not two months after entering Alaska. I want to understand my dad, the poacher. That's what he was, more than once, and at first look that doesn't match his character.

It is not that poaching was a rare crime. Homesteaders harvested moose when they needed meat, and they did it with little regard for hunting seasons or game laws. Often neighbors became accomplices by taking a quarter of meat in exchange for help with butchering just as Dad did. The game wardens were supposed keep a watch for poachers, but the wardens were few, the land was large, and the same guys enforcing game laws also had to look after fishing violations. Since the fishermen were confined to the streams and rivers, the game wardens knew where to look for illegal salmon fishing, while moose could be taken literally anywhere. In such an environment as this, it makes sense that my Dad would worry more about being nabbed for fishing without a license than for possession of ill-gotten moose meat.

Accustomed as we were to home-raised beef and pork, we were particular consumers of meat, and moose meat was a big hit with the Walkers. From here on out, moose—the homesteader's "beef"—would be a major focus of our search for food. The meat is dense and a dark red color with little fat or marbling. Even today I love having moose in the freezer to make into burgers, meatloaf, or stew. Best of all are steaks from the backstrap, sliced thin, breaded in salt-and-peppered flour, and fried in a hot skillet. The drippings make a fine skillet gravy to finish the dish.

For people like us without electricity, storing fresh meat was not as simple as slipping it into a freezer. The animal had to be butchered, cured, and prepped for canning. This started in the field where the moose was usually cut into four quarters for packing out of the woods, and it sometimes arrived at the house with the hide still on. The meat would be hung for a few days to cure, and then the excess fat and sinew was removed and the butchering began. It would keep for a while just hung in the smokehouse or shed, even in summer, but most of the meat had to be processed and preserved. Some of the meat was butchered into steaks and roasts to be eaten right away. Some of it ended up with some unlucky child who cranked a meat grinder clamped to a table, making pound after pound of hamburger. Some was chunked into stew meat. That and the burger were packed in glass jars that had to be processed in a pressure cooker for over an hour.

Mom made the canned ground meat into hamburger gravy that she served over biscuits, rolls, or mashed potatoes. She also worked it into spaghetti sauce or meatloaf. The cubed meat was usually the basis for stew, which we ate a lot of. I also remember school lunches of hearty moose sandwiches on homemade bread. The filling was a meaty spread of canned ground moose, pickle, mayonnaise, and, I bet, some mustard.

Dad always said that the best meat came off a barren cow or young bull taken in January, and this was also a nice time to store frozen meat. Local folklore stated that any moose taken out of season would have rich flavor. In spite of proverbs about the taste of forbidden fruit, there is some science behind such suggestions. Males taken during fall hunting season are sometimes tough and gamey due to hormones and stress. Out of season was often midwinter when the bulls were not stinking up their meat with testosterone. Barren cows are often fatter than rutty males or cows feeding a calf or two. Winter is hardest on cows and their new calves, and they were rarely targeted by the out-of-season hunter.

The discreet hunter would approach a moose in a wooded area out of sight of house or highway and shoot it with a small caliber rifle. It would require a close and accurate shot but it made a smaller sound than a big bore rifle. Timber and brush would hide the hunter and his kill from prying eyes. A well-prepared hunter would also be packing a chainsaw or ax to drop a tree or cut brush to cover the gut pile. In less than an hour, a moose could be butchered and evidence hidden. In winter, quarters of meat would be buried in snowbanks behind the homesteader's cabin, a secure freezer for illicit game. This was true subsistence hunting.

Harvesting "Alaskan beef" was an example of how the frontier populations interpreted law and resource management. A man with eight mouths to feed was bound to be tempted by meat on the hoof wandering through his yard. Homesteaders tended to be independent people accustomed to making decisions for themselves, including what to hunt and when. The moose was theirs for the taking, much like the land they filed on. The whole homestead philosophy was based on the idea that the earth is a garden for man's purpose. On the frontier there was little difference between harvesting a moose feeding in the forest and harvesting a steer raised on a pasture in that same land.

While the homesteader's view of resource management might seem selfish, they probably saw themselves as an addition to the local ecology. They were using a bountiful resource that was relatively easy to acquire, and it seemed that their god had put the moose and salmon here for their use, manna in the wilderness.

In 1958 the salmon and moose seemed to be in abundance compared to the number of humans, but that was temporary. The lifestyle of the subsistence homesteader gathering food and fuel right out the back door could not last, not with a highway outside the front door. Even in the short time we were on the homestead, this ethic of a homesteader's open season changed so that most people began following the game laws. With a chest freezer and some planning, homesteaders could get their year's meat during regular hunting season and had no need to risk losing their meat, rifle, and hunting license.

This is all part of that brashly condescending phrase "opening the wilderness." The first settlers in a new place always lived a different life than those who followed, and that lifestyle was temporary, usually because game and other resources were overused to a point of depletion. The saying that you can't make an omelet without breaking eggs has applied directly to the homestead movement since its inception in 1862. The settlement of the West ran roughshod over habitat and ravaged the game population, breaking eggs right and left in order to dish up the homestead omelet. Traditionally, frontier governments didn't control hunting and fishing or protect critical habitat. As a result, many areas of the United States lost important wildlife species like the American bison and the passenger pigeon.

By the twentieth century, people knew enough to protect fish and wildlife, and there was a serious attempt to preserve the native species of Alaska. Wildlife managers, then as now, were trying to balance the demands of homesteaders using moose for food with sport hunters who knew that the Kenai was the place for trophy moose. Luckily for Alaskans, millions of acres of Alaska are still public land and managed as habitat for wild species.

In spite of all this protected acreage, the homesteaders, in silent alliance with their neighbors, began to reduce, remove, and replace the very natural history that drew them here. It is the unwritten mission and the true intent of the Homestead Act to convert the frontier from the "wild" state to a cultivated state; to change from moose-ranging willow thickets to cattle-ranging hayfields; from berry patch to potato patch. We homesteaders cleared the land for gardens and pasture and in the process destroyed the habitat of the very moose and bear we wanted to harvest. For example, by hunting and logging for cabin lumber, one homestead family could easily eliminate several acres of habitat and collectively deplete game populations in a much larger area.

Wholesale clearing of wild land, a big part of homesteading, radically changes the land forever, and only the failure of agriculture on the Kenai kept that from happening here. Without the incentive of a cash crop, most homesteads were not completely cleared for farming. Even today, much of the private land is in a generally wild state, partly because there was no economic motivation to farm. Most homesteaders, now as then, clear land for a house site and gardens, leaving the rest as a woodlot and privacy barrier.

When the land didn't pay off, there was the sea, and a lot of homesteaders turned to fishing when they realized that farming the Kenai would not be economically practical. Yes, the land was good for big family gardens and even small-scale animal raising, but no one was going to make a go of farming without some supplemental income. Many families joined the commercial fishermen working the rich North Pacific, harvesting the five species of salmon as well as halibut, clams, and crab.

We ate a lot of seafood, especially salmon. The salmon was caught by sport fishing, or we traded for it. Maybe there wasn't much salmon poaching because they were plentiful without poaching.

Even today, most of the people I know, from homesteaders to oil field workers, spend part of the summer trying to fill freezers with fish, and I still do. People paying twenty-five dollars a pound for salmon in a Denver grocery store would be awestruck to see the scores of pounds of it in the pantries and garage freezers of Alaskans. Today three interests battle for access to the Kenai Peninsula salmon: sportsmen, personal use, and commercial salmon harvesters, all wanting their interests protected when shares of the resource are meted out.

The hunting and fishing patterns of fifty years ago did not persist on the Kenai; they couldn't. The change in the habitat of the salmon and moose as well as pressure by legal hunting and fishing made it no longer okay to hunt and fish at will. The frontier way can't continue after the frontier is gone. Even though we may complain about bag limits and tight regulations, we know that we can only keep these animals in our lives by protecting them, and that is more important to most of us than access to protein. While there are probably a few modern-day homesteaders still taking what they want whenever they want, there aren't many.

There is no indication that Dad went through a deep psycho-emotional introspection when he got the chance to go in on an illegal moose. Like his neighbors and forefathers, he saw a resource and used it. One only has to read the list of meals and canner loads to know they were using the whole resource and appreciating the bounty. They planned to live off the land, and at least in some part they could. I must bring myself to think that he was not so much a scofflaw as he was a practical provider. He acted to fill a need and an act against nature could be justified by the needs of man. My father was a religious man, and in the tradition of the American Christian values that he followed, we are all Adam in the Garden of Eden with dominion over animals and fish. I must infer that moose hunting was between Dad, the moose, and God, and the game warden was part of the hunter's gamble.

Nine

Hardpan: A cemented or compacted, often clayey layer in soil that is impenetrable by roots, water, and even shovels.

While Dad and Tom are digging the cellar, I am excavating these letters. Foolishly, I thought by reading them I would I find an autobiography of my father. I thought a profile would show itself, letting me see his tastes and tendencies, letting me laugh with him, and allowing him to speak to me from the past. He speaks, but the voice is muffled. I must dig through the words and paragraphs for clarity. So far I have found a man who's good with words, a man with a dream, a man who left his parents behind but doesn't leave them out.

The other things I know are the stories we've told and retold since Dad's death—stories we repeated until they morphed and grew and became a legend, the tall tale of our father, remembered anytime two or more of his children were together. He was Dad, a soft-spoken man with an explosive temper: "Once he was working a tractor and a part broke in his hand. He swore and threw it so far that he never could find it." He was the man who faced his own fears: "He didn't like heights, so when he finished setting the rafters on the garage, he walked the full length of the ridge board like it was a high-wire—just to do it." He could fix or build anything, outwork anybody, and joke about it when everyone else was too tired to talk: "If he fell in the pigpen he would come out vice president of the hogs." People said he looked like John Wayne, and my family elevated him to the level of a cultural icon. We saw his flaws as beauty marks, small and quaint. We seem to have rejected any evidence that went against the myth, the legend, the legacy.

Dying at an early age seems to have given Dad a waiver of judgment by his children. My siblings and I talk freely about the failings, flaws, and foibles of our mother, yet we maintain a kind of truce of criticism about our father, remembering only the good and strong elements of the man's character. It was as if he became our Abraham and can only be remembered fondly; anything else would be irreverent.

Ask one of her children about Mom, and you will hear about her tyrant-like mothering, frequent spankings, and vicious tongue: "That will be an elegant sufficiency of that!" Ask about Dad and you get an example of his humor, his kindness, his nobility: Amy came home once in tears because her teacher called the students' parents a bunch of drunks who live in dumps. Dad said, "Go back to you teacher and tell her Daddy's trying to quit drinking, and we're moving out of this dump next week."

August 2, 1958 raining

Dear Folks —
Had another letter from you Thurs. They are coming along very nice. We are still getting a heap of rain—had two nice days and more rain today. Had a load of wood to haul today but can't get it out in this rain. We are all fine but I think we as a whole have more sore muscles than we've had for a while. Took our "steak" sandwiches over to the "place" yesterday and finished the well for now. May have to dig deeper this winter. It is twelve foot deep and thirty inches across, had at least fifty gallons of water in it before I finished out the bottom. It is about ⅓ bigger now so it will fill up more. It's cold as ice runs in these places. Kids and Briar cleaned up old log stumps and then I cut six trees, the biggest one about twelve inches, and they piled the brush, cut part up in wood (and one made a house log), left the rest in long lengths.
We dug the cellar 7½ x 10½ feet deep still going down another foot or so. Some of us dug all day on the cellar. The well is in one end of it, will shore it all up with slabs or boards. Will put sills and joists and floor down before we lay up the logs. The rain sure clobbered things up. The trees, spruce are just like Christmas trees, one long tapered pole with limbs not very big nor very long. I cut one twelve inches at best about forty feet tall. Trimmed it and blocked it up in wood in fifteen minutes. It was dead, not good for lumber but sure burns good, lot like pine. The green don't burn so good but works pretty good mixed. Mom you asked if the range would heat the cabin, it does now too good but

we brought our little heating stove too. You see several stoves up here made of old oil drums. Put a door in one and the stovepipe in the other. Lay the drum down and put legs out.

The cook is baking cookies and bread, Mike reading, Bill running errands and reading, Amy and Peggy washing dishes. Tom is out somewhere probably at our neighbors. We ground the last of the "hamburger" for dinner, have a fresh roast for Sunday dinner then that's it. Mike has a spruce hen in the oven for dinner too. Had some more fish yesterday. Tom and I went with Jim Trent Thursday and got some swell trout eight inches or so long. Danny, he's putting cookies in a pan for his mother. Rainy days sure have their problems keeping the small fry happy. Peggy is cleaning up the sausage grinder. Think I've told you the news for now. Your last letter was dated July 27, postmarked the 28th and we got it Thursday the 31st, not bad at all.

Bye for now—will let Briar put in her two cents worth if she gets to it. She is still hanging stuff up. Had to put a hole in the roaster handle so she could hang it up.

As ever, Chet and family

A homestead cabin had to be put together like a space capsule for it would need to stand alone in a hostile environment. It had to provide protection from the elements with a dependable heating system and food storage. It needed an area for tools and for food preparation, sanitation and water, and a place for the family to gather and then to sleep. And like the spaceship, the homestead cabin is only temporary because most homesteaders dream of replacing this rustic shelter with a permanent and grand house. Someday.

Our cabin started as a hole in the ground, a rectangular cellar hole dug where the house would sit. When covered with a cabin floor, this was a cool, dry place where we accessed the well and stored root vegetables and canned goods. A ladder led down to it from the cabin floor, and a little boy sent to store canning jars or bring up potatoes for dinner would be spooked by threatening roots twining out of the dirt walls and daddy longlegs crawling across his hands. By spring the last of the potatoes had long snaky sprouts growing up from the bin, reaching for sunlight and finding only me and my flashlight. Years later, when I revisited that cellar as an adult, the crib boards had rotted and the walls had sloughed in, but the loamy smell of the earth was still rich and the daddy longlegs were plentiful.

Since this ground is mostly a dense brown loam with a few pebbles mixed in, it gives easily to the shovel once you get beneath the grass, moss, and tree roots. It's easy to dig, but it's a mess when it's wet. Even a little rainfall when digging in this earth makes one feel like he is wrestling a wad of potter's clay. Dad was getting a lot of rain when he was working on the foundation, so he would have been quite a sight by the end of the day. After digging down through mud for about three or four feet, the work would suddenly get harder. Here Dad was facing hardpan, a layer of crumbly mudstone that would defy the tip of his number two shovel and force him and Tom to use a pick to bust up the rocklike layer and keep digging. If they didn't get through the hardpan there would be no well. Down past the hardpan, they reached the layer where groundwater percolated through the gravel.

Because it had to be wide enough for a man or boy to climb into, a hand-dug well had to be more than three feet in diameter. One well digger was in the well filling buckets and another pulled the buckets up and emptied them. This process went on until the well started serving up water fast enough to keep a reservoir pooled in the bottom.

Luckily, Dad and Tom only had to go down twelve feet before water was pooling around the digger's feet fast enough to provide water for a family of eight going on nine. The upper portion of such a well had to be cribbed—lined with vertical boards that formed a box or casing—to prevent the dirt from sloughing. Then, once the pump and line were installed, the well had to be covered to keep out mice and voles. We learned that the hard way when Dad went down into the cellar one day after the cabin was built and found drowned rodents floating in our drinking water. He fished out the tiny carcasses and made us kids pump out water for a solid hour while he built a tight wooden well cover.

The well was shallow enough to be used with an old-fashioned pitcher pump. Ours was cast iron and about the size of a large milk pitcher with a big spout on one side and a handle on the other. As soon as Dad had the pump installed on the kitchen counter, he set up a big pot to store water and taught me how to use the pump. Sometimes a few pumps of the handle would bring water flowing, but if the prime was lost, a pitcher of water had to be poured into the top of the pump while someone started pumping. From that day on, it was my job to keep that pot full at all times.

One only has to live for a time without household water to appreciate what a luxury it is, even with a hand pump. Dad was planning for homestead finery when he put the well under the house with a pump in the kitchen. No more toting buckets down the road with a yoke. No more melting snow or chopping ice in the winter as some people had to do. In most of America, this would have been an archaic system, but in the homestead communities of Alaska, we were cutting edge.

August 5, 1958 Rain Rain Rain

I am a day early for the mail but this way maybe I'll get it written. Always seems like mail day is busy. It has rained steadily here since early Monday morning. Never rains hard just a real gentle drizzle and you can walk a mile in it and not be wet. Also wet is all you get. The only place there is mud is where it has been cleared for a road or garden. Otherwise there is about a foot of vegetation and you never touch ground so no mud, just water. Chet said to tell you he is screwing for a pastime. When he made the table he had no screws only nails. So today he went to Homer, and while he was there he got some screws and is now putting them in. it's a pretty good table but I knead bread on it every other day so it has to be sturdy. It's the handiest size table we ever had. Our fresh meat is all gone now but we kept it for 6 days in the basement and it was warm days too. I guess the spruce chickens are nearly ready to fry. I'm anxious to smell up the skillet with one or two or three of them. I've had one, a hen, and I made gravy over her was real good.

Oh yes, quit worrying about us not getting mail. I have got at least one letter from you every mail day since we have been here. Keep them coming. Even when they are short we are glad to get them. Mother has outdone herself. We've had two or three from her. We have sent you a letter every mail too so you should get a pile of them sometime. Catherine has been writing regular too. And I've heard from Lois twice. I've heard from Aunt Daisy and Aunt Mabel too.

Today is Amy's birthday and Esther Trent gave her some material odds and ends. So I made her two blouses and two doll dresses (one for Peggy). Have another 2 yard piece of strawberry colored sports denim. Have a notion to make her jeans out of it. I believe two yards would do it, it's 36 in. wide. Have things pretty well in shape for school. Must send an order to Sears for some cold weather boots etc, tho. Up here school even furnishes pencils and paper. They have to take their lunch though. Well, guess this is it for now.
Love always,
Briar

Though sometimes we probably seemed remote as a spaceship, our homestead maintained a tether of communication with Highland County, Ohio, and the rest of humanity. Like anyone, we wanted all the news from back home that we could get. And all we could get were letters, the occasional telegram, and the hometown newspaper. Even when we finally got electricity, there was no TV, so the radio, magazines, and letters kept us close to the Outside (an Alaska term for the continental United States). While a few antisocial homestead families would head for the hills without leaving a forwarding address, most of us didn't leave home to get completely away, just far enough to be missed.

This was a world as different from present day as it was from the end of the nineteenth century. Imagine a family in a log cabin without electricity on a remote dirt road in Alaska exchanging weekly letters with grandparents in rural Ohio more than four thousand miles away. Mail came and went regularly with only a few days of wait time for the answer to a question or the delivery of a critical set of hair barrettes.

In the twenty-first century, when people seldom write personal letters, it is a stupefying contrast that Mom and Dad were writing letters almost daily, and Grandma was doing the same. These letters were often passing in the air between Anchorage and Seattle after traveling first by truck from both directions. The envelops may have said "Air Mail," but our letters and those coming from the other direction never went airborne until they reached a major airport, which meant a two-hundred-mile ride to Anchorage before heading to Ohio. Letters from Grandpa and Grandma probably traveled all the way to Cincinnati from Hillsboro before they took wing. Even then, the letters were arriving rather quickly. Of course, "rather quickly" is a relative term. This was 1958 when people weren't flying from Los Angeles to New York for a meeting and back the same day. In fact, 1958 was the first year that more Americans traveled by air than by ship, and the same year that Boeing would debut the 707 jetliner as the first viable passenger jet.

It is easy to imagine that our smartphones and Wi-Fi gadgets are keeping us connected like never before, and that only with electronic media can we maintain the bonds of family. In reality, fifty years ago, and long before that, people were just as keen on staying connected and did it with more effort and less technology. They wrote letters and depended on a delivery system as old as our country to get them to their destinations quickly, consistently, and efficiently, all for the price of a six-cent stamp.

August 5, 1958

> *Dear grampa,*
> *I learned to tie my shoes. how are you? I've been seeing much moose. I went down to the muskeg. I have much friends up here. It has been raining a lot up here. Jim got a moose and he gave half of it to us. It was a cow moose. I heard you had some Alaska potatoes. I haven't seen any bears. Tom saw three coyotes on the way up here. Mommy saw a bear but we were all asleep. The coyotes were out in a field. That's all for now.*
> *Yours,*
> *Danny (written by Bill)*
>
> *PS How are your chickens.*

Today I don't write many letters, and personal letters are rare indeed, in contrast to my dad who was a prolific letter writer. The letters in this volume are just one collection sent to me in Gramma's shoe box. Other letters from Chet Walker are stored in binders on my closet shelf.

One three-ring binder is full of letters written home when Dad was in Panama during World War II, and another thick notebook holds love letters to Mom written while he worked "doodlebuggin'" for Western

Geophysical, an oil exploration job that paid little and took him away for weeks at a time. He was the father of seven by then and married nearly twenty years, but he still called Mom *Darling* or *Sweetheart* and signed his letters *Peabody*, a private name she'd given him. Once when she called him that, little brother Dave said, "Don't call my daddy PEA POTTY!"

Several times a week, he sat and wrote of his day, his work, and sometimes his frustrations. Mostly he was a writer looking outward not in, rarely reflecting on the man behind the pen, writing more about what he saw than what he felt.

In my first letter, I was writing to Grandpa Walker, who I called Papaw. I find it interesting that the rest of the siblings wrote to both him and Grandma, but I wrote only to Papaw. We had a special bond that was closer than others in the family, as if we shared more than the Walker lineage that made us soul mates. Bonds like that happen in big families; two people come together a little closer than the rest of the tribe. I am like that with my sister Amy, bound in a way that is stronger than the obligations of being family.

Papaw had been a farmer most of his life, and he grew up not knowing how to read until his wife taught him after they were married. As a young man he cooked for a railroad crew and got nicknamed Pus because the previous cook was named something like Pusowki, and his nickname was passed to the next cook. Pus Walker chewed Red Man tobacco and spit into a coffee can. By the time we left Ohio, he was retired to fishing and raising chickens and night crawlers. I think he got sick that same summer we left, but neither of my sisters can help me remember anything about that. I have always thought we were a lot alike, Papaw and I, though I have little on which to base that except the warm feelings I still get when I look at his photo, and he looks right back at me. As I age, I look more like him with a long head covered in thick hair and a hawk nose leading the face into the future. From stories my mother told, I figure he loved a good laugh and took what life served him. I have to think that he must have shown some extra special love to me for such feelings to carry on across the years and miles.

After we left Sugar Tree Ridge, I saw him again in 1962 when he and Grandma drove the Alcan and spent part of the summer with us. I made sure he had a coffee can to spit tobacco juice into when he came, and I don't recall that I ever let him out of my sight the entire time they were here. Even with that small amount of time in my life, he was my Papaw, a big tender man with a nose and a sense of humor to match my own.

Papaw came again when we buried Dad. With all the letter writing, I think they were closer than many dads and sons. To this day, it makes me ache to think that this man had to bury both of his sons, and I am glad it was one pain that my own father never had to experience. I remember Papaw and me sitting together in the basement of the Methodist Church full of the people pot-lucking after Dad's funeral. We sat on the cold metal folding chairs picking at our plates of casserole and cobbler, like men on a riverbank without a boat watching the current of people swirling past us. I was eleven years old, and it is the first time that I remember experiencing empathy, truly sharing someone else's feelings. Amid the rattle of plates and platters and the prattle of mourners, we were both as forlorn and out of place at that moment as any two guys could be. I knew then that we shared a common vacancy, and it was so distinct that I will never lose that feeling, nor would I want to.

Ten

Coho salmon (*Oncorhynchus kisutch*): Anadromous fish of the North Pacific salmon stocks. Also known as silver salmon, prized as a sport fish with acrobatic fighting style; fished commercially; thick body with silver scales. Secondary protein source for sourdoughs, cheechakos, bears, and gourmets.

Dad was a literate man who liked to work with his hands and that is something I have in common with him. He loved to read, and now I know that he wrote a good letter, but put a broken vehicle in his hands or show him a stand of timber, and he really shined. I enjoy that kind of balance in my own life. To work with the brain at my desk in the morning and then be physically active out in my yard in the afternoon is a good day for me. I'm not the mechanic he was, but I can build a house and fix most of things that break, from water lines to snowblowers.

    I need to be active whether I am chopping and stacking firewood, working a building project, or burning trash. It calms my mind and clarifies my thinking. A man can get a lot of thinking done when his hands are busy measuring, cutting, and fitting boards to build something, and if a fellow thinks real hard at it, the mind is too busy to be fretting.

    Some of this "thinking when I'm not thinking" helps me see the man in Dad's letters, often long after I lay the letters down. When I back away for a time, I can see him out of the corner of my eye, like when you drop a tiny screw in the gravel of the yard and you try looking at the ground sideways not straight on because that's often how things catch your eye.

    First, I must see what is easy to see, to know the known. He was an airplane mechanic in the war, and since then he had spent a lot of time with his head under the hood of a car, sometimes because he had to, but a lot of times by choice. In that way we are different. I would just as soon work with wood or cook than work on an engine. Brother Bill was real handy with machinery and Tom too, but once I open the hood of a car it is nothing but dirty drudgery. Dad spent a lot of time in our two-car garage the last couple of years before he died. He built one bay to park the station wagon. Another bay was for working on cars, for my brothers to keep their jalopies running and for bailing them out when they got in over their heads. I am jealous of those times my brothers had, those times that letters and photo albums can't replace.

Fortunately, Dad had his mechanic skills to lean on when he went looking for work. Even though he was doing his own building, a cabin took money, and there were school clothes to buy as well as the staples like gas and flour and coffee. Dad had to figure out how to build a tight cabin and stock up on firewood before snowfall, hunt and fish for food, and work enough to pay the bills. It was interesting to read about opening a garage in a hardscrabble homestead community where most everyone was in the same boat. I'm sure there was a need for his talents, but was there money to pay for them?

Peggy and I pose with Dad and Bill inside the first rows of logs that begin to shape the cabin.

August 13, 1958

Dear Pop and Mom,

Wed night mail goes out tomorrow so we will try to answer all our letters. Wrote some last night, will finish tonight. You asked about the kids' school. They will all go to Ninilchik 8 miles. They will have to walk out to the bus, it is a mile out to the lane but not half as far across country. It starts September 2nd.

The well will be walled with boards halfway down. The rest is just like concrete and won't need wall. The top 4 feet is real loose from then on it's like rock. The well is on one end of the cellar and both will be under the house.

I have been fishing a few times, caught two. I seen three fellows yesterday carry out 6 silver salmon all over 18 inches long. They come in with the tides sometime, lots come in other times none. You have to fish with the tides right now around noon is the best "I hear." There is sure fish here and you can catch them if you are there at the right time. It takes time and know how.

Tom and I cut trees Monday then it rained Tuesday til about 4:30. So I went work hunting. Found a garage in Ninilchik that no one is working. The man who owns it has a service station and store next door so I am going to try getting some cars to grease and repair and make grocery money. It's a cinch, it won't come walking in the door, you have to go out and get it. Work up here is very scarce. The road work and such just hasn't been for two years I guess. There is no garage for 20 mi. either way, also its next door to the post office and school house so there will be some traffic all winter so I try it a while? I won't be out much, only time, and I have plenty of that. Guess that's the news for now will let Briar finish if she can think of anything.

Briar: Chet has a sore wrist so writing is sort of a job for him right now. He sprained it or bruised it a little or something. He may have done it lifting coal. He's been gathering coal down on the beach. They aim to use it to heat the shop this winter. Also brought some home to us. It's free, you know, and you can get just as large a piece as you can pick up to as big as the side of a hill. And you know Chet. All kidding aside, the hill that overlooks the Inlet is nearly solid coal. There is a falls where Happy valley Creek runs out to sea and all the way down water runs over coal. It's scattered all over the beach.

We had fried chicken (spruce) for supper and it was really yummy. We had four and they made plenty. I didn't save the ribs, neck, wings and back. They *are nothing but bone, but you should see the breast. Got a couple of these this evening toward tomorrow night. Sure good.—Love Always, Briar.*

The Walkers made a lot of meals from the spruce grouse that populated our woods. The meat tends to be dark, even the breast meat, and old birds or those taken in the winter can be tough and strongly flavored with spruce needles, but a young bird is a real treat in the hands of a capable cook. And Briar Walker, with her barefoot Kentucky roots, could take about any kind of meat laid on her new kitchen table and make a tasty meal of it.

The spruce grouse is the most common upland game bird of south central Alaska and has many names: spruce hen, spruce chicken, spruce grouse, fool hen, but officially, *Falcipennis canadensis*. It looks much like the ptarmigan, its cousin of the tundra and mountain willow thickets, but it hasn't the need to change wardrobe in the winter. It spends the entire year in a feather coat of brown and black with white accents. The spruce grouse is a forager, making its nest on the ground and scenting its meat with the needles of the spruce tree. Their need to gather gravel off the roads for their gizzards made them easy targets for young Walkers with guns or even rocks.

I once brought one home alive. I spotted it on the lane where the grouse come down to pick up gravel to put grit in their craw. When I went to investigate, the bird just walked away slowly, and I was able to walk up to it and scoop it into my arms. I know now that this was probably a mother hen protecting her little ones and putting herself in harm's way as a decoy. It got my attention and lead me away from its brood and then, as wild critters often do, froze as if camouflaged, and I was able to pick it up and tromp off back home to present my prize to my mother.

I don't recall if we ate the bird I caught or turned her loose, but considering my mom's respect for such things, she probably sent me back to turn my prisoner loose where I found her. Mom would have been more interested in harvesting the hen's brood when they were cooking size than braising up a tough, old hen.

With my brothers shooting "chickens" and Dad finally getting at the fish, the Walkers were living pretty high off the hog. We didn't have many meals of store-bought meat except for bacon, hot dogs, and bologna. Even they were rare treats served sparingly. We arrived too late in the year to start a garden, so Mom gathered wild plants and berries to put fresh greens on the table. It must have been hard thinking that they would have to wait a full year to be harvesting from our own garden. Until then we thrived on wild meat and fish, home-baked bread, canned goods, and Mom's "rabbit food."

The Walkers' weather reports from this year don't make you want to rush to the Kenai Peninsula in August, not unless you're testing raingear. Weather archives support their claim that the sunny days were few and far between. I don't envy Dad and Tom digging down into the earth in that mess. Foundation work is hard enough without water running down your back and mud clogging everything.

I don't remember a rainy childhood in Happy Valley, although I do recall many cloudy days with a cool wind blowing off Cook Inlet. The air chilled by the adjacent sea creates an onshore wind that runs up the inlet over the bluff. That wind is cooler as mid-August portents the coming of fall, a coming that is a lot earlier in the north latitudes than we experienced in Ohio. Fall is gathering and hunting time here as elsewhere, but rather than the crisp, colorful fall common to most of North America, in southern Alaska, the fall season is usually wet and early. The coolness of fall and the dense foliage of the forest conspire to collect and hold water. Yesterday's rain and last night's dew hang on the grass and bushes, and the woods dry so slowly that even warm sunny days can be wet, making hunting season notoriously soggy.

Fall moose hunters generally wear raingear or hip boots in this water-filled land of streams, ponds, lakes, and muskeg. It's hard to keep feet dry when walking across spongy moss that blurs the distinction between land and water, but the long-legged moose is well built for traveling and foraging in just such country, so the hunter must follow.

A lot of anticipation preceded moose hunting season, especially after the Walkers had grown to value moose meat as a happy replacement for our farm-raised beef and pork. We had tasted the Alaskan beef and found it lean and hearty, not as "wild" or "gamey" as some venison is known to be. Modern science tells us that with moose you get healthy red meat that is lean, natural, and nutrient laden. In 1958 we just liked the way it tasted.

Fifteen-year-old Tom was jittery at the prospect of shooting a moose. He was eleven years older than me, so it is hard for me to think of him as the gawky wide-eyed teenager that came to life in these letters. He has always been a grownup in my mind, so I am stunned by his voice as I read this letter reminiscent of Tom Sawyer or the teenage Travis of *Old Yeller*. If I had written this letter as part of a novel, it would seem too contrived and clichéd with words like "yonder" and "doggonest," but here it is pure and raw. Within the timbre of language from this young man two months short of sixteen, we get the wild wonder of all that he has clearly embraced.

August 17, 1958

Dear Grampa and Grandma,
Thought I would break down and write after all. I am going hunting Wednesday, "Legally" with Al Sanborn and Glen Veator, don't hope to get anything myself. But I can help them and get some winter meat.

Dad has got a job finally. I don't know if he told you or not he is running a garage in the big city. He has been there since Wednesday and has two cars in there tore down now.

Boy Danny is big stuff. He saw a cow and calf moose the other evening out in front of the "house." Boy that calf was the doggonest lookin' thing, it had ears that look like a full grown mule and hump the size of a basketball.

Me and Mom have been working our tails off this week. We have been working over yonder digging holes for pilings and cutting wood. I guess I cut about cord yesterday. Our well is sure rough on mice. Every morning there is at least 3 in the well.

I was over to Bell's this afternoon till seven. They have a boy just about my age. He has been working for a commercial fisherman this summer. I think me and him are going to build a 17 foot dory this winter. "I think!"

Well we'll close for now, Tom PS Please excuse the writing.

I was always told that Tom came to Alaska kicking and screaming, protesting his exile in an Arctic wasteland, far from a life of baseball, dates, and FFA. For all intents and purposes, leaving Ohio was forever, and there would be no jumping onto a plane next summer for a visit back home. Two months later, he was won over as if the sheer adventure of it all had worn down his resolve to be miserable.

Late in life Tom was struck down by Alzheimer's, so he couldn't answer my questions about how he felt back then. And I am such a fool that I didn't ask when I had the chance. I wanted to know more about Dad, and I lived for years just miles from a man who got to grow up with him, who worked side by side with him on the cabin, who overhauled cars and learned to swear and joke with him. And now it's too late to sit at his table and say, "So tell me about Dad. What was he like?"

Ironically, the last coherent months that Tom wandered around his house, half lost, would have been the perfect time to ask him these questions. Like many in this stage of Alzheimer's, the past is the clearest part of his life. While he couldn't store recent memories, old ones were vivid and fresh. In his last years Tom talked mostly about Ohio and the people back there and of his boyhood. I was too much the fool not to get him talking about Dad. He would have loved it as much as me, and my regrets for lost opportunities linger long and are hard to shake.

It would have been rich to retrace our steps together, the eager teenager and the wide-eyed child, walking back through Tom's memory unshadowed by the present. Can anyone really recall, with or without a failing mind, not only the memories but the feelings from over fifty years in the past? I should have tried to find out.

I know Tom didn't have the same romantic recollections of our homestead years that I did, but he took a lot of pride from what he helped to build in that clearing in Happy Valley. Just like the teenage boy recounting his first moose hunt, Tom never lost the thrill of the chase, even though moose hunting is a sport that many people find more work than pleasure. I also know that when he left to join the army, he never looked back (so he said), and he never wanted to go to the woods and build his own place. Tom left behind things like canned salmon, firewood, and hand-me-downs.

"Kinda lost my taste for it," he told me once. "It all just lost its appeal."

Eleven

Sockeye salmon (*Oncorhynchus nerka*): Also known as red salmon, prized as a commercial fish of high quality and value, a staple of personal-use fishing in Alaska and Canada. Another major protein source for sourdoughs, cheechakos, bears, and gourmets.

In an old leather satchel that was Dad's, I found check stubs and a farm record book where he recorded his work and farm sales. In Ohio he never made as much as two dollars per hour. His notes are short and mostly numbers that I couldn't quite quantify, but I could see that he kept detailed records of farm income and expenses, and once he arrived in Alaska he did the same, leaving me stacks of receipts for nails, fuel, and groceries.

In that same satchel was a magazine-sized booklet from the Department of Agriculture entitled *Farming in Alaska* and another from the University of Alaska called *Land Occupancy, Ownership and Use on Homesteads in Alaska's Kenai Peninsula, 1955*. Both of these publications suggested a rosy future for farming in Alaska, but the numbers were pretty bleak for the years 1950 to 1955. In 1955 only about 2 percent of the homestead land on the Kenai was being farmed, and almost half of the land with homestead claims was left unoccupied.

Dad's sense of numbers and pragmatic thinking surely brought him to the same conclusion I made after reviewing these booklets. Farming the Kenai was only successful for a few people in prime locations, most homesteaders weren't farming, and trying to raise cash crops would be a good way to go broke. The Walkers didn't need to travel four thousand miles to live hand-to-mouth on a farm. One reason they left fertile, temperate

Ohio was because they couldn't make a living farming. Why would one think farming remote land at sixty degrees latitude would be a better bet?

Dad had researched Alaskan homesteading, looked over the prospects when we arrived, and decided that this was not a place to farm. I know this because he only filed on 40 acres instead of 160. If he had plans for farming, he would have filed on much more than that. I think Dad must have figured his other skills were a lot more valuable in Alaska than his knowledge of farming. It comes to me that he'd rather be turning tools than farming, so that's what he tried to do.

Today when one looks at the Kenai Peninsula, it's obvious Dad made the right choice. Fishing is a much bigger part of the economy than farming. A few farms on good ground raise hay and livestock for local use and a lot of folks keep fowl, rabbits, goats, and horses, but the land is not as rich as it would need to be for farming, the summer is short and cool, and the market is small or distant. We did well with gardens to put up turnips, cabbage, and potatoes, and hardy chickens can be raised economically just about anywhere, but an Alaska farm was never to be.

With farming out of the question, I wondered why Dad didn't make a stab at commercial fishing. Commercial fishing was in transition at the time because fish traps had just been outlawed, and many homesteaders who came to the Kenai to farm became fisherfolk instead. The fish trap was basically a corral of nets and poles that trapped the fish in a maze as they charged into the mouth of their birth stream or along the shore. These were replaced by fisherman using nets from the beach or off boats to gillnet salmon. You only have to read a couple of Dad's letters to know he liked sport fishing, but he never explored that option for making a living. If he did, it was never part of his letters or conversations passed down through the family's oral history. All three of my brothers ended up working in fishing during their high school summers, but not Dad. With a cabin to build, maybe he didn't see time for learning a new skill set and maybe that was enough. Sadly, Dad would end up working far from home for low pay, depriving his family of his last years so he could put something other than moose meat or salmon on the table. Again, a question that I would like to ask Dad, but I fear it will go unanswered.

August 17, 1958

Dear Pop and Mom,

Sunday afternoon again and letter writing time. Seems like I forget something every time I write that I meant to tell. We'll see how I get along this time. Did you get the letter when I ask about the starter? I'd sure like to get one started. Several others up here would too. Danny says to tell you, I didn't tell you he got new shoes, high ones with hooks like Papaw's. Also he looked out the window the other evening and said, "Daddy, there's a cow moose." Sure enough there was a cow and calf. No farther from the window than from your side window to the board fence.

We are all fine here and it's still raining off and on. Sure slows cabin work up. Tom and I got the holes dug for pilings (for foundation). Also Tom and the others of us worked up about 10 trees Saturday. Chet cut them down before he went to the shop; just mowed down a row of them in about 15 minutes before he left for the garage. So Tom used the chainsaw and blocked them up. Mike & I trimmed them, and I burned the brush. Bill and Mike and Amy carried and ricked the wood. We really enlarged the clearing. The trees were not large enough for lumber but we sure have a pile of wood.

I think Chet told you about his garage deal. He's doing a little now. He gets $5.00 an hour when he works so it adds up pretty fast. Moose (and all big game) season opens Wednesday, so there should be traffic for a while. And up where there's traffic there's flat tires aplenty.

I meant to tell you the other day. There are two books that really tell about the country here and Homesteading, if you could get them: (1) Wilderness Homesteaders by Ethel Cavanaugh published by Caxton Printers, Caldwell Idaho; (2) Go North, Young Man by Gordon Stoddard, published by Binfords and Mort, Portland Oregon.

The first one is really the best and more true to life. The other one though is written about this area right here. The man's place is only 6-7 miles from here. However, he's sort of a smart aleck drunk, so we didn't like his book as well but it sure gives a lot of good pictures & maps & and descriptions. Well I guess this all for now. Maybe Chet will scratch a few lines when he comes in.

Love always,
Briar

Well, I came home and brought four cans of salmon, two smoked and two just canned (for free). I tore down a Jeep this afternoon, a fisherman ran without oil. It needs all new bearings and new crankshaft. So it ought to be a pretty good job. Also have a '57 Plymouth to fit a new radiator on as soon as it comes for it. Guess I'll get a little work at least. Still rains nearly every day guess it will till it snows. Tom is all hepped up to go moose hunting Wednesday. Since he is not sixteen he can go without license. I can't see $50.00 for license. I'll hunt illegal. It tastes just as good anyway. I hope he gets one anyway. My fishing is not any good. I never get there at the right time. It goes by the tides unless you go way back inland. Guess that is the story —

Bye now
Chet.

More than moose, more than bears, and more even than razor clams, salmon was the richest animal resource of the region. Cook Inlet and the streams that flow into it are a breeding ground and nursery for salmon, and of all the predators that chase it, humans are most successful. In fact, humans had learned to harvest salmon with near perfect efficiency with the fish trap, and until 1958, that method was at work on the streams of the Kenai. Since the fishermen knew where the fish were going, and that place was the mouth of the river, the trap was pretty simple. Commercial fish traps have killed off the salmon runs in many streams of the Pacific coast, which is part of the reason that they were banned in Alaska starting in 1958.

Being from Ohio, we didn't know much about the ocean or the fish in it, so the life cycle of the salmon was a peculiar one to us. We learned that these fish spend a life of several years at sea and then return to their birth stream to spawn and die. As a result, the streams and rivers of Cook Inlet are inundated with returning salmon populations every year. All summer long, starting in mid-May, at least one of the five species of salmon is making its way back into the Anchor River, Deep Creek, and Ninilchik River. The migration starts with king, or chinook salmon, and, as the name suggests, these are the biggest and richest of the five. Red, or sockeye, salmon is rich in oil and is the most plentiful, making it the bread-and-butter catch of the inlet. Humpback, or pink, salmon are easy prey, but they are smaller and less flavorful than the other salmon. The salmon season continues through September with chum salmon, called dogs because they were often dried for dogfood, and late arriving silvers, or coho. This giant delivery of protein supported the Dena'ina villages and the Russians long before the homesteaders came, and it still feeds families and pays wages today.

With the demise of the fish trap came the age of gillnet fishing in Cook Inlet. This fishery uses nets that hang vertically in the water and trap the fish by the gills as they try to swim through it. Fisherman work nets anchored off the beach from beach sites or drift in the deeper water using boats. Many of my friends were children of fisherman, so I got to spend time at some beach sites where families fished for salmon and lived a setnet lifestyle. My brothers were old enough to be paid hands at beach sites, really getting their hands dirty as fisherman; I only got to visit.

Life at a beach site was roughing it in a way so wild that even the clock was ignored. Once they moved down the bluff to the beach, the fisherfolk's life followed the six-hour cycle of the tides, and they could be working, eating, or sleeping at any time of day or night. I was amazed one day when we visited a fishing family at their beach cabin. They lay abed asleep in the middle of the day. That was something I had never seen before—adults sleeping in the bright noon of a summer day. The fisherman's shelter was a tarpaper shack or a canvas wall tent set on driftwood logs at the base of the bluff. Water came from springs that trickled down the bluff or was dipped from shallow pits dug into the beach and filled by springs that ran down to the saltwater below the gravel beach surface. An outhouse was the only toilet.

The tide set the pace for life on the beach. Nets were tended at slack tide when the power of the Cook Inlet tides weren't pulling at them, a tug-of-war the fisherman couldn't win. The tide changed regularly, flooding for about six hours, then ebbing for about the same. The nearly constant motion of the tide loaded the nets with surprises like broken crabs, jellyfish, or even the occasional whale. The waves and tide worked the beach so that it changed every day and it stank of faraway places.

Fishermen and their helpers went out in wooden skiffs to pick fish from nets set offshore, while youngsters like me would pick fish from beach nets that were tethered to big stakes far up the beach and went dry at low tide. Fisherman wrestled the salmon from the nets and then dropped them into the bottom of the skiff. When the boats came in to the beach, the salmon were offloaded into the wooden bins and covered with wetted burlap. Each day, a big six-by-six truck, a veteran of World War II, would moan slowly down the beach and stop by the fish bin. We could hear it coming from a long way off as it growled through the sand and gravel and stopped at each site. The driver and the fisherman would toss the fish into the truck box with spiked poles called pews, counting as they went. Then the truck crawled along through the loose beach gravel and moved on down the beach to more sites and eventually to the cannery.

Once when we visited a setnet site I helped an older boy who was sent to walk the shore and look for fish washed out of the net. I found two bright fish at the tide line that were too weak to escape in the saltwater. I brought them back proudly and the fisherman gave me two silver dollars. When Dad protested, he said, "That's what they are worth." It was even more of a reason to like the salty fish smell of a setnetter's life with the fish hitting the nets that stretched out from the shore with only their corks visible, making a dotted line across the rolling surf. When fish swam into the net, a big V might form in that line or it might disappear below the surface as they dragged it down. Sometimes, fish struck right at the cork line where they would flash and dance in the sun as they struggled to free themselves.

I wanted my Dad to be a fisherman, so we could spend most of the summer at the beach like other kids. The waves and tide sorted the sand and gravel and delivered logs, fish, and trash; it swept the beach one day and took it away the next. I envied my brothers who were old enough to live that life each summer and come home smelling of the beach.

August 20, 1958

Dear Folks,
Chet is doing some at the garage now. He did two little jobs less than a day and half of work and he made as much as week at the Farm Bureau. But of course some days he doesn't have anything, only maybe change a tire or

maybe even nothing at all. He got up early this am to help Tom go after a load of wood he's hauling up to Clam Gulch (twenty-five miles) for Mr. Trent. Before he started working, Chet hauled some of it for him himself. Tom is to go moose hunting with a couple of men today. He & Mike went yesterday. Only saw one legal bull, and Tom had buck fever so bad he missed two shots. When he came home he could have walked under a duck with his hat on. We went down to Whiskey Gulch last eve to get pilings to put under the house. They are fir, soaked in salt water and heavy as lead. Don't think they weren't a job. Bill and I helped and of course, Chet and Tom laughed at us, but they didn't tell us they didn't need us, so there.

Got another good deal too. The man who owns the garage runs the grocery and gas station there. He will order groceries and we can have them wholesale and pay the freight. We have been having quite a bit of fried (spruce) chicken. I have been deep frying them and they are really good. Also, a neighbor gave us some smoked salmon. It's quite a treat for change. Sort of like home smoked ham. I am sending for some more winter doodads to Sears. Long johns all around and long red and blue socks for me and the girls. We picked blueberries enough for eight pints of jam Monday. We don't care too much for them plain but like jam. Well must close for now.

Love always,
Briar

August 24, 1958

Dear Folks,

Just got in and ate a bite. Had well stayed home but never can tell. I am still trying to get the garage on a paying basis. Have had some small jobs and a Jeep tore down now to put in a new block. That is the best job I've had; anyway I am staying even, not losing anything.

Now as to the cellar, it and the well will be under the house, at the west end right under the kitchen. The big room will be 20 x 14 kitchen, living room, dining room and the girls bunks. The cabin will be about 50 feet or so off the road. with some trees in front and within twenty or forty feet all around. The flues up here for the most part is roof jacks a galvanized plate nailed over a hole in the roof. And the stove pipe goes inside the bottom and more stove pipe on the outside above guyed with wire. Once in awhile you see a chimney, not often.

There is very little farming did here; one dairy herd about 15 miles from here. Then a few on down around Homer. They raise gardens and truck patches for their own use and that's it. Cows are practically unheard of and only a few have goats. Grain cost $7 to $8.00 a hundred. There is only one bunch of chickens around here. People clear the ground they have to and sow oats to prove up and there it lays from there on. There is not much market for the things you can raise. The road is too rough to haul anything to Anchorage. The road is to be paved soon, was to have been done this year but up to now it hasn't. I have seen three horses and mules here and they were turned out on range. Most of the "farming" is done with garden tractors, hoes, and big tractors, caterpillar and wheel type. No we haven't got Danny a dog team yet. They eat too much. Guess that's it for now. Will try to answer more questions when we get your next letter. Happy birthday Pop as ever, Chet

August 24, 1958

Dear Grandma,

We are putting in pilings now on the house. How are you I am fine. I am having fun in Alaska. Peggy's kitten plays with our toes when we eat breakfast dinner and supper. I thank you for the barrettes. Tell Grandpa I said hello to him. Tell him I hope grandpa is not very sick. Us kids take turns getting pancakes. Danny has a Blazo box, a Blazo box is what gasoline for irons and lites (comes in). Daddy has another Blazo box out in the tent for Peggy.

Daddy got two big fish and we threw the heads out by the backhouse and when Daddy went to the backhouse before he went to bed a bear got it. Good-by Amy

Blazo was a brand of white gas and the name became generic for all white gas in Alaska (and the wooden boxes that fuel came in). The white gas, fuel for gas lanterns and camp stoves, came in five-gallon metal cans. The fuel is volatile and the cans were thin skinned, so for security they were packed in wooden boxes, two cans per box. In 1958 Dad paid $6.61

for a box with two cans of Blazo, working out at about 66 cents a gallon. The cans, of course, were also used for everything from gas cans to water pails or even cobbled into temporary woodstoves. Roofs, car fenders, and tractor hoods were patched with flattened cans, and some handy fellows would construct makeshift stovepipes with them.

Amy treated the Blazo box like it was some treasured find, and in a way it was, a homesteader's treasure of many uses. The box was comparable to today's ubiquitous five-gallon plastic bucket. Blazo boxes became book or kitchen shelves when nailed to a wall, served as wood boxes, and became vegetable bins for the root cellar. Some folks took the boxes apart to build furniture, dish racks, and tool caddies from the smooth, light wood. For a kid, the Blazo box became a dollhouse, a garage for a toy truck, or a table for art projects. Many bedrooms never had nicer end tables than the Blazo box. I used mine as a pulpit when I preached to my sisters in my child's play church, and the boxes were desks when my sisters took turns teaching school. This inspired Mom and the girls to use Blazo boxes to build a writing desk out of three of the boxes. Nailed together, then shaped and painted—turquoise is the color I recall—this piece of furniture served many good years in useful service at the homestead and was discovered by my own children thirty years later.

Last summer I found some wooden fuel boxes at a garage sale. On the end of one, the bright chevron logo and the words *Chevron White Gas* was still clear, and another was labeled as aviation gas. The guy had a bunch of them, and his shop, a throwback to fifty years ago, was lined with shelves and bins made from disassembled Blazo boxes. I had to take three home just for nostalgia, two ended up as bedroom end tables in our guest cabin. Every time I see them they remind me of another time when a used wooden box was something to be treasured.

Twelve

King salmon (*Oncorhynchus tshawytscha*): Largest of the salmon family, commonly weighing over thirty pounds and as large as ninety pounds. Black spots on tail and upper body. Prized as a trophy or meat fish with rich, oily flesh. Also known as chinook, or can filler.

August 24, 1958

Dear Grandma and Grandpa —
I'll start out answering questions; this is best way to find out anything. We don't know what you wonder about otherwise. We are all fine. We have been ever since we got here. Yes, we got the Lynchburg News and enjoyed it a lot but it sure did cost you enough to send them didn't it? I think we may have told you but maybe not. We got the girls' barrettes last Thursday, Aug 21. Seems that was a pretty big 50 cents worth. Thanks a lot. We aim to take care of them. They should last a long time. Peggy is wearing pigtails now and looks real neat. It sure makes a change in her looks. I had a time finding ribbons but finally did, first black and white Grosgrain. It's the best kind.
It is about one and a half miles across the muskeg to where we are building. That is how we go when we walk. When we drive it is about four miles. The kids will go to Ninilchik School. That is about 8 miles from our homestead. If we stay here they will walk to the road about a mile and catch the school bus and ride ten miles. If we get the cabin up, they will walk 1000 feet to the road and catch the bus and ride about eight miles. Tom will get his last year right here at Ninilchik. They start a week from Tuesday, the day after Labor Day.
We went up to register the kids last week and they have a grand school building. It was built in 1951. Has all the newest designs and features. All new and modern material. And is even so much better equipped than any of the

schools around home. The govt built this you see, not bond issue or such so they spared no expense. It is really nice.

I canned seven quarts of salmon this week. One fish made a BIG mess for us and seven quarts to can. The two cost us $1.00. When you got no time to fish that is pretty cheap eating, we figure. Want to get more this week. Also want Tom to get us another moose to can. I personally have my mouth set for bear meat, but we'll have to see.

No it has not stopped raining and probably won't until the snow flies. Heard someone say there had been a light touch of frost on the beach and don't doubt it. It's been pretty nippy here mornings. You ought to see the potatoes and turnips up here. They are unbelievable. Well I am about to run down so will close for now.

Answer soon.

Briar

P.S. We and two other families on this road now have home telephones. We can only talk to each other but would be a help in sickness. They are old army field phones and have flashlight batteries and a crank.

August on the Kenai is salmon time, and Mom was up to her elbows. If I do the math, seven quarts of salmon is about fourteen pounds, and if we ate salmon for dinner that night, she would have used another four pounds easily. This was probably a twenty-pound king salmon she was butchering and packing while feeding and tending kids, doing laundry, and baking bread. Salmon do tend to arrive home in large bunches, and anyone processing them is generally looking at spending the day with pound upon pound of bright pink meat on a silver skin. Within twenty-four hours the fish needed to be scaled, gutted, butchered, and either canned, frozen, eaten, or smoked. Mom spent a lot time in the summer putting up food, and much of it she had never seen before.

Putting up salmon was a skill she had to learn fast, and guided by neighbors and her *Kerr Canning Book*, she figured it out. Already she could butcher any animal from a quail to a steer and fit it in a canning jar or cook pot. I'm sure the first razor clams she ever saw, cleaned, canned, or cooked were that summer in 1958. She was a quick study, and clams, available at low tide once a month, were a consistent food source for us. She also fried or braised snowshoe hare, spruce chicken, and even porcupine, which is tastier than one would imagine.

One of her favorite things was to wander the woods collecting edible plants that she made into salads or steamed or sautéed. Our forest was carpeted with a variety of fast-growing, succulent greens, and Mom made good use of them. Some of these plants were edible by her definition but not by her kids'. "Rabbit food," my brothers called them. From this forest salad bowl, I learned to enjoy wild cucumber, a tender plant that grows with a fat single shoot that tastes very much like cucumber. As it grows it makes a good salad green and eventually produces watermelon berries, only good for eating raw. She collected the sprouts of fireweed and fiddleheads, the coiled sprouts of ferns. And even a bland tasteless green called miner's lettuce. She fed us wilted dandelion greens and steamed nettles, which were never tasty for me. Although they were plentiful, I don't remember Mom bringing back mushrooms from her forest ramblings; she must not have seen them as worth the gamble of killing one of us with a wrong taxonomy.

Mom made bread, rolls, and noodles from scratch and soap from lye and animal fat. She sewed, knitted, mended, crocheted, darned, and embroidered any manner of cloth goods from curtains to dress shirts. We put our heads on pillowcases made from flour sacks and decorated with embroidery. We stood off winter's chill with wool quilts that warmed us with a weight like the earth itself.

By the time my brothers and sisters were picky teenagers, Mom was looking at pictures in catalogs and copying the latest fashions for teens on her Singer treadle sewing machine. Bulky Cowichan sweaters with the rolled collars and pictures of wildlife knitted in them were all the rage, and she knitted these to order for cash. She did make one for me of dark brown with a mountain and a canoe on it. With a lining cut down from a cast-off coat, that sweater became my winter coat for as long as I could fit into it. Mom knitted mittens and socks as she read aloud from Hawthorne or Dickens with the book spread on her lap beneath the clattering needles. As she read I was often seated at her feet rolling skeins of yarn into manageable balls.

Even in a dry cabin without electricity, amid all that flurry of labor, my mother always wore a dress, whether working in the garden or hauling brush. Come evening, she'd don a clean apron, brush her hair, and dab on some lipstick before Dad came in for supper. Mom carried delicate white hankies in her purse, if for no other purpose than to give a spit bath to any of her children who needed a touch-up before walking into the sanctuary. Mom always said, "It's no sin to be poor, and some folks can't help it, but you don't have to be poor white trash."

Growing up poor, my mom had learned some of the telltales that proud poor people learned to hide. She learned early that poor people who knew proper English, dressed neatly, had good manners, and were clean could walk about the world like they had a ticket to the big show. She was right, so right that she even fooled her own kids. I was a teenager before I knew that we were poor back then and for a long time after as well.

For most of that time spent in Happy Valley, we were living hand-to-mouth, what folks now call a subsistence lifestyle. What we didn't gather ourselves, Mom or Dad traded for. We were living off the land and the sweat of our brow—although I doubt my brow had much to offer. Most of what capital we had we brought from Ohio, and the proof is in the reading of how every dollar was carefully spent. The foods we bought were staples like flour, sugar, oatmeal, and coffee. There was rice, macaroni, and spaghetti on the list and canned vegetables by the case as well as fruit cocktail, pears, and pie apples. The rest came out of the sea, the sand, or from the forest beyond.

Never having much is a good way to learn the value of things. We were poor, but we lived well in spite of it because Mom made sure we knew that comfort and joy came from energy and effort more than from material things. It is as if the material world mattered, but more for its lack than its plenty; those who have little, value what they do have.

Thirteen

Pushki (*Heracleum maximum*): The only member of the genus *Heracleum* native to America; endangered in Kentucky; also known as cow parsnip; annual plant that grows four feet tall or more with large leaves. The sap will cause blisters on skin when exposed to sunlight; traditionally used for medicine, food, and toy swords.

Besides his tools and a talent for fixing and building, Dad had one powerful asset, the two-ton truck with a stake bed on the back and dual rear tires. In this truck we moved all our gear and much of Butlers' up the highway. Once we settled at Happy Valley, Dad used the truck to make money or trade services for hauling coal, fuel, lumber, or anything else in the area. Everything we bought was a long way away, and not many people had a rig that size.

Unfortunately, Dad was partnered with Tom Butler on this truck, and he had to square with him, and the only way to do that was to sell the truck. That truck could have been the start of a freighting business or at least a way to put money in his pocket while he built the house. I just want to sit him down—I realize he would be younger than I am now—and say, "Listen. You love driving that truck, and you've made some good money already with it. Do a little advertising and put a For Hire sign on the door. Don't sell it. Let Tom Butler wait for his money." I wonder if Mom gave him the same argument.

August 27, 1958

Dear Folks,
Well P. M., The mails goes tomorrow so will answer your letter we got Monday. You no doubt will get two at once as we missed the mailman Monday.

He went a little early. They don't stick to the schedule very close. The mailman here drives a big covered truck and hauls freight at the same time. He will bring a 50# bag of flour from Homer for 50 cents. He hauls bread to the stores along the way.

We are all fine, not much new. Tom has been cutting some wood and they all went and picked blueberries this morning. Haven't hit a lick on the cabin this week. Monday afternoon I started to put a new block in a Jeep. Got it ready for the pan and the flywheel. On the way home I met a fellow who lives the next cabin out. He said he needs to talk to me, to meet him back at his cabin. That was all he said, I couldn't imagine what he wanted. I went back to his place and met him. He said I have a couple of days work for you down at Homer, with the truck he thought they would pay $9.50 to $10 an hour. I sure went down, worked 14½ hours, $145.00 burned $8.00 worth of gas. How is that for two days? I sure could use more of that. They pay $3.80 an hour for common labor.

We had two nice days in a row it only rained a little dab here today it didn't rain at all down at Homer. I hauled lumber and mill work for a house from the dock then hauled two loads on a mountain north of Homer about nine miles, five miles was like Fort Ancient Hill, low gear all the way. You never seen anything like the scenery. On one side was hillside with some cleared fields and a little timber, some houses. On the other side you can see clear across Kachemak Bay to the mountains and see glaciers and snow. On top I seen my first hog since we got here and some cows. Fenced fields. I seen a small field of oats cut and shocked.

Also I seen crab fishing boats come in. They had a pile that looked about the size of a 100 bushel pile of corn. The crabs leg and all look like a spider about 2 foot across some weigh 10-15 pounds; they sell for $1.50 each to the cannery. They can salmon at Ninilchik. We've not got a moose yet. They hide pretty good. We are still hoping though one will walk by the cabin and sort of commit suicide. Guess I've told you the news up to now. Will go back to the shop tomorrow and finish up that Jeep engine. Take care of yourselves and don't work too hard.

as ever,
Chet & family

(Briar) Those crabs are a real pretty bright pink color. Sort of coral. They are so pretty they look artificial.

As I follow Dad driving his truck up to the high country above Homer, I realize that while there may have been a lack of luxury or modern convenience in our life on the Kenai, we had traded that for a bounty of experiences unattainable in Sugar Tree Ridge. Back in Ohio the land rolls over the horizon with little change in any direction while the coastal lands of south central Alaska seem to change over each hill and around every turn of the highway.

The southern coast of the Kenai is a primeval maze of mountains, islands, glaciers, and fjords, while great lakes, rounded peaks, and alpine valleys dominate inland. The chain of rivers and lakes that make up the Kenai River drainage bisects the peninsula, traveling through jagged mountains and coastal rain forests in the east to rolling hills and black spruce muskeg in the west. The Sterling Highway follows the river to Soldotna and then turns south to follow the shoreline to Homer. This coastal topography is relatively tame until steep bluffs drop dramatically into Cook Inlet. Beyond the inlet the horizon is lined with volcanoes and soaring peaks, white shouldered even in the height of summer.

On its southern tip where Homer is located, the peninsula's mountainous backbone undulates down to a round high country that tops out at about tree line (a thousand feet at this latitude). Several homesteaders proved up here well before anywhere else, and many of these people were already making a go at ranching and truck farming when we arrived. In fact, some still do. The high meadows make good pasture for beef cattle and the land gets a lot of sunlight. According to the Department of Agriculture and the University of Alaska, this was better soil than what we had at Happy Valley and was the basis for the optimistic publications about farming on the Kenai that Chet and Briar read while planning their move to Alaska.

The views Dad enjoyed along that drive were dramatic because one looks down on the Homer Spit—much more attractive than its name—and Kachemak Bay, across to Halibut Cove and Peterson Lagoon with their scattered islands, and into the glacial valleys of the Kenai Mountains. In the far distance to the west, Augustine Volcano rises out of the waters of Cook Inlet. In Dad's time, Kachemak Bay produced Dungeness and king crab in commercially harvestable quantities. Halibut and salmon were also abundant, so many folks were making a living fishing or at least bringing in enough cash to let them live this wilderness-embedded lifestyle.

Homer was and still is a bustling seaside town with fishing and cargo docks on the shore and farms and homesteads on the bluff and up into the hills. This town, where most people on the southern peninsula went to buy fuel, hardware, and groceries, was a rambling sprawl of a frontier town with muddy streets, more than its share of rattletrap frame buildings, and a unique finger of land that reaches out into Kachemak Bay. A remnant of a glacial moraine—gravel a glacier left behind—the spit stretches out past the typical Cook Inlet mudflats into deep water. Along most of Kachemak Bay, a boat beached at low tide will swamp with the high, and a boat beached at high tide will be left high and dry for twelve hours. At the end the of the spit the water is deep enough that docks, fish processing plants, and a boat harbor are accessible even at low tide.

In Homer my dad found odd jobs hauling with his truck, which allowed him to buy building supplies, groceries, and fuel. It was here that brother Dave was born the following year and here that brother Tom got his first job processing crab. Homer was "the city."

Even today, Homer embodies and epitomizes the frontier town. Homer is literally the end of the road, and one often finds people here who are not comfortable or welcome anywhere else, people trying to find a place where the music matches their step. They might be leaving failure, or pain, or unattainable expectations. They might have been pushed out from the confines of middle America or maybe just drawn to the libertarian openness of Alaska. For whatever reason, they are *here* because they couldn't be *there*.

When I was first in Homer with Dad, he told me about the Barefoot Boys, a religious cult that started a colony in Homer. I wanted to see these guys with long hair and beards who didn't wear shoes, and they were quite a sight to see walking the streets of Homer, Alaska, in the fifties. Twenty years later they wouldn't even turn a head. The group was active in the local volunteer fire department, and when I first saw some of them, they were fighting a brush fire on the edge of town. Although I found their long hair and biblical beards amazing, I was disappointed because they were wearing shoes, a requirement for firefighters.

The cult, which was officially named Wisdom, Faith, Love, Knowledge Foundation of the World, was started by a fellow named Krishna Venta who said he was Jesus Christ. Homer was the site of one of his two colonies of followers. Coincidentally, Krishna Venta died in 1958, and the cult didn't last long after that. His teachings were influential for two notorious characters, Jim Jones and Charles Manson.

September 3, 1958

> *Dear Folks,*
> *You asked about how long it would take to get a package from Sears. We got one Monday that had been sent out just 10 days. I thought that was pretty good. There are 3 ways they can be sent. The slow ways cost less. The 10 day one was the middle one. This next one is coming the slow way. It has real cold weather clothes and we weren't in too big a hurry. Also this package will weigh about twice as much.*
> *We went to Homer today and got some shoes for the girls. Sears didn't have the ones I ordered for Amy Sue, and Peg's didn't fit and had to be sent back. Also got some hats for Chet, Tom, and Mike, <u>and</u> established a bank account. Got back at noon and Chet went to work. Yes, he is still getting some work along. Not getting rich, but we have quit spending our backlog. Have around $200 worth of groceries laid in for winter so we feel pretty darn good about the whole thing.*
> *We ordered (and got) little cotton vests and panties that come just above the knee for the girls. The vests have short sleeves. Knee high nylon socks. They have good jeans, boots and sweaters. I made each of them woolen hoods to wear under their parka hoods on their coats. They had good knitted mittens and I made extra large woolen ones to pull over their knitted ones. Makes a real cute outfit. Peg's is brown and Amy's is black. The boys all had good heavy mackinaws. So we got new hats, long underwear, heavy wool socks and shoepacks for them. Shoepacks are knee high laced boots. They are rubber over leather about as far up as a slip on rubber overshoe covers. The rest is leather. They wear inside them a felt insole about a half-inch thick. If they are large enough they wear two insoles also one*

or two pairs of wool socks. These socks as heavy as those felt house slippers. They have plenty of warm shirts and sweaters.

The neighbors wear ordinary heavy overalls like our boys are used to. Chet is getting long johns too. He has plenty of old wool pants etc. Also, Mama is going to wear long ones too. Difference is mine will be pink and only come to below my knee. And, I am getting knee high heavy nylon socks for me too. Most people up here say you need these extras the first year but after that you are used to it, and they don't wear any more than we did back there except for their feet. They need to be pretty careful about their feet to keep them warm.

So far, Tom has not had any luck moose hunting, but they got lots of spruce chickens. About the chinking for the logs, there is a thick cottony moss that grows on the muskegs up here. it is plentiful and grows everywhere. When it dries it looks for all the world like excelsior only a little finer. They use this for chinking in the rough logs. Chet plans to get fiberglass and cut it into narrow strips for ours. Occasionally, you see one that has mortar between the logs.

It gets daylight about four am (I guess, I'm never awake at that time) and gets dark about 8:00 pm. It gets dark in a hurry too. And black as Satan's heart. But the stars shine just like they do anywhere else. The big dipper is in the west instead of north. I don't know about the north star. It's supposed to be part of the big dipper so it must be in the west too. the kids started school and are all excited and very happy about the whole thing. Answer soon.

Love, Briar

Part of making a new life in a new place is facing the unknown, and, for my family from the mild Midwest, winter in the true northern latitudes must have raised some palpable trepidation as we prepared for the long dark night of that first Alaska winter. Fall is short in Alaska. The season seems to be just a long, damp pause between summer and winter that descends like a dark, wet curtain on the bright, endless days of summer. Sometimes, it is so soggy that even people who don't like winter are glad to see the first inches of real snow.

It is only September in our narrative, but at sixty degrees latitude that means the days are shorter and cooler, and leaves are starting to turn. The fireweed is going to seed, for this harbinger of winter will warn before all other plants that fall is here. The fireweed is an annual plant that stands three to four feet tall in thick stands. Fuchsia flowers are arrayed in rings around the top third of the stem. The flowers transition in August to pink seedpods that soon burst to release white parachute seeds into the wind. That's when we know the first frosts are soon to come. Two other early casualties, pushki and devil's club will turn brown and gold, respectively. Pushki, with stalks that dwarf the fireweed and leaves the size of pizzas, are topped with clusters of white flowers and turn brown in mid-August. Under the trees, devil's club adds color to the forest with clusters of bright red berries and golden leaves the size of trash can lids. Overhead, the massive flocks of sandhill cranes will be calling with their clattering voices.

In Happy Valley, the Walker kids were talking school, and boxes packed with flannel shirts and practical school dresses and shoes came in the mail from Sears and Roebuck or Montgomery Wards. Other boxes arrived with long johns and wool work socks. The first snowfall was two months away, but fall in Alaska could be harsher than winter elsewhere in the United States, and we would be ready.

This was an intensely busy time. Blueberries and crowberries were ripe in the muskegs; cranberries and raspberry in the forests; and, after the first frost, the lowbush cranberry would be ripe in the mossy carpet under the birch trees. The men were afield at dawn and dusk trying to bag a moose. Trucks and station wagons were driving to the beach to stockpile coal to supplement the wood supply.

The Ford Country Squire station wagon served as the homestead carry-all, hauling kids, coal, lumber, and harvested game for the Walkers in the early sixties.

Anyone still building, like Chet Walker, felt the chill in the air. We were straddling the seasons during this time when the bounty of summer collided with the threat of winter. It was time to prepare, but any warm day lured us back to summer pursuits like salmon fishing, clam digging, or picnicking on the bluff above the inlet.

The days were only twelve hours long, which felt short after the endless daylight of July when we seemed to have all the time in the world. Those who had gardens started harvesting with diligence since the first hard frost was due, and the leaf crops had grown all they were going to. Some folks dug potatoes. Others waited until the vines died with that first frost and dug potatoes when the ground was cold enough to turn their hands numb.

As September progressed, kids went back in school, so the yards were empty until late afternoon. The fishermen put up their boats except for the few still scratch fishing for cohos or long-lining for halibut. The tourists and summer folk headed north to Anchorage or south with the sandhill cranes, so there was less traffic in and out of Dad's garage. The air was damp and chilly, and we were crowded into a one-room log cabin with Tom and Mike bivouacked in a tent. During this short time, Dad had to get a twenty-by-twenty log cabin up, roofed, and sealed against winter. I bet he wasn't sleeping much.

September 3, 1958

The piling we got is fir that was used for piling on a pier or something and worked out and floated up on the beach here. It's been soaked in saltwater for ages and lasts indefinitely in the ground. We let them set, and tomorrow we start hauling logs to the mill, will get some sawed Saturday if nothing prevents. We are going to saw the logs on three sides for the walls. 2x6's for floor joist and rafters. 1 inch boards for floor and sheathing. Roll roofing in top.

I have been hauling some coal off the beach to heat the shop this winter. There is chunks that will weigh a ton or more. You split it with a wedge like wood. It burns a little slow but gets hot and holds a fire good. Lots of ashes but no soot and it don't get you dirty to handle it. I'd better get to bed, so long now.

Chet

Fourteen

Alaska yellow cedar (*Cupressus nootkatensis*): Common evergreen tree of the coastal rain forest of the Pacific Northwest and southeast Alaska, known for rot resistant oils and attractive grain. Common driftwood found and used on Alaska beaches; piling material.

Around 1988 I removed some of the wooden piers that Dad and Tom had set thirty years earlier. These pilings had been standing in wet, poorly drained soil without protection from the elements. The wood had rotted and allowed the cabin to sag, so I replaced them with dunnage—short chunks of power poles treated with creosote. Dad might have been wrong when he said what kind of wood they were. At least some of them were cedar. Wood of any kind lasting in this soil is impressive, considering that the only preservatives were their own natural chemicals and the salt they collected during their time adrift.

Replacing the pilings was part of a bigger restoration project that Madelyn, the kids, and I undertook over a couple of summers. I had told Madelyn stories for years about the place we built at Happy Valley, painting the stories in the rich and idyllic hues that I remembered. When we returned after college and I took Madelyn there for the first time, it was impressive but not in the way I'd hoped.

The place had been rented out for years and showed the marks of people who didn't care for it the way owners would. Besides the ugly blue paint on the logs and the rampaging weeds, the cabin itself was sinking into the ground. Madelyn and I stripped the interior down to the old log walls and tore down the lean-to addition that Dad made a year after the main cabin went up. It joined the house to a two-car garage and had a bathroom, laundry room, and bedroom for us boys that Dad called the boars' den.

Apparently, this part of the house didn't have the good driftwood pilings, for I found the supports were a fading memory and the floor was fast becoming part of the earth beneath. Without a solid foundation, the lean-to was pulling the garage and the main cabin down into the earth as well. The only option that made sense was to remove the walls and rotting floor and save the roof, which was in pretty good shape. We used temporary posts to support the roof until we added a new deck of rough-cut spruce and stood four posts to support the roof, creating a long, open porch. I shored up the rest of cabin by replacing several pilings. In the end, we still had the cabin and beside it the garage sat still plumb, if a bit forlorn. The windows were broken, the roof needed tarpaper, and there were rotten boards in the floor and on the eaves; but the building had some life left in it. The garage was of frame construction rather than log, but like the cabin, it was built from rough-cut lumber taken from trees felled on this land and milled just down the road. It too could be lifted out of ruin with a bit of hard work.

The homestead cabin was a summer getaway for me and my family (here with Carlyn and Luke) in the eighties.

After a summer of weekends, the old cabin was filled with another generation of Walkers sleeping in the bedrooms, a covered porch overlooking the old garden in the clearing, and a thirty-year-old outhouse sitting over a new hole. We furnished the place with garage sale finds, spare cooking utensils, and handmade projects. Our two kids came in from the woods long enough to stock it with books and board games. The homestead once more was filled with life and vigor, and the boy who ran through the weeds in the backyard was the same age that I was when I first came to this place thirty years before. What had been a homesteader's abandoned dream settling into the earth was now a four-square little cabin sitting in a field of wildflowers ready for more Walkers to make stories of their own.

I have always been closely bound to this place and the memories it conjures. Of my siblings, only Amy seemed to share my tender sentiment for this plot of land that shaped us all. With her husband and kids, Amy lived at the homestead for one winter, and they made their own memories to add to the old ones. Today she lives only five miles away. My younger brother's lack of interest I can understand since he was only five when we left. But I've always wondered why the older brothers never found a way to connect to the land or the cabin on it. Some holidays they'd drive by and maybe stop to walk out into the clearing behind the cabin where they'd stand and tell stories and then take a photograph before loading up with a silent shake of the head. As they moved down the road, they seemed more injured than uplifted by the place. I guess the memories of the good times always come with some regret.

September 10, 1958

In case you're wondering why you haven't heard from us, we goofed up and forgot to get stamps. You have to get them at the post office and have the letters all ready to go. And you know he only goes two days a week. We got the first two Lynchburg News Monday. They were Aug 14 and Aug 21. thanks a whole lot. I expect it's much less expensive this way. We all enjoy them a lot. I also got a raft of birthday cards including yours. It was really cute. I let the kids play the game but didn't let them cut the markers out. They used buttons. I don't remember that I ever did get so many cards. Even from Katie, Naomi, and Clara. Heard from Mother last week but nothing this week. I don't know what I'll do with my dollar but I'll let you know when I do and thanks a lot. Also for the ribbons. The girls were really pleased but to keep pace you better hunt some little gimcrack for Danny. He's really been having a time lately.

Tom went to school the first two days and now doesn't go anymore until his course comes. They teach the juniors and seniors by correspondence course from Juneau. The courses are made up by the University of Nebraska. Anyhow, Chet and Tom have been working on the house. Danny and I sort of fetch and carry. I told him I would write you and tell you he's Daddy's flunky. They have the pilings all leveled (and believe you me that is a job) the posts up in the cellar (for support) and all but about ¼ of the floor joist laid. They ran out lumber though, so now tomorrow they are off to fell some more trees. Friday they will haul them to the mill and Saturday saw them. Quite a lot of work, but darn little expense and a whole lot of fun.

I really had a time over the weekend. Sat a.m. Chet and the 3 boys went over to Bell's to saw lumber. They had been gone nearly an hour when Tom came back and said Renee Bell had some exhibits to take to Ninilchik to the fair and wanted me to take her. So I went on over and she said, didn't I have anything at all I could exhibit just to help fill in. Well, I had baked a kettle full of old fashion lemon cookies (Leona Cornahan's recipe) on Friday. So I came back over and got a plate of them. They were real fancy too. I just baked them to have something to put in their lunches. Also I had a little hood and mittens I had made for Peggy Ann. I know the whole thing hadn't taken more than 30 minutes to make. And a hanky case (not really new) and hankies I'd edged. So I took them in, and we unloaded & came back.

Sunday PM when Chet went to work, I took the kids and went to the fair, and, lo and behold, I got a second prize on my cookies and 3rd prize on both the hanky case and hood and mittens set. But I got left out on the hanky. I'm sending you a ribbon for a souvenir; I was never so surprised in my life. If you see Leona tell her what her recipe did. She gave it to me when Bill was a baby.

I really had a celebration for my birthday Monday eve. Chet brought home ten big silver salmon, so I canned thirty-five quarts yesterday. I'm really proud *of them too. Tom is still hoping for a moose, but we haven't had much hunting time lately.*

I want to tell you a funny. A week or so ago Chet, Tom and I were out walking. We went about a mile or back in the woods and came upon a cabin and clearing. There were a few outbuildings too all in good shape. It was evident that no one lived there anymore, so we looked around. I went to the toilet and it was really something. It was lined on three sides with black bear skins and had only one hole and that hole was a perfect heart shape. Just as smooth and pretty as a valentine. So I showed it to Chet and told him that's what I wanted for Valentine's Day. Couple of the neighbor women had seen it, and we got quite a laugh out of it.

Briar

While sorting some old family letters, get well cards, and tax records, I came across some fair ribbons from the Ninilchik Fair. They weren't dated, but the tags showed that Mom had won blue ribbons for carrots and knitted socks, while her dinner rolls only earned a second-place ribbon. It must have been a shock to her pride not to win a blue one for her baking, considering that her dinner rolls were always the highlight of any meal, and she took great pride at being a real standout at baking.

When our kids were young and we were spending a lot time in the summer at Happy Valley, we took in the Ninilchik Fair every year. Sometimes we would enter our own canned salmon or raspberry jam. I think the attraction of a small-town fair like the one in Ninilchik is the unabashed, unpretentious fun of it. Just a little more formal than a birthday party in the backyard, the Ninilchik Fair is one of those places where a person doesn't have to be a star to stand out in public. Being good at making biscuits or growing rhubarb is enough to get a person a ribbon and a little local recognition. From homemade beer to hand-carved chess pieces, it's all there to see along with games, food, and music. Out back the 4-H kids show off the livestock they raised by hand in the backwoods and homesteads and that they finally sell at auction.

A fair has been held in Ninilchik since the early fifties. Somewhere along the line, it became the Kenai Peninsula Fair, but regardless of the name it has always been a showplace for the south peninsula people who live off the land. Even in the twenty-first century, one can admire the homemade smoked salmon and the jarred or canned moose, sourdough bread, wine, and hand-knit socks made from hand-spun dog-hair yarn.

Visitors won't find a field full of carnival rides; they'll be lucky to find some ponies taking kids around in circles. The booths are rustic and simple, often local fund-raisers for the swim club or the Girl Scouts, but there will be hearty clam chowder and steak sandwiches sold by the Legion Auxiliary and music by my old friend, the Singing Fisherman, and any of his cronies who are in the right frame of mind. A room full of quilts will create a flood of color, and Smokey Bear will terrify some kids and give balloons to others. If it rains, and it probably will, people put on their raingear and keep going. Just as it was fifty years ago, the fair is a perfect excuse to have a parade, strut your crafts, eat too much, and listen to both good and not so good music.

Any local fair gets started as a way for folks to celebrate the richness of rural life and a chance for people who live scattered wide across the land to gather and look each other in the face over a piece of pie or a bowl of chowder. When people live remotely, the fair is a chance to come out and put the work of their hands in front of their neighbors and say, "Here it is, and I feel pretty good about it." Today, fairs are big shows of commercial marketing, carnivals, and concerts. But somewhere out behind the midway there is still a building with the 4-H kids and their livestock, and another building with all the craft and vegetable entries made by people who just want to say, "Here's something I'm proud of."

Fifteen

Bog blueberry (*Vaccinium uliginosum L.*): A low bush six to sixteen inches tall with small oval leaves and a sweet, dark-blue berry, round or barrel shaped. Also known as an alpine blueberry, or gegashla; found in tundra, bog, muskeg, pancakes, and pies.

School started at Ninilchik not long after the fair closed, but the school had no kindergarten, so I was left at home. While the other kids were at school, I got to tag along on adventures with Mom, Dad, and Tom. Until I read these letters from 1958, I hadn't remembered how much there was that I got to share. From trips to Homer to moose hunting, I was front and center for the great drama of homesteading in Alaska. I'm sure it was a little extra work taking me along on all these tromps through the woods or walks down to the creek for water, but I made myself useful as a game and berry spotter.

It must be hard for parents of big families to spread the recognition around, and it seems Dad and Mom really tried to be even with this, but in this time, Tom stood out as the golden boy, and it was well earned. He was big enough and old enough to actually help Dad. He was energetic enough to rise early in the morning to hunt moose in the cold and damp woods of an Alaska autumn.

Lucky for Tom, moose hunting was in its zenith during the fifties, and this fifteen-year-old farm boy was hunting in the premier trophy moose region of Alaska, and perhaps in the world. These qualities combined to make Kenai Peninsula moose the prime source of protein for the Alaska homesteader and the prime target for trophy hunters. Even if they didn't bring home a trophy, hunters were usually successful in bagging one of the plentiful bulls.

Today we continue to hunt moose on the Kenai Peninsula, but not with the success that Tom experienced in his first hunting season in Alaska. Moose hunters have to go farther and longer and often still come home empty-handed, and those who are eating moose meat probably spent top dollar getting it to the table. Very few moose are shot before breakfast a mile away from home.

Some people blame the proliferation of bears, especially brown bears, for the decline of moose in this area. Others point to the destruction of the forest by homesteading, highway road kills, and over-hunting by sportsmen. In a recent report on the decline of moose on the Kenai, biologists suggest that the cause is not human hunting, not marauding brown bears, or rampant road kill. They say the biggest factor in the drop in the Kenai's moose population has been the loss of habitat or, more accurately, changing habitat. Again, this isn't land being used up by people but the process of forests maturing. Moose prefer an immature forest, where browse is plentiful.

It turns out that the bear that has done the most damage to the moose population is Smokey Bear and his "Only You Can Prevent Forest Fires" program. Fire may be the enemy of man, but it is the friend of moose habitat. Fire kills off a mature forest and lets the succession start over with fireweed, willow, alder, wild rose, and birch. The dominant spruce trees take over only after decades of growth.

Moose have a varied diet. In the summer they eat a lot of water plants, which explains why they are often seen standing in muskeg ponds or lakes. The rest of the year they get by on brush and small trees such as young birch, willow, and cottonwood that are found in land that has burned. Early in the twentieth century, the fires on the Kenai Peninsula were big and common. Hundreds of thousands of acres were scorched and millions of board feet of timber went up in smoke. The result was not pretty, but after ten or twenty years the moose browse developed into a giant moose pasture. This was the Kenai Peninsula we were hunting in 1958.

Late in the twentieth century, spruce bark beetle, taking advantage of mature forests protected from fire, invaded the Kenai Peninsula and decimated acre upon acre of spruce forest, leaving trees standing but dead. Some were logged, and the firewood gatherers had a heyday, but this didn't help the moose. Rather than restarting the forest like a wildfire would, the bark beetle took out complete stands of spruce, leaving scattered mature birch and willow. With the ground unshaded, the grass grew denser and taller—not a welcome meal for the moose. So we are left to look back longingly to the time when Alaskan beef was common and relatively easy to get.

September 13, 1958

> *Dear Folks,*
> *Received your letter and the red and yellow ribbons. Thanks ever so much. You asked about Amy's hair. It's real long and she wears it most anyway. Sometimes braided or pony tail or just tied back with ribbons. They are both awfully proud of their ribbons.*
>
> *We had aimed to saw lumber today but got our minds changed. I'll start at the beginning. Yesterday am it was raining & couldn't do anything so Chet was sleeping late. He and Tom together had banged up one of his fingers about right, and it had thumped all night so I was glad he could stay in bed. The kids left for school and Tom and Danny started out to the spring for water. They had been gone about five minutes when Tom came running back and said there was a bull moose on the trail. We woke Chet up (I figured he was a better shot). He jumped up and grabbed the 30.06 in his shorts and tee shirt and barefoot and off he went. Got to where Danny had first seen it, and just as he got there, it took off. He missed and started right out through the woods and muskeg after it, half naked. And it was cold, nearly frost cold. The darn moose got away, and I had by that time got to him with his shirt and pants. Danny was about half way mad. He said, "I went and found you a moose and you had to miss it."*
>
> *Tom and Danny went on back and got the water. Saw on the trail where had been two moose and a calf there. In the meanwhile we were eating off a haunch of moose Bells had given us. They shot two one am. Last evening, Tom went back the same way to Jim Trent's and saw the same moose on the way there and again coming back. He was really put out. "Standing there laughing at me," Tom said.*
>
> *In the afternoon, Danny got artistic and drew a picture of Chet chasing the moose in his underwear. He didn't leave out anything either, including the*

front opening in his shorts. I asked him what it was and he said, "You know, that's Daddy!" We really had a laugh over it.

Chet got home and Tom told him about the moose laughing at him. So Chet gets down his skinning knife, his whetstone and says all right we'll get him in the morning. So they left the house at 6:00 am and at 6:20 I heard two shots, and at 6:35 Tom came in grinning from ear to ear and said, "I didn't miss him that time, you can tell Grandpa I just pretended he was a frog."

So we all went back to help butcher. Had to do it all flat on the ground because it was out in the middle of a meadow and no tree near. And it was a big one too. When we hung up the hind leg it was twice as big as the leg Bell's had given us. Chet guessed it would weigh half a ton. He let Tom shoot it. I guess he figured he owed it to him after letting him get away yesterday. I don't know who was the proudest Chet, Tom, or Danny. Took just about two hours to butcher and cut him up and load him in the trunk of the car.

No one had had breakfast so I fried up the biggest platter of thick steaks (off Bell's moose) you ever saw and they really ate. Tom said, "Dad, I didn't figure you'd eat any breakfast."

Chet says, "It's this Alaska air. It's different."

So, we are real proud of ourselves. Aim to share with a couple of neighbors who don't have any yet, but I'll have a great plenty to bottle up. We were sure glad Tom got it. The other day, he shot four times at a black bear and missed. He was so mad he bawled (just like old Bob Walker). The day before he shot the heads off three spruce hens, and their head is no bigger than Pop's thumb. Mike is really best at Spruce hens. He's got more than all the rest put together. Bill does pretty good. Danny is the best to see things. He never yells when he spots anything just grabs a pants leg and pulls. They have learned to take him along too. He and Tom and I were coming home from the homestead the other day. Danny found a thick patch of lowbush blueberries. We didn't have any bucket but picked enough for a pie in Danny's hat. The cranberries are ripe now but by the time I take care of this moose they will probably be frosted.

Mike has his initiation this next week. He'll be a sight with all they have lined out for him to wear, high heels, skirt, blouse, makeup, diaper and carry bottles and spare diapers.

We left the offals where they lay and Tom is going to try and get a coyote eating them. There is a $50 bounty on coyotes, but they are hard to *hit and harder to kill. Well, I guess this is all for now. Chet may write some tomorrow.*

Love always, Briar

PS I never remember to tell you the time difference. We are 5 hours behind you. I think it's Pacific Standard Time.

The moose that Tom shot was just down the road from the cabin where we were squatting. The letters brought the kill site out of the back of my memory to the front of my mind. A patch of open meadow sat uphill where the road made a bend around a hill. Standing on the road and looking up toward them, I could see Dad and Tom, but the moose was down in the grass and brush where I couldn't see it. The two of them had already started butchering when I got there.

I remember carefully holding Dad's rifle, a full stock Springfield bolt-action veteran of the U.S. Army. It shot bullets as long as Dad's fingers and weighed so much I could not imagine holding it up to shoot. This was one more time that Tom got elevated to adulthood in my eyes. He could lift that heavy gun and kill a moose.

My big brother was a man, and even now I find it hard not be jealous of him. Who would not want to be Tom Walker in this story? He was the long-suffering teenager dragged from his friends and his baseball team to go off to far Alaska, but once there in the north country, he was about avoiding going to school and instead worked like a man with his father, went off moose hunting with grown men, and shot a bull moose. Of course, I probably had it second best. I was the tagalong, the moose spotter, and sometimes even my brother's sidekick. Too bad I don't have perfect memory to recall those days in the fall of 1958 when we were moose hunters, Dad and Tom and I.

We never hunted together again, but here I find a precious moment in time that I remember only from reading a letter, but it is mine just the same. I look at my grandson, now about the age I was in 1958, and that helps me get a picture of myself moving through these scenes, the questions I would have asked, the wonder that filled my mind at the things I saw around me.

Sixteen

Subbituminous coal: Flaky brown to black coal with about half the carbon of anthracite coal; considered low grade; may be susceptible to spontaneous combustion due to water content; known to leave a lot of clinkers and sore backs when used as stove fuel.

For Tom, school seemed to hang in the distance like a threatening storm. One day he would have to set his rifle down and put feet under a desk with the rest of the kids, but for now he was having his time working and hunting like a man. On top of that, he was the big brother to five siblings who looked up to him whether they wanted to or not, and only Mike could even dream of standing shoulder to shoulder with the great hunter.

In 1964, when Dad was in the hospital, Tom and Mike each killed a moose on Thanksgiving morning. They were hotshots and the moose had been close to the road, standing together as if waiting the for a pair of brothers to come along. The shots were easy, but the pack out wasn't. They had to pack the moose down a hill into a gully and then back up the hill to the road. I can still see the whole back of the '56 Ford station wagon packed full of moose quarters. Tom never liked the work of cutting and hauling firewood, but he was willing to pack moose meat, any day, anywhere.

Tom kept the rifle (Dad's military surplus Springfield) that he killed his first moose with. Eventually, when he had money for such things, he had the gun customized with a sport stock and a telescopic sight. He always liked hunting Happy Valley, and many years later, he would return to hunt and harvest in the same places where he hunted during his man-making year of 1958. I don't know how many moose he killed with that rifle, but I know it was plenty.

Moose hunting remained a passion for him and any year he brought home a moose was a good one for Tom Walker. Later, when Alzheimer's—he called it CRS, "can't remember shit"—was eating his brain, some of the last stories he told were about moose hunting. His favorite was a tale about when he and a friend went hunting at Happy Valley on the old road just below the homestead. They spotted a moose and split up to find it. At almost the same moment that Tom fired, he heard his buddy's rifle. They each shot a different moose, thinking they had spotted the only one. It was nearly as special as his first moose.

September 16, 1958

Dear Folks —
At last I will take time to start you a letter. It has been a little while since I had written. Just been too busy trying to do too many things at the same time. I've quit the garage work. Since school started traffic had almost stopped so there wasn't much doing so I am going to finish the cabin or bust a gut. I've got the floor joist all down and started first course of logs. They are sawed six inches square on three sides like a D. They will be 15 logs high. The bottom course is even with the top of the floor joist. There is a 2x6 plate goes on top to put ceiling joists and rafters on. That will make the ceiling seven feet. The gable ends will be board and batten. That will make an attic to put stuff in. We only hope to get in under roof before the weather gets bad. I can finish it up this winter inside. So much for the cabin.
The cook is canning moose. I came in at noon and she had been working on half the ribs and neck of one front quarter. She had worked all morning and had 12 quarts of meat and god knows how much hamburger and couldn't turn it over it still was so heavy. Now that was only half the ribs on one side and the neck. She had canned today 54 quarts off the two front quarters without the front legs. I cut the legs off first. Took off shoulder blade and all. Cut back legs off at the hip joint. That was all I could carry.
When Tom kills a moose, he don't mess around. It was as big as a horse. I'd say it would have weighed about 1200 pounds at least. He sure is a proud kid. I'm proud for him. I could have got one too, but one at a time is enough to can. There was another bull and cow staying around while we butchered it, just like

an old inquisitive cow. They seem awful stupid sometimes. They sure do make good beef and hamburger.

Tom is still out of school until his books come. He helped a man dig potatoes yesterday and today made $20. They dug, or rather picked, 1500 pounds one day and 1900 today two of them. Potatoes did real well this year for all the rain and cool weather.

It's daylight now at 5 am and still light at 7 pm. Then it gets dark right now. The last two days have been fall days there. Frosty in the morning and sunny and warmer during the day. They cools off quick in the evening. the mountain across the inlet is white with new snow. the birch trees are yellow and the leaves are falling even the weeds are pretty colors. The spruce trees, that is what most of them are here, are evergreen and cones like pine on them. The little squirrels sure make them rattle and fall. The trees were full of them around the cabin this morning while I was working. They don't get much excited about people. They are red squirrels but at smaller than the grey ones there. No one ever kills them to eat they are so small.

Briar rendered out about 15 pounds of suet. She used some in bread this afternoon and it did just fine. It's almost ten o'clock and two cookers of meat to come off in 15 minutes. Still two more to go don't know if she will do them or not. This leaves us all well and the kids in school. Glad to hear you are getting along and Dad is back taking care of the chickens. Briar will most likely add a little tomorrow. this is Tuesday and won't go out until Thursday.

By now,
Chet and Family

September 17, 1958

Hi folks —
This will be short and sweet because the old lady is sure done in. I canned altogether 60 quarts yesterday and 50 today. And we didn't can either of the hind legs up to the hipbone. Gave one away and are keeping one to eat steaks off. We figure four families can use it before it spoils. Tom held the shoulder blade and attached leg up to him that darn moose was as tall as Tom at the withers. We'll say good-by now and write more when I'm not so tired. You didn't say if

your last shot helped as much as usual. Does rainy weather seem to hurt? I got both the starter recipes and it works fine, thanks. (Briar)

Moose wasn't the only thing we hunted; they were just the most common target since we lacked deer or caribou in the neighborhood. The only deer in Alaska are in Prince William Sound and the southeast panhandle. Even though the foothills of the Kenai Peninsula are called the Caribou Hills, the caribou population on the Kenai was almost nonexistent in the fifties and sixties. Black bears were eaten as were grouse, of course, and migrating ducks. We ate a few porcupines, but they were easy to catch and kill, so people usually left them for when meat supplies ran out. Squirrels, on the other hand, were pests that we shot for target practice. Sometimes you'd see their napkin-sized pelts nailed to the outhouse wall. These Alaskan tree rats have a penchant for storing spruce cones in attics and lining their nests with valuable building insulation. I've seen the cones stacked a foot deep in an attic around the chimney where heat could ignite them and the squirrels mining for insulation open holes to bring in the cold. These little fellows have few supporters on a homestead.

Not much bigger than a chipmunk, our American red squirrels are very different from the meaty, gray squirrels that folks back in Ohio and Kentucky could turn into a meal. When I began reading stories of backcountry heroes, I couldn't get my head around how someone like young Davy Crockett would go out and hunt up a squirrel for dinner. A one-squirrel dinner for the whole family made no sense to a kid where squirrels were so small, they wouldn't feed a child. I was a nineteen-year-old college student when I first confronted a squirrel the size of an alley cat. I really understood then how different a gray squirrel was from our little red devil.

Another homestead pest was the black bear, and it is still one of the most common wild animals prowling around peoples' backyards. They came around our place often, looking for an easy meal of garbage, dog food, chickens, or hanging moose meat. Once, some friends were bringing their rabbit hutches to our house while they went Outside for a few weeks. The road was thick with spring mud, so the hutches only made it part way up the lane instead of to the house where the dog might guard them. Nobody liked leaving those hutches out like that, but in a couple days the road would be dry enough to move them. We went out to feed them the next morning and found them slaughtered and eaten. Tracks in the mud showed that a prowling black bear cleaned out the hutch full of rabbits, killing all but one old rabbit. The hutches were far enough from the house that nothing alerted us, not even the dog, until it was too late.

September 21, 1958

>*Dear Grampa and Gramma.*
>
>*Well by George, I didn't miss this time, I just pretended he's a frog Grampa, Ha. Me and Pa went out last Sat. morning and was just walking down the road and they heard us first, but I heard them take off through the weeds, and boy I took off. I came up over the hill, there were three so I picked out the biggest one and busted him in the rump I thought, but I hit him in the shoulder then he stopped and looked at me and I shot him right in the hump in the spine and I think he was dead before he hit the ground. Pap said he would weigh 1200 lbs on the hoof. The top of his shoulder blade came right up to the top of my head with his knee bone right at my knee. I thought he was a monster but Al Sanborn said it was an average sized animal.*
>
>*We sawed 23 logs yesterday for the house. We will peel them tomorrow and cut some more trees tomorrow, "I think."*
>
>*There was an Awful wreck down at Anchor Point Friday night. One boy was killed and a girl seriously injured. The drivers and another girl weren't hurt. All four of them went to school at Ninilchik.*
>
>*I guess maybe I'll start to school Tuesday 'cause two boxes of books came Friday but Auten didn't open them during school. Well I guess that's all, all that I can think of anyway.*
>
>*Love always, Tom*

Sometimes these letters leave us confused when we only hear the punch line of an inside joke. I can only assume the frog reference between Tom and Papaw had something to do with frog gigging since it was a popular activity in Ohio. Bullfrogs were tracked by their loud call and when found, speared with a trident, called a gig. Gigging is a night sport, so the hunters use flashlights to spot their prey. Breaded and fried, the legs are a tender delicacy.

Al Sanborn, whom Tom mentions in his letter, was a Happy Valley neighbor, and he lived just down the road from where we got our first moose. Al was one of the characters who became part of our family history.

Al drove a green-and-black Chevy pickup and lived in a one-room tarpaper cabin just a few steps off Happy Valley Road. He had been around a few years, so he was glad to offer opinions and advice to our cheechako family. I don't think Al worked, and he didn't have much to show for it if he did. As far as anyone could tell, he had the pickup truck, the cabin, and a few tools and a gun. I think Dad would have called him one of those fellows that's "too lazy to work and too nervous to steal."

His cabin was littered with paperback books and smelled of tobacco. He rolled his own cigarettes, a common habit among folks on the peninsula. Every time he came by for coffee, I waited eagerly for him to take out his can of Prince Albert tobacco and roll a cigarette, because he was missing a thumb, and it seemed to me that rolling a cigarette with only one thumb would be just about impossible. He could do it though, and I had many chances to watch him because he liked to "stop by for coffee," which meant he'd sit around and talk Mom's ear off until mealtime came around and she had to ask him to stay and eat.

In this place where bears were more common than dogs, Al Sanborn was afraid of bears. In fact he felt that the black bears of Happy Valley were on a mission to disrupt his life with particular alacrity. And he saw many of them because they were attracted to his strawberries. He had a fine strawberry patch, and one day a bear visited the patch and got close enough that Sanborn felt threatened even though he was in the house behind a sturdy door. Even with a high-powered rifle in his hand, Sanborn was terrified and too scared to step out onto the porch to shoot it. He stayed inside and shot through a window. This was not an open window, not even a Visqueen window. He was so afraid that he shot out the glass windowpane to avoid going out on the porch. Then he calmly told that story to his neighbors and anyone who would listen, unabashed by his own fearfulness. Even as a boy, I thought it was foolish that anyone terrified of bears would live in a little shack in bear country and grow food for bears to snack on. I smugly affirmed that if I were that afraid of something so common as a black bear on the Kenai, I would have to find another place to live. I wondered how he ever got to sleep at night.

Actually, I was one to talk for I was afraid of bears myself when we lived in Happy Valley, and I would have nightmares about them. Those are the only nightmares that I can still remember, and I know that they recurred, embedding themselves in my recollections. They tended to be scary with a touch of silliness. In one version, I was running in slow-motion in a dream-state, panicky kind of run, the kind that is so slow you can't seem to get anywhere. I was running toward our neighbor's front door with three bears in hot pursuit. In my dream I always made it to the door, but then I had to struggle to pull it open, desperately fighting against the weight of that heavy wooden door. The bears always stopped at the base of the steps as if they couldn't climb them, and the largest suddenly turned into the Quaker man off the oatmeal box, complete with a flat-crowned black hat and emotionless smile. Maybe he symbolized home or something safe, but I still woke up scared and confused, hating the darkness closing in around me.

Almost as bad for me as the nightmares was when a real bear tried to get into our garage where moose meat was hanging. I lay in bed, literally with covers over my head in sheer terror of the beast at the back door even though I knew a plain old black bear could not breach a door built by my dad.

Though I respect them, bears no longer terrify me. If a black bear is prowling around my yard, I'll step out the door and throw rocks at it to run it off. At the same time, I have learned that there were things that give us terrors that won't be pushed aside, and we cannot resist their ability to paralyze and sicken us. I am that way about standing or driving on steep cliffs or being in close places like closets or elevators. I don't choose to be panicked with my heart racing and sweat running down my back. The reaction is as involuntary as shivering when I'm cold. I see Al Sanborn differently now, not as a silly, frightened old man but as someone who faced real terror. And by choosing to live where he did—in a bear's playground—he was facing a mighty demon every day because he wanted so badly to be where he was.

In today's world, there is a great effort to make our surroundings safe and free from harm. Helmets and pads, seatbelts, airbags, cellphones, and GPS weave a safety net around us, giving us security and peace of mind. We have become so protective and protected that we develop a fear of being scared. Yet a man like Al Sanborn made an explicit choice to live with a certain level of dread, one that could not be ignored, only survived. There is much in common with the fears that must have run through Dad's mind when he took six kids out to this wild place and put them up in a borrowed cabin and a tent. A cabin had to be built in six weeks—not *could* or *should* or *might*—but absolutely had to be built in six weeks because winter was coming and winter can be a bear.

September 21, 1958

Dear Folks —

Here I am again. Sunday PM We will try to get a few letters written. Went to church this morning and had a picnic lunch at the end of the lane on a bluff along the beach. It is the place where Rex Hanks had his water power sawmill a few years ago. You will read something about it in the book, <u>Go North Young Man</u>*. Also there is a coal "mine" there. The coal is just on top of the ground. We got there the other day. It rained Friday and part of the night, quit yesterday morning about nine. Thursday I cut some trees and then some more Friday. Got the logs hauled in and sawed them yesterday so have them to peel on one side and lay up. I am going to cut more first and get them in and sawed as fast as I can. Will lay them between times, they lay one on top of the other and eight-inch nails countersunk two inches in drove down through them. That should hold them. last week was pretty until Friday. Today is beautiful; we had bad freeze last night, was down to twenty-four degrees this morning. Makes us want to get our house done as fast as we can.*

The logs we cut for "house logs" are eight inches at the small end. They sometimes run twenty-four feet long, but they are awful hard to handle that way. Twelve to Fourteen feet do very well. If they're crooked we cut them in two and make short logs for between windows and such. We cut twenty-one logs that are from twenty-two to eight feet long and sawed them Saturday.

We still have some moose, fresh I mean, and our neighbor Bell killed a black bear and gave us a ham off it. It's real good eating. Had bear sandwiches for picnic dinner. It was a young one. Looked for all the world like your dog buster. The ham may have weighed 10 pounds, not too fat. Briar ended up with about twenty pounds of moose fat. She uses it for anything you use lard for. Even made a raisin nut cake "your recipe" and it turned out fine.

Tom still isn't in school as his books haven't came yet but he heard they came Friday but not from a reliable source. So he will be home tomorrow at least. We plan to cut trees and burn brush.

The days have been getting shorter, it's 6:30 now and almost dark, but its daylight by 5 am. The temperature is 36 degrees, everyone is well and getting along fine. Glad you are getting along and traveling about. We need a wick trimmer for a Aladdin lamp, would you send us one?

By now,
Chet and Family

The southern Kenai Peninsula is underlain with a layer of coal several feet beneath the fine-grained soils. This vein of coal is exposed along the bluff overlooking the beaches of Cook Inlet at Happy Valley and Ninilchik. The continuous erosion of the bluffs leaves chunks of coal on the beach, waiting to be collected by homesteaders like us. The layered coal breaks into chunks of every size, and coal gatherers need to be ready to bust the bigger piece with sledgehammers or crowbars until they are small enough to be loaded.

As they got older, Bill and Mike got to drive to school some days, but the trade-off was that they had to drive to the beach and load the back of the station wagon with coal. This subbituminous coal is low grade without the shiny black luster and chunky character of anthracite coal. It burns with a brown smoke and a strong odor, leaving the ashpan full of clinkers, the unburned contaminants, but it was free for the taking, full of BTUs, and plentiful. Many people in the area would start their morning fires with wood and add coal to hold the fire through the night.

Even today, a family who wants the fuel can drive their truck down to the beach and load up on coal. When I was a kid, the houses in the village burned a lot of coal, and whenever I smell coal smoke anywhere, I am transported to cold winter days in Ninilchik when the brown coal smoke lay like a wool blanket above the rooftops in the village.

Where Happy Creek breaks over the bluff and into the Cook Inlet, water has excavated a small canyon through the soil to expose this seam of coal. Here Happy Creek becomes a waterfall the color of weak coffee as it tumbles across the black ledge of coal and crashes down to the beach. With Cook Inlet below and Iliamna and Redoubt Volcanoes in the distance, it is quite the setting.

It was here on a late September Sunday that we came for a picnic. We ambled down the dirt road to the highway and crossed the highway where it passed over Happy Creek. My brothers carried the food and some blankets while Dad supervised the parade and teased us about hauling coal home on our backs at the end of the day. The meadow above the falls sloped gently toward the creek and gave a little shelter from the wind, and though it was a sunny day we were in jackets and sweatshirts against the fall chill. A couple of weeks before, we had declared this our family picnic spot as if we owned it and could keep it all to ourselves. The older boys chased us little ones through the meadow and down the steep trail to the beach, while Mom laid out the lunch. Soon we were sprawled on blankets with plates of potato salad and coleslaw. We lunched on sandwiches of salmon salad and fried moose steak. We drank hot cocoa from Dad's thermos and he complained that there was no coffee, but on this day we could laugh at his misery because it was a picnic. We ran wild, playing hide-and-seek and then returned for cookies and pie. We decided that next time we would have a hotdog roast and bring marshmallows too.

Soon Dad was snoozing with his head on Mom's lap. These picnic Sundays were the only times I remember Dad napping or even laying down. He was the first one up and last to bed, and in between he was fully dressed and on the job. A leisurely Sunday with church, a good dinner, and a nap were part of the Ohio lifestyle he wasn't ready to give up.

Today, the Sterling Highway has been moved a few hundred yards to the east, and the old road is now an alder-lined lane that ends in a rough trail that winds down through the cottonwoods to the creek and a grassy meadow at the bluff's edge. Alders and young spruce grow up through the skeleton of an old pickup truck, and floodwaters have washed out the old highway culverts. The fireweed and wild geraniums still color the overlook and frame a view of the falls created by the creek crossing over the ledge of coal. Happy Creek Falls is still a fine place for a picnic, but it's been used hard over the years by campers and picnickers with a heavier footprint than ours.

Seventeen

Autumnal equinox: Occurs on or about September 21; the period during the year when the sun passes over the equator and the length of day and night are equal; traditionally the last day of summer; in Alaska, mid-fall.

Now that there was moose meat in the larder, Dad focused on cabin building. The first frost of the season had come before September 21; so on the last day of summer, winter was already knocking on the door, and the days were getting short fast. Dad could hear the pages of the calendar flipping with each day bringing the hard freeze closer. The sourdoughs had surely told him that in October the days would be gray, cold, and probably wet. By Halloween, winter would be here for real.

Anyone who has ever built anything knows the truly fun part is putting up walls. While it is a rich experience to turn the first shovel of dirt and fell the first tree, the real excitement comes on that day when the actual building begins. The planning and design process is so full of decision making and logistics that the joy of building can be lost in the drudgery of details, but planning is an important time when the builder is making materials lists and structural decisions. Do I want two-by-six or two-by-eight rafters? How long is the eave overhang? Should the windows be thirty or thirty-six inches? How many twenty-penny spikes do I need? How many sixteen penny, ten penny, and eight penny nails?

Every question must be answered with enough information to be sure the answer is correct. But once things are started, it is like leaving on a trip. What's done is done, and we have what we have. In this case, the cabin was where it was, the dimensions were what they were, and every log spiked and countersunk was another step away from turning back. Having built two houses and a cabin myself, I know that the planning and staging seems endless, and a builder is so relieved when it's time to start putting pieces of wood together. The two favorite logs in cabin building are the first and the last.

Once Dad started laying logs, he'd be able to see the end point and knew he could get there. After felling trees to make lumber and logs, helping the sawyer mill the logs, and staging them onsite, Dad would finally get to make them into a building. Not only does the act of building begin forming a concrete, tangible structure but it is also a commitment that prevents turning back. Each step eliminates more second-guessing.

In the thirty days after equinox, Dad, with the help of Mom and the rest of us, had to lay sixteen courses of logs, frame in doors and interior walls, mount rafters, and layer up a roof. He had to build doors and windows, install a wood heater and cookstove, and enclose the gable ends. When this was all done the cabin would be considered move-in and winter ready. There was no paint for the logs, no glass for the windows, and no insulation for the ceiling. Shelves, kitchen cabinets, and closets would all come after we were moved in.

This was a heap of work even for him, and it must have been tempting to keep Tom out of school for the extra help, but it never seemed to be a consideration. Never in these letters do we hear a doubt or a hint of regret. Dad and Mom seem comfortable and confident in the plans and the commitments they have made. This would be their home.

Maybe this is part of what's missing in my attempt to profile this man who left me so young. There is no complaining from Dad. He won't tell us his worries and woes. His anxieties and trepidations are kept inside, leaving me to guess what, if anything, is eating him. If Dad would just go on one tirade in a letter, I might get to peek under the mask of his emotion. This propensity for projecting the positive is part of the Walker way. One doesn't air dirty laundry in public because our problems were no one else's business. Just because you are sick, tired, or out of sorts doesn't mean people have to hear about it. I'm sure there were days when things didn't get done, when we kids were being brats, and when plans fell through, but these don't have to be sent par avion to Ohio for grandparents to fret over.

One thing I can learn about Dad just from reading his and Mom's letters is that he's not afraid of work, and he likes things done right, not just done. Dad was not an emotionless or insensitive man, quite the opposite in fact. He was playful with his kids, passionate with his wife, and when he was mad there was no doubt about it. All this I remember, while the letters tell me of a man who is not going to show the downside. He comes across as the eternal optimist. That's a hell of an asset when you are bucking weather and time with nothing but your own two hands and a sense of humor.

Like my dad I followed a dream to build my own house and luckily married a woman willing to help. In 1982 Madelyn and I built a house in Seward, where we raised our two kids. I framed the forms for the concrete basement, built the shell, raised the rafters, and sheathed and roofed it. We hung windows, siding, doors, and sheetrock, working so long and hard that sometimes I slept in the trailer rather than drive the short six miles back to town in the evening. Everything but the electrical, plumbing, and carpeting we did ourselves. The house was strong and straight and warm, and all the flaws and mistakes were ours without apology.

Ten years ago, we built a log cabin off the road system, out in the woods and across a lake at the end of a crude, muddy trail. I had always wanted to build one, and it sort of replaced what we lost at Happy Valley. During that process, my wife got to experience the aching arms and blistered hands of a log peeler and savor the ease of peeling a green log after having peeled dozens of cured ones.

We seemed to make building this log cabin as challenging as possible. The property really didn't hold enough good trees for building logs, and we didn't have the equipment to fell and mill full-size trees into cabin logs, so almost all of the materials had to be brought in. That meant the logs and everything else were hauled over a hundred miles of highway and then fourteen miles of logging road—under construction at the time—then off-loaded onto a sled or ATV trailer depending on the season. These loads were bounced and dragged a mile and a half over a long mud track through the woods. At the end of the trail was a lake to be crossed in a seventeen-foot canoe. Finally, one by one, each log and stick of lumber was toted by hand up the trail to the cabin. Every nail, every log, and every window was handled so many times by the time it reached the building site, each had its own personality.

With the materials on site, putting our cabin together seemed like the easy part, or if not easy as least more fun. I think that was where Chet was at this point; putting these logs together to make a house would be pretty simple. I know the logging certainly wasn't.

September 24, 1958

Wed night and the letters to answer so we try and get all answered. The last letter we had came Monday. Aunt Mabel's was in it. Briar is answering aunts and we will send both together and you can see she gets it.

We are all fine, the kids all in school, Tom started today. They all seem very happy in the school here and like the other kids fine. They haven't had to walk out more than one morning as I go over to the homestead every day and they ride out with me. They sometimes get off the bus over there and others walk in. That makes it pretty good for them.

Tom was ready to get started to school. He has worked pretty hard lately on the cabin. He says he has had enough digging for quite a while. He and Mike still sleep in the tent. They have sleeping bags and a bed. They say it's warm as toast. We had a hard freeze last night but was beautiful today till about 5:30 or 6 o'clock. We are all enjoying the cabin building; it is at last realizing one ambition we had, building our own house.

You asked about Mike, he is here with the rest of us, seems to be doing all right in school. He is pretty good at spruce chicken hunting. He writes to Billy Bell's sister yet. Danny is quite the log cabin kid. He stays over there and gets back here all petered out. He can't wait till we get it done, neither can the rest of us for that matter.

It rained Monday all day, Tom and I peeled logs till noon then came home and dried out that afternoon. Tuesday am we went back and we laid what we had sawed. That makes 4 logs high. I then cut 21 more logs and we drug them in. The Bell boy with his tractor, Briar and I loaded 17 of them in the truck, hauled them onto the mill, put them on the ramp, loaded a load of slabs, hauled them back to the clearing this morning, unloaded the slabs. After dinner she and

Danny went back to the cabin and washed and baked bread. I stayed there and cut more trees, cut and trimmed 12 more logs. Then Bell came home and we got nine sawed when it rained a little shower. The tail end of a storm at sea. They call them williwaws here.

Guess that about it for now. Briar may put in her two cents worth. Hope she don't overdo it like she did water in the noon coffee.

By for now, Chet and Family

Tom's near perfect autumn must have been hard for Mike, the second brother. Mike was just a year and half younger than Tom, and they had been thick as thieves growing up in Ohio. But while Tom was out being a young man and not even going to school, Mike was boarding the school bus each morning feeling young and left out. He never bought much into school, although he was probably the smartest one of us. On one hand, he was a bookish fellow who kept to himself. He read voraciously and never forgot anything he read. On the other hand, he was wild and reckless with a fascination for guns and cars. He was probably pretty happy when Tom finally had to go back to being a school kid.

For Tom, it was hard to leave all the manlike grownup things he was doing, but it was nice to be meeting other teenagers and working a little less. We all know that as much as youngsters want to be adults, being a teenager is really a pretty good life most of the time. School was going to feel like a vacation after working side by side with Dad and Mom on the cabin, and they surely were missing his help, though they still had me for what that was worth.

Tom was doing what we now call distance education, basically correspondence school. He was attending school, but his class assignments came by mail. He would be one of two in the first graduating class of Ninilchik High School. He may have been spending his days at school, but I bet his evenings were spent helping Dad lift logs in place as the walls of the cabin rose.

Setting the three-sided logs on a cabin like this is pretty straightforward. One needs a long level or other guide to keep the walls plumb and an additional guide or homemade tool to keep the corners square. Then the logs are stacked and nailed with long spikes and alternating butt joints at the corners. Today, it's common to drive long rods down through the logs in a wall but this isn't necessary or possible in a one-story wilderness cabin. Sometimes a builder will frame doors and windows as they go. Other times they wait until the walls are up and then cut out the openings with a chainsaw. When this part starts, it goes fast and the logs get used up pretty quickly. Figure that each row of logs is six inches thick, so one would need sixteen to eighteen rows of logs, depending on the wall height. Four walls at eighteen high makes seventy-two logs. It's seventy-two if the logs are long enough to span a whole wall; many wouldn't be. I bet Dad estimated he would need about a hundred logs. That's a lot of trees to fell, limb, haul, mill, haul again, and peel.

We peeled our logs with either a drawknife or a spud. A drawknife is like a long knife with a handle on each end, and a spud is like a large chisel on the end of a shovel type handle. Green logs will peel easily, giving up long strips of bark with little effort and leaving a slick white wood beneath. My brothers used to laugh at me when I would brag that I peeled one of the logs, but I can distinctly remember not only peeling the log but also where it lay in the cabin wall. Dad used it as the header log above the west window in the living room. It stood out because green logs peel slick and white, so it shone brighter than the logs around it. I'm pretty sure that this is the kind of peeling job that I took on, one that a little kid could strip pretty easily. After a log has had time to dry and age a bit, the bark bonds more tightly to the wood and must be chiseled off bit by bit. Mom, Mike, and Bill did most of the peeling, a task that raises blisters and makes the forearms sore for days.

September 24, 1958

He could have written quite a lot and left out about the coffee. Guess he doesn't realize he needs so much water every day, and it won't hurt him to get some of it in coffee. You ought to see us hunker down over an "Indian Fire" and eat. And I do mean eat. Mike actually eats more than Tom. One year ago I'd have said impossible, but he does. Good thing "beef" is free. It would break Rockefeller to buy the platters of meat I cook. And I swear I've baked three barrels of cookies since we've been here. But they always disappear. We ate forty-five hot rolls for supper with Mulligan stew. Jim Trent, an old logger taught me to make it. They like it fine as long as I go easy on the turnips. I peeled a turnip the other day that before it was peeled just fit in my 4 quart stainless steel mixing bowl. Well I still have to write Lois Jean so I'd better close and get at it. Let us know how this last shot treated you and is Pop's incision still so sore? Did Dr think that was normal or no? Hope this finds you as well as it leaves us.

Love always, Briar

I didn't know that there was recipe for Mulligan stew, since Mulligan stew is traditionally thrown together with whatever is in the kitchen or at the fireside come cooking time. I can't remember which of my mom's recipes that would have been. There never was much fancy food on the table at our house, but there was always plenty, and most of the time it was really tasty. Something I do remember, and still love, is a pot of pinto beans cooked up with a ham bone or hocks. We ate many a bowl of beans at our table, usually served with cornbread and a dollop of cottage cheese. Sometimes we poured beans over the cornbread, and often there were no ham hocks just the skin off of slab bacon. Dad taught us to save a piece of cornbread for dessert. We would crumble the cornbread into our milk glass, add a spoonful of sugar, and top it off with milk. It made a milky, sweet kind of poor man's pudding. Miguel de Cervantes said, "Hunger is the best sauce in the world," and log cabin building was a great way to prove it.

Eating cornbread and milk out of a glass at the dinner table was not acceptable behavior in Mom's house, and only Dad and kids under his protection could get away with it. Mom always had a thing about manners in general and table manners specifically. We ate with cloth napkins on our laps (something else to iron), and it was always, "Sit up straight, don't talk with your mouth full, keep your elbows off the table, don't put your knife in your mouth, and keep one hand in your lap and eat with the other." When you wanted something from down the table, "Your tongue is longer than your arm." And, "If you can't say please, don't bother asking." We learned to set a table with the silverware in the proper places next to the plates, and how to place our knife across the back of a plate when finished using it instead of flopping on the tablecloth. According to Mom, good table manners were part of making dinner a pleasant repast. When one of the older brothers would chime in with a sarcastic, "One foot on the floor and no stabbing above wrist," Mom would look over the top of her glasses and reply, "Someday you will thank me." And I have to admit, I do.

Most of the time, meals at the Walkers' were taken the old-fashioned way, at a table with everyone eating at the same time. Breakfast, the first meal, would be pancakes, biscuits and gravy, oatmeal and toast, eggs and fried potatoes, or any combination of those. Cold cereal was rare, as was orange juice or any fruit. Breakfast was a quick meal and usually followed some chores that included a made bed and clean bedroom.

At midday we ate dinner, usually a hot meal served to whomever was at the house. We never called a midday meal lunch unless we were away from home or out in the field, where the meal was usually cold. Lunch was cold dinner. Most people today would call the evening meal dinner, but we called it supper. I guess that's a Midwest thing.

On Sunday, dinner was usually a little fancier meal with company and top-drawer manners. We brought a lot of southern Ohio farm traditions with us, and a formal Sunday dinner served right after church was one of them. Usually it was fried chicken, but in the early years, it was more than likely a moose roast with side dishes from rolls to sweet pickles, and it ended with cobbler or pie fresh from the oven.

Back in Ohio, if dinner was at Grandma Walker's, the table was always fully set when we arrived and covered with a clean white tablecloth until mealtime. When the meal was over, rather than clear the dishes, or "rid them up," she draped that tablecloth over the whole mess and left it until later. I couldn't understand why Mom went to all the trouble she did with dishes. I asked her once why she didn't have a tablecloth like Grandma Walker's. She didn't know what I meant. "Well," I said, "whenever we go to dinner at Grandma's she just covers the table full of dirty dishes with a tablecloth. When we come back the next time the dishes are all clean. Why don't you have a tablecloth like that?" I figured that magic tablecloth was a lot better deal for cleaning dishes than what Mom had going at our house.

From an early age, it seemed that Amy and I were the last two to leave the table: Amy because she was always talking and ate slowly, and me because I was a big eater. Usually, I was still eating when there was nothing left but the last of the gravy sopped up with bread. I was a teenager without older brothers at home before I ever saw leftovers; there has to be something left to have leftovers. Before everyone ate there was a prayer and as everyone ate there was news time, debate class, story hour, work update, and school reports all rolled into one. After supper, Dad sat at the table entertaining the dishwashers with stories, advice, and whimsy.

Mom didn't approve of snacks between meals. If you were hungry you waited until the next meal and made sure you ate enough not to be hungry too long before the next one. Needless to say, there was no tolerance for special diets, finicky eaters, or food allergies. We ate what was served or we didn't eat. "Shut up and eat what's put before you" was the response to most complaints. I have gagged on enough fried moose liver to prove that rule; there was no leaving the table with food still on the plate.

Those bites of liver would grow larger and larger in my mouth, and my throat would refuse to swallow as if the stomach had been warned of what was coming. There was no possibility of spitting it out because what went into your mouth never came out, especially at the table. So I sat with that growing wad of liver crowded in the behind my teeth, trying to convince the throat to take it in. Bill said we should try holding our noses as we chewed because that was supposed to keep us from tasting. It didn't work, and we usually ended up giggling and then Amy laughed and Peggy too, until we were all in trouble. I can't tell you if we really ate our full portion of liver, or if we just had to suffer through enough to be miserable, but to this day I will not eat or serve liver. Enough is enough.

I said that there were no snacks between meals, but Mom writes about baking hundreds of cookies, and those had to have been eaten some time. The reality was that we didn't have free access to the larder; food was controlled and distributed by Mom, and that was that. I also have to admit that we had two other snack foods, roasted marshmallows and popcorn. Even after the house was up and the garden cleared, we often had some kind of fire going in the yard, whether it was brush, roots from the garden, or tree limbs. When the fire had burned down and all the charred ends raked into the coals, we got to roast marshmallows. Little brother Dave wasn't very big when he learned to ask if he could fetch the marshmallows anytime someone started a fire in the yard.

Popcorn was an evening snack. We ate it while playing board games on Saturday night or when Dad, Mom, Tom, and Mike would play pinochle and we younger ones played Fish, Jacks, and Steal Casino. Someone would get out the cast aluminum pan and pop up a bunch, and it would have to be a bunch, because no one could get after popcorn like the Walkers.

September 29, 1958

Dear Folks —

How is everything with you? We are all fine. Still working on the cabin. Cutting trees, dragging logs and laying them up. We now have them six rows high and ready to leave out the space for windows. There will be eight all together. Two on each of the four sides. Thursday and Friday we, Briar, Danny and me, laid up logs. Saturday the big boys and myself took the truck and helped Bell and his boy Jack mine two truck loads of coal. Cutting wood is real easy compared to that. We had to shovel off about eighteen to twenty inches of dirt to get to the coal then pry it out with bars. Some blocks come out I know would weigh 500# then you split them up so you can handle it. You really earn it to get it, you can bet on that. It's real nice coal though, holds fire good, not very fast but does good after it starts.

Today we went and helped them get their potatoes dug. PS: Mrs. Bell planted 400 pounds of seed potatoes and I know they dug 5000 pounds. I never dug potatoes any time that were as good. Not many little ones either.

It has froze pretty hard three times now. The nights are just real cool. Yesterday and today were beautiful days. Tomorrow we, Briar, me and Danny and Mrs Bell are going to Homer and get a truckload of gasoline, kerosene and groceries. Gas at the stations is forty cents a gallon. You can take drums and get it in bulk for 30 cents a gal. I'm getting three for us here, about 700 gal altogether.

I'll get my roofing and so forth at the same time. The coal mining and trucking is to pay the Man (Bell) for sawing my lumber and dragging in logs. It's really a pretty good deal. We had hoped to get it up to the square this week, but we will see how we make out and try. We want to at least get it under roof before snow.

Mike helped a neighbor here today get his potatoes dug and banked dirt around his house. Made a little spending money.

Bye for now, Chet and Family

Eighteen

Cheechako: A newcomer to Alaska; a term generally applied to anyone who had not yet wintered through. A tenderfoot, an inept amateur. The term is of disputed origin as are some sourdoughs.

October 1, 1958

Hello Folks —

We sent you a package today with a little something for both of you (birthday present) hope you get them and like them. This leaves us all fine, kids in school and apparently doing all right. Car license up here cost $20 a year. We got ours Sept 1. They are half price then.

We went to Homer Monday, really spent the day at it. Homer is thirty miles south of here. Took the truck and brought back 16 drums of gas, kerosene and Blazo (Blazo is what they use up here for gasoline lanterns; it's a naphtha gas). It's cleaner than white gasoline. Kerosene here in five gallon cans is $4.25 for five gal (85 cents a gallon) by the drum it's 36.5 cents a gallon. Blazo is the same in five gallon, by the drum 37 cents a gal, gasoline 40 cents a gal. at station 29.3 cents a gal. down there so we saved heap many dollars. I also got my roofing and black building paper and clear plastic for windows. It's not wise to put glass in a new log house as it will twist and heave and rock and roll 'til it dries and settles and break the windows. It rained on us all the way home. Then about all day yesterday and is still drizzly today. Not much logging weather.

We are going over this pm and clean out the well, put in a pump, and cover the well to keep out the chips shavings and sawdust. Maybe I'll get some logs in this evening after Jack comes from school. We also got a few groceries Monday for ourselves and Bells. Mrs. Bell went along. Most of the gasoline was for them. He works on the highway, drives to work everyday. Besides the sawmill, they saw with an A.C. tractor about like the one we used to have only a newer model. That is what we drag logs with. I don't seem to be able to keep much of a schedule on building as the rain sure makes it slow.

Chet and Family

After supper same day ... We cleaned the well. We had kicked mud in it and shavings and that sort of thing. It filled back up in an hour, course it was pretty oily. I got the pitcher pump ready to put in and found out I had the wrong valve leather so we didn't get that done. It rained again about 4:30 and then again since then so we didn't drag any logs. Thanks for sending the wick cleaner and ribbons and curlers. That was real good service.

We've been thinking and talking about Christmas. If we may suggest, some magazine subscriptions would be really welcome. Briar would like "Good Housekeeping" or McCalls. McCalls preferably. The boys would like Popular Science, "Highlights" for the little kids. Opal Eaglin could tell you the particulars about it. Now that's only a suggestion. You do as you like but if it is any help, you are welcome. Guess that's the story for now. Oh yes, we got two letters Monday. From you that is.—Chet

October 1, 1958

Hi Folks,

I'll put in a word or so here. This envelope will need 50 cents in stamps if we keep on. Thanks a lot for the ribbons and so on. That fixes the girls up in good shape. We are all pretty well set for winter now. It will be handier if we get the cabin done before snow but we are so much better off here than a lot of people are for their first winter. It sure makes for easy housekeeping. Looks like a shambles every morning but only takes about an hour to do everything. If I ever get everything built in the way I want over there at the new house it will be even easier. I'm getting lazy enough for anybody. People up here do their housekeeping the simple way. Only do necessities and not much "foofarah," but they have plenty of time and enjoy it too. Well, must write to Mother. She sent me dress material for my birthday and Tom two pair of socks. We got them Monday.

Love, Briar

While Dad was focused on getting the cabin built, Mom was his right hand every day after she put things in order at home. Many a morning, Dad would leave the Goggins' cabin at first light to walk a mile-long foot trail across Happy Valley to the unfinished cabin, leaving Mom to ramrod the kids off to school with lunches, then put the cabin in order and maybe do a bit of baking or laundry. When all that was set straight, she would drive over to give Dad a hand. Somehow, in that time she would have the house clean and tidy.

In stark contrast with most of our neighbors, cleaning was Mom's passion. Contrary to what she says, these causal housekeepers would never convert her to the Alaska approach to housekeeping. She would mop and wax a dirt floor if that's what it took, and kids who didn't do their part to keep even a squatter's cabin spit and polish clean would get a whippin'. It would not have been a "foofarah" but a fate worse than death.

The house and the yard would always be in apple pie order, as Mom put it, not just for company or on Saturday when everyone turned out for

The seven Walker children—(clockwise) Mike, Tom holding David, Bill, Peggy, Dan, and Amy—are ready for school pictures in the fall of 1959.

chores, but every day, all the time. Such a showcase is only maintained with constant vigilance, tireless labor, and standards higher than anyone else's. For Mom, the "simple way" was to keep it clean in the first place, put things where they belong, and never go to bed with a messy house. It sounds simple, but you just try it, even for a month or so, and you'll find that it requires not only energy but also focus and priority, all three of which Mom must have been born with. She must have gotten over the laziness she referenced in her previous letter.

Life in the new cabin was business as usual with Mom and that meant we got up, got dressed, made the bed, and cleaned our bedroom before breakfast. After every meal someone immediately did the dishes, usually one ridding up, one washing, and then someone drying and putting away. This included sweeping and mopping the floor with the last of the dishwater. I never remember going to bed with dirty dishes in the sink, and we kids never left for school or anywhere else without a wash up. "Face and hands and neck and ears" (Mom said it like it was all one word) all got a good scrubbing before a meal, before the school bus, before leaving home, and before bed. Baths came once a week, routinely in the kitchen where enough water was heated on the cookstove to fill a fifteen-gallon number two washtub. We scrubbed with homemade soap and stepped out of the tub onto a dry, clean towel in front of the warm oven. We took turns in the tub until the water was used up, then it was dumped and refilled. My mom and the girls washed their hair over a washbasin.

I used to think that everyone, except bachelors like Al Sanborn, kept things clean and orderly one way or another. Not everyone lived like we did, and in fact I discovered that the spit and polish regime of my mother created a unique island of clean and tidy in a rather messy world. I visited houses when I was a kid that weren't like that, and I was amazed. Many of them just seemed to camp among their belonging with no order to their possessions or the flow of their life. Some people just piled dishes on the counter or in the center of the table to be taken care of later, or tomorrow. Sometimes I would visit friends, and I'd have to move laundry off the couch to sit down. Never would one ever see that at the Walkers', only over Mom's dead body or the body of the kid who didn't get the laundry folded, ironed, and put away.

This same penchant for a clean and orderly world led my mother to a career in professional housekeeping, a world away from the backwoods of the Kenai Peninsula.

Nineteen

White spruce (*Picea glauca*): A widely distributed evergreen that grows to sixty feet tall throughout much of North America. The bark is thin and scaly, the leaves are needle-like. Commonly used for lumber, less commonly for firewood and Christmas trees.

October 5, 1958 Sunday pm

Dear Folks,

Well we sure had a rapid change in the weather here the last two days. It had rained all week, as I think I told you when we wrote Thursday. Friday night during the night, the rain turned to snow. Everything was wet and the snow clung to it and left all the trees, grasses, bushes and so on coated with a layer of white. It was really a winter wonderland. But the craziest thing was it was not even cold. We, the girls and I, were baking and had just a normally hot fire but had to keep the door open.

Chet and boys and Denny Bell and his boy Jackie sawed 26 logs and drug in 26 more ready to saw. Then Chet an the boys peeled 16 of the sawed logs. The snow was half melted by afternoon, and they were not at all cold except where their hands got wet from the snow. They didn't come in until after dark last night. They were surely a tired bunch. Mike especially. Seems he got sort of put out at the other boys and did lot of the log rolling by himself. Ordinarily, he is not much of a worker—spends most of his time getting out of work. But he was really done in last night. They put away a big supper and it wasn't long before they were ready for bed.

They got up about 8:30 this morning. Tom got up earlier because he was going to church with Jack Bell this morning. We are going into Ninilchik at 2:00 to the Methodist Church and Sunday school. It is a lot closer than Anchor

Point where we have been going and will be even closer, only six miles when we move. There is not much else to do on Sunday anyway. I don't know if this will be a permanent arrangement or not. We did like the church there at Anchor Point a lot.

When we got up this morning, the ground was frozen hard. It has begun to thaw slightly right now on top and the sun is shining so bright it hurts your eyes. Chet is delighted. He likes to work in weather like this. He thinks he might have to cut about 8 more logs and that's all. Then he will need to cut some saw logs for rafters, sheathing, flooring etc. He has the trees picked out and a few saw logs down so we begin to see the beginning of the end anyway. He'll never see the end of all the cupboards and closets and so on we want to put inside, but he can do that inside when the snow is flying. Danny said to tell you he's taking his new hanky to church. About the girls baking, Peggy made "hermit" cookies. They turned out especially good. Amy made some from a recipe she altered to suit herself. They ended up a combination oatmeal raisin and peanut butter. They were fair but would have been better if she had watched them closer in the oven. But she'll learn (I hope). I made bread and pumpkin pies.

We heard from Butlers this week. They are still in Oregon but intend to stay only until spring I guess. Dennis didn't go to school. He failed last year and is 17 so he figured it wasn't worth it I guess. I think so too. He never would graduate at the rate he had been going. He is working on a ranch. I'm not sure just what sort of work but I guess he likes it.

Let me tell you a good one on Tom. They had a ballgame the other day with Tustamena School. Here the boys and girls both play on the ball team. The pitcher in the Tustamena was an Hawaiian girl. She was a real beauty I guess. Tom said she went to Ninilchik last year and all the boys fought over her all year, and Tom says she's worth fighting over. Two days later, they came home in a dither. The girl, her name is Verda Bice, had written a letter to Mike. I don't know what was in it and I don't know if Tom ever found out or not but it sure got him. (Briar)

(Chet) Hi, I'll add a little dab to let you know I'm still kicking. The boy and I went out scrounging a little coal at the "mine" to hold fire at night in the range. We don't have the heater up and don't think we will till we move. This wood here don't hold fire like oak. It either burns real fast or goes out. We didn't do much this week up to Friday. We got some licks in Thursday and yesterday.

Must sign off, Chet

146 / Dan L. Walker

October 6, 1958

Dear Folks,

Monday night, had two letters from you in today's mail. Glad you are getting along. Winter had really hit here but it sure is a welcome change. The snow is practically gone tonight. It was about 17 degrees this morning and the ground stayed froze. A few more like that and the mud will be gone 'til spring thaw. We worked over at the cabin today. Peeled the rest of our logs we have saved, hauled a load to the mill, and hauled back a big load of slabs. Tomorrow we lay up logs. We have twenty-six ready to go; that should lay up four rounds. We will see.

About the logs, I'll draw you a picture. and so on up. You see they don't lap at the corners but the alternate ones that go clear through. The long ones are nailed through to the one below that runs the other way at the corner. It's a cob-house sort of. The nails are eight inches long and counter sunk two inches. That makes four inches in each log; you nail them every five feet or so all the way along. When it's all up, there will be over 100 pounds of those big nails in the walls. The corners will be like they had ⅜ rod clear down through them. They hold alright. I seen one where they had a 2x8 laid under the bottom log and the floor joist set on that two inches that stuck in under the log. The center rested on a double 2x4. I didn't go for that. I have a 3x6 on edge on the outside edge and the center sill is a 6x6 like so.

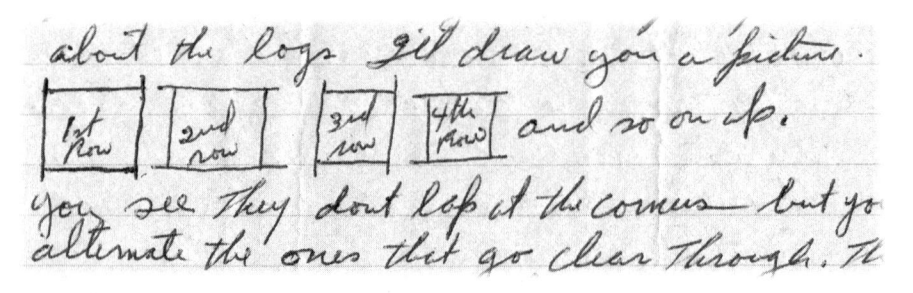

The Ceiling Joist will bear the outside walls with a 6x6 beam down the center of the house with posts down directly over the pilings and posts below. There is two posts in the cellar. There will be one post in the center of the big

ends and the center sill is a 6x6 like so [sketch] 3x6 notched in 6x6 3x6 logs The ceiling joist will bear on the outside walls with a 6x6 beam down the center of the house with post down

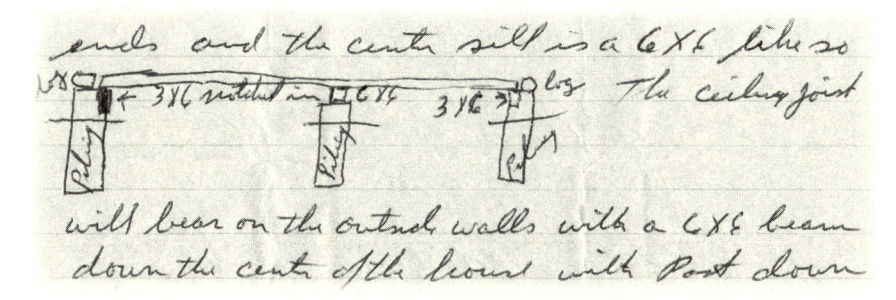

room behind the cook stove. The others will be in the partitions of the bedrooms. We got our pump working, a pitcher pump Bell gave us.

Oh yes, Bells came from Pennsylvania eight years ago. They built their cabin in the winter and he cut all the logs with an ax, some in deep snow and the stumps are still there three to four feet tall. He hauled his logs to the sawmill on a little trailer behind a Montgomery Ward garden tractor. They had their truck shipped from Anchorage to Moose Pass by railroad. There was no road then. Some people came by barge.

The children at school are a duke's mixture; some are Russian some are Eskimo some Indian, some are "damn Yankees." Tom says about a third of the children were born in the states; the rest were born here or at least in the state.

Briar came home at school bus time and did a washing after 4:30, hung them up too. It's not eight yet and supper over, dishes done, and writing letters with electric light. We only use the light plant to wash or iron. I'll move it as soon as I start the rafters and roof to use the electric saw. Will continue this later on in the week.

Monday night, had two letters from you in today's mail. Glad you are getting along. Hope the hula-hoop don't get you down. Winter had really hit here but it sure is a welcome change. The snow is practically gone tonight. It was about 17 degrees this morning and the ground stayed froze. A few more like that and the mud will be gone 'til spring thaw.

Thursday AM. Sun trying to shine. Kids on the way to the bus. We are being a little lazy this morning. We took our heating stove over yesterday and put it in the house to warm by and warm our dinner; felt real good. It's been down below twenty degrees every morning this week up till this morning. We've run out of sawn logs. Need four rows and about ten feet more to be up to the square. We are going to fill in under the house today between the pilings and between *the joist around the cellar. We bring nearly all our water over here from the well now. We've got nearly enough logs cut and hauled in from the woods to finish the logs but most likely won't get anymore sawed till Saturday. Will sign off for now. Behave yourselves and let us hear from you.*

As ever,
Chet and Family

Folks today usually build with log for the aesthetic but not so with pioneers' and homesteaders' log cabins. In a place with plentiful resources a young, strong man with an ax, chainsaw, and a couple of chisels can put together a log cabin in a clearing in the woods. If it is possible to mill logs into lumber, a frame structure is a more practical choice.

While using the trees on our property for building lumber was convenient and cheap, it also meant a lot of work. After a tree was dropped and limbed, it had to be dragged a few hundred yards to Bells' sawmill. After being run through the mill and coming out as a house log or several boards, the wood was stacked again, then hauled to our place and probably stacked once more, then finally cut, peeled, and fitted into its part of the house.

Without the mill right next door, there is a good chance that Dad, a practical man, would have built a frame house instead of logs. He was leaning that way only a few weeks before.

Maybe having the Bells' sawmill just down the lane helped make the choice for this particular piece of land to prove up on, and Dad was able to pay off this service by hauling cargo, including coal and lumber, with his truck. In fact, the benefit of local logs could be lost if they had to be trucked far to be milled. One might as well buy lumber already cut. There is nothing like distance to make any job tougher, but with the mill right next door to square the logs, he didn't have to mess with sealing joints between raw round logs. They made log building fast and tight.

The Bells were important in our success at cabin building, not just because of the mill in their backyard, but also for their friendship and advice. In contrast, I remember the Bells as rather glum and dark people, without much laughter in their house. Denny and Renee Bell were followers of Herbert W. Armstrong, a radio evangelist who lead the Worldwide

Church of God, a Christian sect. I can still hear the radio show playing in their house, "This is Herbert W. Armstrong coming to you with the World Tomorrow!" His messages, even to a young boy like me, were pessimistic and bleak, warning us all to prepare for Armageddon and pleading for us to leave our evil ways behind.

In spite of these differences, they were the heart of kindness to us in those first fragile months and good friends in the years that followed.

Besides the log work, we often socialized with the Bell family, and Dickie, a couple years older than me, was a handy playmate. Their house would be almost within shouting distance of ours when we moved in, so kids could play easily in the woods and along the lane between the two places. The Bells seemed quiet in contrast to the Walkers' frequent laughter and noisy banter. They did bring music into our house; Renee played the mandolin, and none of us played so much as a harmonica. In the frontier though, the friendship between neighbors is essential to facing the routine challenges of life, and our friends are the neighbors that come with the land, and the best friends are the ones sharing a common experience.

I don't remember any playmates except Dick Bell until I went to school and met other kids my age. I'm sure that I played with other kids at church and such, but at five years old, my family was the center of my world.

What kept this world on its axis was Dad. He also kept it bright and hopeful. He was romantic, and by that I mean that he looked hopefully toward the future and savored the rich qualities of life. Mom was more sentimental, prone to look back at what was or wasn't in the past. Romantics are full of hope, and the sentimental are prone to cynicism. The unity of those two forces made a strong team that was carrying us forward in the autumn of our big first year in Alaska.

October 12, 1958

Dear Pop and mom —
Sunday PM. Supper over and another day shot. I put helper springs under a neighbors pick up this morning, and we all went to Sunday School and church at Ninilchik this afternoon 2 till 4. Went down to the beach and picked up a

little coal to hold fire at fire. Then home for supper. Also stopped at the homestead and picked up 15 gallons of water.

Tomorrow morning we will unload the truck and haul a load of coal from the mine for Bells. They dug it out today. If it lays there very long someone else may haul it away. We sawed enough logs to finish laying up the cabin yesterday.

So will get at that as soon as we haul coal. there is 33 logs to peel bark off of before we lay them. We won't do them all at once though. Peel a few then lay them. We have enough lumber saved for window and door frames and make the doors. I hope to get the rafters and sheeting sawed next Saturday. I'll have to cut the logs but that won't take long. The Bell boy will drag them in after school with the tractor. The rafters will have to be 11 ft the rest can be 12 or less for sheeting, the ceiling joist will be 12 ft.

We had a little more snow but it is about all melted again. Yesterday and today were beautiful about 20 degrees of a morning but soon warmed up and it thawed more this afternoon but gets chilly about 5 o'clock and is dark by 6. We don't need a light mornings after 6:30. We are all ok and the cabin is coming along. We got eleven rows up out of 15 rows of logs. We put slabs and logs under the logs between the pilings and banked dirt up to keep the wind out from under the house. I'm sure we have a weeks work with the the material we have ready and logs to cut. If I can get enough sawed next Saturday, we could get it under roof in the next two weeks. that is our goal at least. there is lots to do so you can be sure we are busy. Guess that brings you up to date so will sign off for now. Be good and write.

As ever,
Chet and family

Twenty

Bush: Wild, remote, or uncultivated land; the part of Alaska inaccessible by road; also known as most of Alaska.

It is easy to think of Dad building a cabin in the woods as an isolated construction project, and one then easily shapes an image of the cabin as the whole homestead. In reality, the cabin was shelter, and within that shelter we established a center for our life. But *to homestead*, literally or figuratively, was more than that and not just in the clichéd sense of a cabin becoming a home. Homesteaders are land and local resource dependent, self-sufficient, and live off the land. To homestead we had to establish how we lived on this land in this place. What would be our place in the community? Who would be the friends and allies? Who would we avoid and distrust?

Homesteading is a geographic change of place as well as a change of lifestyle. Usually it means becoming part of a community or moving to where there is none. I know that I am a different person because I grew up here in Alaska instead of Ohio. My family had to change the way they lived, and the experience itself changed our sense of the world and how we lived in it. Maybe that is why some people can't live here. They want to change their location without changing other parts of their life. They build the cabin but never really move in. To move in means to move into the community, into the rhythm of the season, and into the realities of the local economy. To homestead is to make a place where no place was before and to make that place permanent. Permanence might be the hardest part of all.

October 15, 1958

Dear Folks,

Wednesday night and letter writing time. At last we have our logs all up. Finished about 3 pm today. Have it up to the square. I cut three trees and we dragged the logs into the mill, seven of them. They are for sheeting on the roof. Tomorrow I'll put the top plate on, a 2x6 laid on top of the logs for the rafters to bear on, and put a 6x6 beam down the center with 6x6 posts under it. Also will cut a bunch of logs for rafters and ceiling joists. Also some for flooring and more sheeting. It sure takes a lot of boards and material. I used about 100# of those big 8-inch nails on the logs. As Denny Bell says, if it falls down it will be from the weight of the nails.

We hope to get enough sawed Saturday to get it ready to move in. It will take a lot of doing but not impossible at all. We had a nice day Monday. Tuesday it rained all day and up till 9 or 10 last night. Then it cleared up and was nice all day today. We worked in the rain up till 4 o'clock then came home at school bus time. The lane had thawed out and we had to walk in then back and this morning it thawed just like the spring break up.

We were both glad to get that last log up. Had three left over, one of them peeled. Briar hated that; she don't care much for log peeling. I don't either far as that goes. The kids got report cards today. All are doing well in school. Amy got all A's but a C in writing. Bill was next then Peg then Mike. He is getting lazy and just don't study. This leaves us all well but tired. Briar says Hi. Be good and write.

Chet and family

My dad wasn't a builder by trade. He was a farmer who volunteered for World War II, and the U.S. Army Air Corps trained him as an airplane mechanic, but there is no doubt that he had good instincts about building and knew that building it well was the way to sleep at night. He had a saying about fences, "Horse high, hog tight, and bull strong." That's the principle he applied to building our cabin too.

For whatever reason, be it ignorance, hardheadedness, or necessity, Chet Walker went against some of the basic tenets of wood construction. First, he used uncured, raw spruce that he felled and dragged to Bell's sawmill where some were cut into boards and nailed in place all on the same day. Most professionals would tell you that any wood needs to be dried at least one year before using it for anything. That is why commercial lumber is milled, planed, dried, and cured before it is sold to the local lumberyard. Lumber like this was available 140 miles away in Seward, but it was pricey and unnecessary when perfectly good trees were available right on site.

Spruce is a wood with a lot of grain, which means that strong fibers run up and down the tree, making it resilient and generally straight. Wood of this nature is highly flexible and resistant to breaking, but it is also highly prone to twisting and warping. A beautifully milled, straight-grained board laying out in the weather for a few weeks will practically tie itself in a knot. Usually, the result is a comma-shaped bowed chunk of wood good for little but a campfire.

Dad's green lumber would shrink, but it would only warp if not nailed in place, and the logs wouldn't warp at all. In fact, for generations, impatient men building shelter for their families have been doing what my dad did. Cut, shape, and use green lumber to build a house. This works because the green wood works both against and for itself as it dries. Dad drove a full hundred pounds of eight-inch spikes into the logs walls. He drove twenty-penny nails to anchor joists and rafters. All these fasteners were gripped tighter and tighter as the wood shrank around them. This allowed, or forced, the joints to draw together tightly as the wood dried, and the tendency to twist and warp leveraged the wood against itself as much as it was pulling away. The result: straight, tight joints.

Dad also left his wood untreated. The logs and board and batten went up without paint, stain, or oil. It makes sense that he built this way. Dad's clock was ticking, and he was thinking about getting his family into a warm, secure house for the winter. Of course, this worked in his favor because the untreated green wood was allowed to breath liberally in all directions. When people talk about wood breathing, they're referring to the movement of moisture, and the goal is for the wood to have the same moisture content as its surroundings. Any paint, oil, or stain would seal the pores of the wood and slow the water's movement out of the wood. The fact is that there is no wood finish that can be spread on green wood with any expectation of permanence. Spruce is a sappy wood rich in creosote, and until the moisture abandons the other chemicals in the dead tree cells, no coating will stand.

The Walker cabin with its tightly fastened frame of log and lumber would sit through the cold, relatively arid winter, slowly giving up its moisture, which is what curing is all about. The wood had been allowed to develop a uniform level of moisture, and the result was a dry, tight, square cabin that stood for thirty years in its parent forest with only a little rot along the base logs where the soil lay directly against the wood.

The rest of Dad's work would prove to be much the same. The joints he formed with logs and lumber were strong and didn't split. He took the same approach to relationships with people, and those relationships weathered the years, lasting longer than he did.

He was so religious that one of his searches in this new land was for a church that matched his way of dealing with God. In my first reading of these letters, I noticed reference to attending one church or another and observations on the way the people approach worship or the tenor of the sermon. That search seemed to never end. If we didn't go to church, we would have a bit of Bible study, songs, and prayer at the house, and I imagine that squatter's cabin rang with song many Sunday mornings. The religion I was raised in was rooted in the Church of Christ teaching of the Midwest, which involved a lot of singing and using the Bible as a guide in daily life. Church was an important part of our lives, because that was where community began. I never sensed my parents holding a preoccupation with the afterlife or being "saved" or of God intervening for us. It was more about living a good life by following the teachings of Jesus and the commandments. When we left Ohio we were still a part of the Church of Christ, and my parents didn't seem to mind looking at alternatives, but the theology had to be right. We had found our land, dug a well, and started a cabin. Dad and Mom needed a church.

The thirty-mile stretch of road from Anchor Point to Clam Gulch held more houses of worship than one would expect. We tried every one of them and got to know many different people since the churches were the social center of the area—and we got along well with most of them. For a time, we even had church in our own home with a minister trying to gather a flock around him. Sadly he did more taking than giving, and that didn't strike Dad as very Christian. I'm not sure my parents ever found a church that fit. Usually, it was not the people that put them off, it was the preaching. The comments in their letters and conversations with Mom when I was grown reinforced the impression that she was constantly searching for a message to match her ear. When we moved to Anchorage after Dad died, my mother settled on the Episcopal Church, where she found comfort in its English roots and ceremony.

October 19, 1958 Happy Valley

Dear Folks,

Saturday night 8:30 pm. Just got in and the stove hot. Had Family Fellowship potluck supper after church and a good time was had by all. Had roast wild duck, moose loaf, roast moose, moose with spaghetti, potato salad, pie, cake, coffee, cookies and Bavarian cream, hot rolls and butter. Had 35 for Sunday School again this Sunday. Next week Mike and Tom are going to Anchorage to church youth meeting. Expenses paid. They will get quite a bang out of it I'm sure. Three of the school teachers were there tonight. The meeting started with Sunday School at 2:00, church at 3:00 then we ate about 5:00 got in home about 8:00. The fire was out. We just used the range and no one fixed the fire before we left so the house was really cool. It was down to 29 degrees last night and windy. It was 14 degrees at the village. It's always colder there than out here in the woods. The wind off the mountains and Inlet hit there with no trees to stop it.

We are all fine and the kids pretty well, kept busy with school and water carrying and wood splitting. Tom cut enough about two months ago that we will have wood to move I expect so they don't have to cut it. We've quite a pile cut over at the cabin and plenty to cut all around the clearings.

We have the logs all up to the square and the center beam and posts in also, the top plate on and ready for rafters and ceiling joists. We sawed the lumber for them Saturday. I guess we sawed close to 2000 ft Saturday. I had twenty-eight logs in to the mill and we sawed all but three of them before it got too dark at six o'clock to saw. I went over this morning and we sawed them. I think there will be enough sawed to get us moved in. It's hard to tell exactly till you get to nailing it up though.

We had a good week as far as progress goes, we got a lot done even though the weather was bad. We are keeping our fingers crossed for it to stay bearable to finish getting the roof on. A neighbor moved the generator over for me on a pickup so I can use the electric saw on the rest. That will help alot. I had the big truck loaded with lumber. I didn't want to unload only as I can use it.

It's cold and a little windy tonight will get down pretty cold before morning. It warmed up and rained last Thursday and road in was impassable back in here till late yesterday so we hope it stays froze up. We had the water cans in the car and it was a mile out, so we (the boys) carried water for a half mile to walk in. You can see why we want to get moved where we have water.

Guess I've told you all the news up to now. Will write to Catherine now. Briar is writing to Billy Bells Mom and Catherine Walker. Be good and don't work too hard.

Bye now,
Chet and Family

From Briar ... same letter
Chet didn't tell you the boys will stay overnight in Anchorage. Up here when anyone is invited to stay overnight, they don't worry about beds. They say, "Bring your sleeping bags." Then you just bed down on the floor. The boys will probably sleep in the church in Anchorage. There will be young people there from all over Alaska.
Briar

A person needs to spend some time without running water, like most of the world does, to appreciate what a luxury it is. Hauling it is time-consuming and usually inconvenient, especially when you are a family of eight. Figure a quart each for drinking, which gets to two gallons real fast. Add in a couple of gallons for cooking and another couple for washing hands and dishes. Wow, we are at five to six gallons per day without considering anyone taking a bath or doing laundry. Come laundry day, the Walkers likely needed ten to twenty gallons.

When a home doesn't have running water or at least a stream out back, water is a daily issue. Rain and snow are convenient, but rain must be captured in a clean way and isn't reliably available. Snow has to be melted, and that is a messy, time-consuming proposition. Depending on the wetness of the snow, a five-gallon pail of snow will probably melt down to a quarter of a bucket or less. It is one thing to melt snow for a weekend camping trip but doing so every day all winter long gets old fast. However, even today, there are a lot of people in Alaska who don't have city water or a well on their property, and they have to integrate hauling water into their lifestyle. I have visited Alaska villages in the bush where people live without running water and part of the daily routine is loading water jugs on the back of a sled or ATV and hauling them from a central pump house. Combined with a laundromat and community showers, they are usually called washaterias.

Even the people in established towns can face the challenge of water. Many subdivisions on the edge of the communities of Fairbanks and Bethel have large modern homes without wells or city water. These houses usually have large cistern systems that collect rainfall, and/or they haul water in giant plastic tanks that fit in the back of a pickup truck. These folks usually only worry about water hauling on a weekly or monthly basis, but it still puts a premium on water that is not found in other places.

The Walkers came to Alaska expecting to rough it. We slept on the ground or packed everyone into a tiny cabin. We ate the wild game that the land gave up and the fish dragged from the water. We lived and worked in the rain, wind, and snow. We settled for mail twice a week and no electricity, and we tromped to the outhouse in below-zero weather. That was all just fine with us, but we would not spend the winter hauling water or melting snow. In-house running water was a major priority for Dad and Mom, and when priorities are reasonable, they aren't hard to achieve.

Twenty-One

Board and batten: Vertical siding composed of wide boards, usually rough cut, with narrow strips, or battens, of the same material that are nailed over the spaces between the boards. The primogenitor of T1-11.

October 23, 1958 6:30 am

Dear Pop and Mom —
Cold and little windy here on top of the ridge. You feel the cold more on top of ridges in the clearings. This cabin sets in the middle of a clearing, 5-6 acres right on top of the ridge. Our cabin is in the woods so it is lots warmer than here. Building is progressing fine. Monday we put the ceiling joist and cut the first pair of rafters. Tuesday we put the rafters up. Wednesday I had Tom stay home and help and we put the sheeting on. So today we put tar paper on the roof. I've had mighty good help or we would not have been so close to having a house. Briar drove nails all day and her right arm was about broke last night. I squared one end of the boards on the ground with electric saw. Tom handed them up and I cut the other ends to splice on a rafter. Briar nailed. We had it done by 3pm. 676 sq ft of it. It is looking like a house now.
We put the door frames in Tuesday after we got the rafters up. Still have the windows to frame and doors to make. We will need to cut a few more logs and saw this Saturday. I need more boards for floor and gable ends and odds and ends, partitions. About a half dozen good sized logs will do it. So it will be about the middle of the week when we can move in. That won't be too soon.
Water is hard to come by here and the tent is too cold, so Tom and Mike sleep in the cabin now in sleeping bags on the floor. It gets a little crowded and

inconvenient. This leaves us all well and busy as beavers, just needed today without snow to leave it whipped. It's clear so we ought to make it. We will have to get the stove up and heat the roofing so we got another big day ahead of us. Will give you the latest Sunday.

Bye now,
Chet and family

PS: the hump on a moose is much like the shape and location of a horse's withers or a Brahma Bull hump.

Alaska summer days are painted with purples, pinks, and yellows on a canvas of green and are filled with a youthful vigor that stretches into the long bright evening, while autumn is a dark and damp time that draws a curtain on the green, bright summer. I was a college student before I would experience an autumn like the ones on the October calendar photos. The calendars show forests of gold and fields full of pumpkins with landscapes painted in yellows, oranges, and browns. In Happy Valley, the days of fall are painted in darker earth tones deepened by the shadow of the sun's decreasing angle, and the optimistic summer vigor develops a certain desperate tone. October brings a hurried sense of the impending winter with its shortened days as the last of the pigments are drained from the cooling land. We rush to complete the final chores like those who find that they have only weeks to live, for the first significant snows of winter are here by Halloween.

Surely the old-timers told my folks what to expect from the weather of October. They wouldn't want to be moving in through the snow; they had enough challenges. Dad wouldn't want to shovel snow off the roof before he put on tar paper. These final steps had to happen before they ran out of October. A little of the desperation trickles through when Dad surrenders the rare complaint: "Water is hard to come by here and the tent is too cold, so Tom and Mike sleep in the cabin now in sleeping bags on the floor. It gets a little crowded and inconvenient."

I can't remember the Goggins' cabin well enough to know what size it was, but I know eight people living and sleeping in a one-room cabin would be far more than "a little crowded and inconvenient." But this is the Dad that I like to remember, a man with his glass half full, a man to emulate, uncomplaining about the present, optimistic about the future, and confident in himself and others. This is the kind of man you want finishing your cabin in October.

October 27, 1958 Happy Valley

Dear Pop and Mom —
Monday morning partly cloudy and not so cold, it's still. The wind has been pretty strong the past few days. We had a busy day yesterday so didn't write any last night. I helped Mr. Bell saw lumber yesterday all day in order to get some sawed for me. He had trouble Saturday and didn't get much done. I needed more boards for flooring. Briar baked bread and cleaned up the cabin. Then went to church yesterday afternoon. Then was invited out for supper. I got my logs sawed, and they came after me at dark around 6 pm.

Tom and Mike went to Anchorage to a church youth meeting Friday night. Got home about 11 pm. Had a fine time. Said it was 2 degrees above at Anchorage and was about 20 degrees here. So you can see we had a busy day.

We had a very busy week all through. The weather stayed nice not too cold, no rain or snow. The ground is froze solid except in the extreme wet places. The temperature has been down at least to 20 every night. It's real pleasant to work out. I cut logs two evenings for Bells and one for us. Worked in my shirtsleeves. We dress to keep warm. I wear long underwear and two pairs of pants, a shirt, sweater, sheepskin vest and light jacket so the cold don't bother. I bought insulated boots last winter and wear them with a thin pair of cotton sox.

I guess that's the news for now except the cabin. I'll give you the latest on that now. Thursday and Friday we put on the roof. It was quite a job—we warmed the tar paper best we could but it gave us quite a bit of trouble at that. We finally got it on, it's a poor job but I don't think it will leak. Friday night I made a front door and hung it. Saturday I closed in one gable end just one course of boards. Today I aim to put in windows. Guess that's it. Will get to move in this week we hope. Lay floors tomorrow. Two neighbors are going to help. I aim to have the boards all cut ready to nail.

Bye now,
Chet and Family

In the last weeks of October the temperature is just above twenty, the heat has gone out of the sun, and sunset each day is six minutes earlier. Not good weather for roofing. The roofing, or tar paper, was about thirty-six inches wide and came in long rolls with cans of tar and bags of nails tucked in the center. The first strip of tarpaper had to be rolled onto the roof along the eave and nailed in place, then a layer of tar was poured along the top edge and the next strip of paper lapped a few inches over that tar, and so on up the roof. In the cold and damp of October, the tar paper was stiff and hard to unroll, so before Dad could start, the tar paper had to spend some hours sitting next to the woodstove while the cans of tar warmed on the stovetop like a hobo's soup. I'm sure the time it took to roof that cabin was tripled by the weather conditions, but it didn't leak, and photos from 1959 show the tarpaper still in good shape and two stovepipes rising out of the roof.

Unlike the Goggins' cabin, the homestead cabin had two stoves, the renowned kitchen range and a humble box stove. Although these were not nearly as efficient as modern woodstoves, they were head and shoulders above the barrel stoves most people were heating with at the time. The barrel stove, a homestead standard, was constructed from a fuel barrel, usually a fifty-five gallon variety, to which a stovepipe and door were attached. The barrel was laid on its side, and either legs were added or the barrel was placed in a bed of sand. Barrel stoves were good at burning wood but lousy at heating houses.

Our heating stove was a rectangular box stove, about twenty-four inches long and twelve or so wide. It was made of cast iron, a more durable and safer stove than the cheaper sheet metal stoves. In the fifties, the woodstove was pretty much the same as those used a hundred years before. The cast iron stove wasn't airtight, so it was hard to keep a fire all night, even with coal. During cold weather Dad would get up to feed the stove in the middle of the night.

With the stove and roofing installed and a door in place, moving day was getting closer. The windows would be double layers of Visqueen with an air space in between, and the gable ends would be sheathed in board and batten rather than logs like the rest of the house. Even with the cold weather, I'm sure leaving windows and gables open to the last was part of Dad's plan. Keeping a fire going in the heater would provide a warmer cabin for him to work in and a place to make coffee or warm food. The fire would also start chasing the water from the green wood, for not only was it green, but the wood was also wet from the rain that had fallen since the lumber was felled and milled. Those first few days with a fire in the cabin, it probably steamed like a locomotive out the open eaves as the moisture began to leave and the cabin started drying in readiness for the eager inhabitants waiting on the other side of Happy Valley.

I was five years old when my family built the new homestead cabin.

Twenty-Two

Good Friday Earthquake: A 9.2 earthquake centered in south central Alaska that occurred on March 29, 1964, at 5:39 p.m. Resulted in massive damage, 128 deaths, and radical modifications of the landscape. It proved to be unrelated to local cabinetmaking.

When Dad took on the task of building a home, it took over his whole person. I know that feeling; I've been there. The cliché is true that a house is not a home; building a home is much more personal. The mind is always working ahead to be ready for the next task, the next step, while at the same time it works in the detail of the moment, the task at hand. There is the management of materials and tools for the next project; the planning of what happens when; the work of the day, the week, the month, the moment; and the problems of the minute are all happening at once. The logger-designer-builder doesn't get time off or rest breaks.

The brain won't quit like the body will. The body will slow down as it tires, and when muscles fatigue, they finally stop, but the brain won't stop. Those times spent not physically working are used for planning what is going to happen next. And there is the worry: worry that the rafters aren't husky enough, that there are enough cross braces, and that each joint is strong and tight. The brain might get stupid, slow down, and become error-prone, but it won't stop chewing on the project—not until sleep, and even then there are dreams, dreams that have the builder facing the insurmountable tasks over and over, so that he wakes exhausted with a head ringing from clenched teeth.

I feel the sag in Dad as the energy that carried him these thousands of miles began to fail. The chore list from day one was backbreaking, and then there was the next day with another list, and so many days like it to follow. Fatigue this deep feels like actual weight, like one's skin has turned to iron so that gravity pulls one down to the nearest sawhorse or stump to stare with interest and humility at the next thing to do, knowing what needs to be done but not able to do it. One can see the tool to be lifted, the next board to be cut and nailed, the next ladder ascended, but instead there is only the stare. The body is held in place by an inertia that threatens even the most mundane of tasks. It is the kind of exhaustion that comes from working the body for twelve to sixteen hours a day and working the mind every waking moment and most of every sleeping moment too.

Most of the time Dad was working alone, so every board, every measurement, every nail was his to cut, mark, and drive until darkness or fatigue finally called it a day. And now with the front door hung against a callous winter, the man's efficient words tell me that he has enough, just enough, to make the final move before he rests.

October 30, 1958

> *Dear Pop and Mom —*
> *Wed. night and letter to write. just writing to you as we are both pooped. We are going to move tomorrow if nothing unforeseen happens. Monday I went over by myself and made a door and hung it and put in three windows. Tuesday we put down the all the floor and I cut some trees for Bells after three o'clock. Today I cut the rest of the window frames and 20 blocks to fill in between the rafters. Then put the other gable end and put in three more windows. We have no partitions as yet but figure we'll have the extra room anyway and not be running back and forth so much.*
> *The past few days have been nice, around 20 degrees in the morning then warm up to about 30 during the day. The days are getting shorter fast, now dark 'til seven in the morning and dark by 5:30 in the evening. The kids will leave about 8:30 and be home by four when we move and not any farther to walk than to your pond. That will be a big relief to say the least. Also water in under the house is real handy. We have a pitcher pump, real modern.*
> *We put black building paper under the floor so we won't have wind blowing up from there. The gable ends are only sheeted with boards crossways. I'll put black paper on next and put 12 inch boards up and down and strip cracks with*

1x4. I put a little window in each end, we expect the boys (Bill and Danny) to sleep up there. Guess that's it for now. Let you know about moving when we write Sunday. The kids are going to a school Halloween party Friday night.
   Bye for now,
   Chet and Family

   I wonder if Dad worried about the details like I do when I build. I remember a nearly sleepless night while building my current home all because I became anxious that I built the house too tall to stand in the wind. Once the trusses were set in place, I was at peace and everything was fine, and I moved on to the next worry. There must have been some things that worried Dad like that. I'd like to build a cabin with him and find out. To work with him all day and then lean on the logs at the end of it and look back together at what we had done. I'd like to go fishing with Chet when the cabin was done and trade strategies for outsmarting the salmon working their way upstream. I'd like to take him on my boat to see whales and porpoises in the Gulf of Alaska. I'd like to bring him to the house that I built and let him measure my work with his eye. I think he would have liked that too, and that makes me proud.

   When I built my house, my father-in-law, Ray, was the huckleberry, a good replacement for my own father. He came to help me build the forms for the basement. We worked for two weeks in that five-foot excavation using rough cut two-by-fours and plywood to build eight-foot forms for poured concrete walls. I think it rained every day, and we slogged home dirty and tired and proud each day until that stage of the project was done, just in time for the weather to clear and bring the fall sun to shine on our work. Ray was hardy and jovial, and for a time it was like having a father in my life, though in some ways it just reminded me of what I had been missing out on through the years spent without Dad. Something I never thought much about until then.

   Growing into adulthood without a dad meant I got used to not asking people for advice. I'd just figure things out for myself. Our house with Dad in it had a garage packed with tools and hardware, coffee cans full of nails and wire and car parts. Piles of spare wood lay up in the rafters, and moving through all of this was an example, a model of adulthood.

Then one day that was gone. First he left, then we left, and the new place had none of him in it. The real him and all that Dad paraphernalia got left behind. No collection of tools in the garage and no tubs of hardware and stray car parts. No years of experience to draw from, just stories and memories, and from that I learned to just be on my own, not always a good feeling.

November 2, 1958 We have moved in!

Dear Pop and Mom —
Sunday morning snowing some big "wet dabbly snowflakes." The ground isn't covered nor is it freezing. We moved in Thursday. Needless to say we are a bit stirred up yet. We moved everything but the range and the tent Thursday. Friday we moved the other stuff.
Friday afternoon I cut ten little logs and we sawed them yesterday. All in boards 12, 10, 8, and 6 inches. A few 1x4's and a few 2x4, 2x6 and 2x8. I think that will be plenty to finish it up. There is lots to do yet and lots of straightening up to do. It's all under cover so I can slow up and breathe a little now. I won't have log cutting or going back and forth to worry with.
I am going to put in shelves and closets first then do the gables. That way we can get things put away and have room to work. I put shelves in the kitchen. Briar will tell you about them. Also moved the pump and put in the other two windows and put in the door locks, only one, and one window has the inside trim on. We were very fortunate that the weather let us get moved, it has been threatening to snow the past few days. Friday morning we had an inch but it was gone before evening.

Dear Folks —
It's been quite a while since I wrote to you so now that I can get my breath I'll try to catch up. Chet forgot to mention that we are now getting the Press Gazette from Hillsboro. We have got three issues more. And the Lynchburg paper is also coming regularly. I'm glad Uncle Clarence enjoyed the card. We were pretty worried about him, I hope Aunt Daisy doesn't overdo. They will have to have someone stay with them now, won't they? Aunt Mabel is the best they could get if she could arrange to stay.

Needless to say we are surely glad to be moved in, clutter and all and we are really proud of ourselves. It is quite a deal to cut a house out of the woods. My kitchen shelves for instance, a week ago, the birds were flying thru them.

Chet built my shelves so that they can have doors put on them for cupboards. I don't know how soon that will be done but it doesn't matter a great deal. The kitchen is small where I work but the end that has the table has plenty of room. And I have plenty of counter space to work on.

We won't get a sink put in before next year but we do have a pump and water and are very comfortable. And the work we have to do now is in the dry and warm and can be done much more leisurely. We plan to make a couple of small bedrooms upstairs but it will be quite some time before they are finished. We really don't need but one but it will give us a handy place to put things and we do seem to accumulate an unholy amount.

I had to quit and get ready for church but here I am about 4 hours later. Thought I would write a few more lines while the potatoes cook. Also must wait for biscuits to bake. they surely do get rid of a pile of biscuits and bread around here. Once you get used to it, though, it is no more trouble than peeling potatoes or anything else.

When we drove into Ninilchik today to church this afternoon they had nearly 2 inches of snow and it was still snowing pretty hard. When we came out two hours later it had stopped and the snow was all gone. But I think it has begun to freeze now at 6:30 pm. It gets dark about 5 now and light about 7:30 am.

Tomorrow Chet and Tom are going to Homer to get Tom's driver license. You asked about voting, I think you vote after you've been here a year but the voting age here is 19 instead of 21. I don't know if it's that low anywhere else in the country or not.

We got a dandy bed for the girls for free. One of the neighbors had one they wanted to get rid of, and we got in the way and we got it. Its Hollywood style box springs and inner spring mattress. The folks here have all been so good to us it's hard to believe. We are invited out for dinner next Sunday evening to one of the oldest settlers hereabouts. They have been here eleven years and have chickens, cows and so on. I'm pretty anxious to see their place. They have six kids, the oldest are outside going to school. The baby is a menopause happenstance, and she reminds me for the world of Lena Champlins.

Have your books come yet? In the one, "Go North Young Man" you will read of Rex Hanks sawmill. That is the same mill that is sawing our lumber and logs. Denny Bell bought it from Hanks. I hope you get them soon for I know you will get a kick out of them. This month's Sports Afield magazine has two articles on Alaska in it. We just got our first one sent up here and its due to expire soon.

The Methodist Church is really active up here. I think more active than any other. It is well supported by missions in places where it is not sufficiently strong to be self-supporting. So you see some good comes from your money. We can see that much. They are beginning construction next spring on a new Methodist College in Anchorage. It is to be ready by 1960. Now there is only one college up here. The University of Alaska at Fairbanks. Tom thinks he'd like to go there and is making plans that way. I don't know how long this interest will last though. Well I must close now and finish up supper. Be good to yourselves and write soon.

Love always,
Jeannette

In mid-July the Walkers committed to this piece of raw land without so much as a human footpath on it. Three months later they had taken up residence in a home constructed out of the forest where it rested. This must have been done with some sense of awe, to realize that the insertion of this family into this forest was an irrevocable transformation of the land and the people. My mother makes reference to the wonder of it, the impressive investment of labor that they had made, and the near religious deference to the honor of being a part of this place: "It is quite a deal to cut a house out of the woods. My kitchen shelves for instance, a week ago, the birds were flying thru them."

So often our homes are spaceships landed on alien soil; they are not part of the place where they rest. Even in a forest, we bring lumber from another forest far away; fabric, filament, and chemicals from throughout the continent; and fixtures from around the world. And although we anchor these alien intrusions and make them permanent, trying to blend them into the local land, the materials are not from this place or of the land. Such houses will be foreign until they are buried within the land. Then, like windblown leaves, some parts will enter the soil, join the circle of life, and become a part of a place. But our cabin was from this place as much as the nest of the raven or the drey of the red squirrel. We had gathered our sticks and made our place.

The cabin was about twenty by twenty feet with a front door near the center of the south-facing wall. Stepping through the front door, you entered the living room and to the right was my parents' bedroom. In the second bedroom a ladder led to the loft where Bill and I slept. The bedrooms took up the east half of the house; the other half was for living room, kitchen, and dinner table. Between the kitchen and the living room was a set of bookshelves up to about waist high with the kitchen stove backed up to it. The box stove was placed near the center of the house between the doors to the two bedrooms.

Almost immediately, we kids had the endless chore to sand the inside walls of the cabin. The rough-cut logs had a flat but coarse finish when they came out of the sawmill, and before they could be oiled or varnished, they needed to be smoothed. For that job we had many small hands with wooden blocks wrapped in sandpaper.

The floor was rough too, which three kids learned early. The girls were playing jacks on the floor and were forced to include me. They explained the rules and showed me how the jacks were cast on the floor, the ball bounce, and a specific amount of jacks were scooped and the ball caught after only one bounce. Each of us in turn cast, bounced, and scooped with the heal of the hand sliding along the floor and picking up slivers. The first game was short and bloody as we cried and wailed for relief. Luckily that floor was quickly smoothed by the endless traffic of eight Walkers, and splinters because a less common occurrence.

Each wall had two windows. The one in the kitchen was high and long so a person washing dishing could look down the lane and perhaps spy Dad coming home. The two in the living room were large picture windows that faced south and drew light into the unlit cabin.

In a year, a lean-to would be added to the cabin, and glass windows would follow. Dad would lay Masonite and Linoleum on the floors, and Homer Electric would set a pole by the lane and bring electricity to replace the Coleman lantern and bring music and light to our evenings. But that first winter we lived a rustic simple existence crowded into four rooms.

The cabin expanded each year. Here the walls of a two-car garage take shape.

When Dad built the shelves and counter in the kitchen, he promised that someday there would be drawers below the counter and doors on the cupboards, a real up-to-date kitchen setup. The shelves and counter he made were plumb and level, strong and functional, but plain and rustic. He promised that the wooden planks covered with linoleum would eventually be a Formica countertop, and the rough board shelves would be hidden not by curtains like most homestead cabinets but by cabinet doors with paint and matching handles.

"These cupboards will have to do until that cold day in hell when your father finally gets around to finishing them," my mom quipped.

It wasn't that long after all. One year later, Dad put in a sink, and then he picked away at doors and drawers for the cabinets. Briar Walker's kitchen could be called complete with all the modern luxuries, including a propane range and hot and cold running water in 1964, long before that cold day in hell. In fact, it was Good Friday about 5:30 in the evening when Dad officially finished the last of the drawers and slid it back and forth on glides to demonstrate the smooth operation and the fine fit of the joinery. Minutes later, the earth moved and we were tumbled about in the cabin by the biggest earthquake ever recorded in North America. The windows and doors rattled and slammed, while outside, the trees lashed to and fro, flinging their spring snow in great showers. Our dog leaped over the Dutch door and crawled under the couch. Shaken but unharmed, we all laughed the nervous laughs of relief.

"Well, it was a bit of a big deal getting that kitchen done," said Mom. "I didn't know it would be that magnanimous."

Those cabinets not only survived the great earthquake but twenty years later the doors closed and the drawers still opened after years of wear and tear and two decade of renters.

November 5, 1958

Dear Folks,
9:30 pm snowing. Glad to hear you have your fall work all done and Pop can concentrate on hauling the women around. I'm sure they can keep you busy. Glad to hear that Uncle Clarence is on the mend also. I expect Ain't Daisy needs Aunt Mabel to help her pretty bad. It's nice that she is not busy and can help her now.

Well, we've been in our new cabin a week tomorrow and it is beginning to shape up pretty good. Still lots to do but we are pretty cozy as it is. I put in closets and partitions today. Have the studs all in one bedroom wall done. That way with two closets with a hanger rod and a shelf, we have room for our belongings. We have one mattress upstairs. And all our canned stuff, a bunch of lumber, tools, and roofing, and so on. We moved the tent and I put it up for storage space that will take care of some of our junk too. We were all pretty well pooped by the end of the week. I've been slow to move. This afternoon, I slept from one 'til four so I feel a lot better. I fired up the light plant and started to work and really got some boards and 2 x ½ nailed up since then.

The weather has been mostly nasty, not cold but wet rainy sleety nasty slick weather. We've found out that the only kind of weather they have here is "unusual weather for up here." That's what the old timers say, so it is really hard to tell what kind of weather to expect.

> *Monday, I took Tom to Homer and he took his driver's test and got his driver's license. Made 100% on his driving and 94 on the written test, good enough, I'd say. He is proud as a peacock you might know. Well, guess I'd better turn in so be good and take it easy.*
> *By for now*
> *Chet and Family*

Finally, written evidence that Dad was as human as the rest of us, that he could be exhausted, so exhausted that he slept in the afternoon. And maybe in there we see the first hint of change, the failing system that would bring him all the way down in the end. Any other person would collapse and sleep all day, and they certainly wouldn't jump up and get after a pile lumber that needed ripping and nailing. Mom would often say, "No matter what else you say about us, we Walkers know how to work." But now Dad showed that he could run down too, could fade and need to seek succor. In the final tally an occasional afternoon nap would not be enough.

Why do we get enormous relief from seeing others show weakness, especially those we admire? Why do we enjoy knowing that others must surrender to time and toil? Does it give us a glimmer of hope that we can do great things, that we can make it to that level? Whatever it is, it also brings us closer to that person. I can feel my dad so much more here than in his other letters.

Dad has written enough letters here that they create a body of work that shows the character of the man, and I see now what was not obvious early on. Dad was not easy to know through his writing because I was waiting for him to tell me how he felt, what his mood was, or why he did this or that. But he was not an introspective writer; he was looking outward. When Dad wrote, the story was not about him, it was about the world around him, the people in it, the work done and to be done. The story he told was not about him.

Rarely does his mood, his aches and pains, his attitude come through. Dad's scrawling sentences describe the people he meets, and his anecdotes are about his kids, "the cook," the work, the land, and the numbers. As Madelyn says, numbers were my dad's favorite adjective. Writers generally use color, image, and sensory detail to tell a story. Dad's letters are rich with detail, but generally those details are numbers. People like Dad quantify the world and calibrate it, qualifying it with quantity. Dad lives in my son that way. Ever since he could talk, Luke has been about counting, measuring, and calculating. As a boy, he would ask people's age, and years later remember their age with the adjustment for time that had passed, "Mister Numbers," we call him. Maybe I should have named him Chet.

It is from Mom that we hear the details about Dad chasing a moose in his underwear and the hand he injured wrestling with coal. In fact it is partially through my mother's letters that I learn about my father. Perhaps the truth of it was that Dad believed a man was formed by the work he did and the place he did it. What was left of any man was his work and his children. He left a log cabin in the Alaska woods, the clearing that goes with it, and the seven children raised up with and in it. That is what was left of that man. And it is no wonder that he was tired.

Chet holds his youngest son, David Kenai, the hundredth baby born in the Homer Hospital.

Twenty-Three

Cord: A measure of cut firewood equal to 128 cubic feet. Traditionally a stack of firewood measuring eight feet by four feet by four feet. Related: a *flat cord*, which is a single row of firewood stacked eight feet long and four feet high, and *cordwood*, which is wood cut into short lengths for use as firewood.

Somewhere in my journey through time via the letters from Dad and Mom, I realize that I will not find what I seek, that I must change my target or accept failure, and let my father remain a lost Dutchman. At sixty-some years old, I am not looking to find myself like a nineteen-year-old Kerouac wanna-be on a road of lined notebook paper paved in Chet Walker's tight script. I am who I am and comfortable with that. What I want and can't have is the man, not his memory or his story, his profile or legacy. What I long for after these decades is to have the years I never had, the years my brothers had as teenagers and the twenty years mom had—time with the man who died too young when I was too young. I want the man who died and broke a family's heart, because he was the heart and, in eerie hyperbole, his heart attack struck us all. Until that happened I didn't understand the world and even then, the learning came slowly like the melting of glaciers, a few precious inches a year. Though evidence to the contrary lines the Sterling Highway, I thought that if people wanted something hard enough and worked for it, that was enough.

The homesteading boom on the Kenai Peninsula was only a few years old when I was a kid, but even then abandoned cabins and unfinished houses dotted the landscape along the Sterling Highway. Some sat slowly settling into the weeds just off the right-of-way and others were tucked well back in small clearings carved out of the forest by their builders. Typically, a small cabin faced the road with a nearby outhouse tilting off vertical. Assets included an old truck, a half-finished outbuilding or two, and maybe a tire swing slung from a sturdy birch tree. The fireweed, grass, and pushki were growing tall where a family had trampled a yard, and the paths to the outhouse were overgrown. Shreds of Visqueen in the window frames and tar paper flapping in the wind signaled surrender.

On summer Sunday afternoons we went tromping around in the backwoods, following abandoned tracks to clearings where someone tried to make a go of it. Some held only a tiny shack with broken windows and a rotting woodpile. Others were extensive clearings with defined gardens, outbuildings, abandoned machinery, and farm tools. Once we came upon a full-sized house and a garage with a car still in it, sitting alone and forgotten in weeds at the end of an overgrown lane. Looking through the windows, we could see furniture and dishes as if this house had been left for the weekend, but the fireweed and waist-high grass growing tall all around the paths and doorways said it was forever.

As a child, I studied deserted cabins along the highway from my vantage point in the third seat of the family Ford station wagon, and I would wonder what happened to make the people break away from all of this. A family once lived behind those cabin walls with dreams of a bountiful forest garden, a locker full of meat, and a bigger house someday. For one summer, maybe two, they prepared for winter with jarred moose and salmon stacked on rough-cut shelves; with firewood and coal heaped against the cabin wall; and with dry beans, rice, and powdered milk stored in some nook, ready for the siege of winter. Now they were gone, gone with the spring, broken by winter.

On some sections of the highway it seemed like there were more abandoned places than occupied ones, as if some great evacuation took place before we arrived. Why would they leave this life that I found so perfect? I always thought of them as quitters because only quitters would leave something this good. That's what I thought until it happened to us, and I learned that things are never that simple.

The studies conducted in 1955 support my estimate. More people abandoned homesteads than stayed, and now I understand that these tragedies and crises were unique and personal, nothing so simple as a family's will broken by the winter. This is not just demographics; these are real people, families who fell victim to some disaster, overwhelmed by a storm of life that swept them on to another place. The people who hung those tire swings and started those outbuildings intended to stay in spite of the long cold winters, regardless of how far they were from family, impervious to the threat of bears and blizzards and cabin fever. But something, something they didn't prepare for, something that couldn't be worked away, traded away, or waited out shuffled the deck and dealt a hand they couldn't play. They had commitment once, but it didn't happen or couldn't last, and the people moved on.

November 9, 1958, Happy Valley

We got a letter from Popular Mechanics saying we'll get it for a year from you. Thanks a lot.

Dear Pop & Mom,
Sunday not quite time to go to church so will start a few lines and while everything is more or less quieted down. We are all fine and getting pretty well settled and straightened up. I put in partitions and closets on the bedrooms so we have a place to put things away. The upstairs, or loft, is still pretty well mixed up but everything is where we can get at it. I've used so many boards off the floor, it is pretty sketchy as far as making a ceiling. Bill and Danny sleep up there, they still have enough "floor" to get to bed on. I put in the window and door trim and the cook has curtains in the kitchen and bedroom.

The weather has turned real nice since it snowed Wednesday night. There is about six inches on the level. I banked it up all around the house yesterday we have the warmest floor we have ever had anywhere.

Tom and Mike took a school party last night. Tom had to try out his new driver's license. They had a nice time. It was an outdoor affair. They went about 1:00 or 1:30 and helped get a log bonfire going. They had picnic supper outdoors in six inches of snow. Can you imagine?

We had quite a battle with wet wood the middle of the week, so I went out and cut a dead tree. Talk about kindling, you never seen the heat; it really takes off. We had quite a pile of wood cut when we made the clearing also we have two big slab piles eight foot high or more. and the tree tops galore all around the cabin where I cut logs. I've got to make a toboggan. To haul it in on a sled with runners upsets too easy over roots and stumps. Well, will fix the fire and go to church finish this tonight.

Home again, cold and clear. Must be around 10 above, was 10 below at Ninilchik this morning. 2 below over where we did live, didn't seem that cold here though. Out in the clear where the sun hits, the snow is about gone, but in the woods it is still there.

We went to Sunday school and church. I have to teach adults. There generally is only four or five, and they don't know any more about it than I do, so I guess I can make out.

I sold the truck last week, was pretty lucky to get rid of it. Most people who come up here usually end up with a truck that literally rusts down in a heap. Come out pretty good on it. Got as much out of it as we gave, guess that's good enough. Would have cost me a hundred dollars for a license and forty more for insurance, so I didn't argue with the guy when he made me a decent offer. I'll send T. Butler his share and make him happy.

I am going to Homer tomorrow and get a drum of gas for the generator with a neighbor in his pickup. We have a drum of coal oil and one of Blazo (white gas for the lantern) so that will keep us lit up all winter. The Generator uses about a half-gallon of gas an hour. We use it when we work or use the electric saw. We do that at night and have lights at the same time. It's a big relief to have all the water we need right in the house. Guess that's about the news for now will sign off and go get some more wood, have the fire's going, and the house warmed up.

By for now,
Chet and Family

Dear Papaw,
We moved in our house. I like it fine.
Danny

Grandma saved this little thing, this sample of me from my beginning that I now hold in my hand once more. So few things that are ours, that we have made, come back to us as this has come to me, and I can look at the letter and say, "these are the first words of this book," for here is where the writing started, and now it continues back through the same words and the same place.

My sisters and I were hatchlings and that cabin was our nest, a warm, sheltering, and nurturing place that would hold us for six years of our young lives. Six years of dinners at the table Dad made; six years of Jacks, Go Fish, and Chinese Checkers on the floor by the woodstove; six years of the Walkers in their homestead cabin. When I climbed into the loft to share blankets with my brother and later when I had my own top bunk with heavy wool quilt, I was safe and content in way that made me think trouble could never get to me. Perhaps this is what is meant by the innocence of childhood, that something could be so good it could never pass away.

November 9, 1958

Dear Folks,
Don't know what I can write that will be any different than what Chet wrote but I thought I'd put my two cents worth in. We just got back from church. We had a work party after church and a potluck supper. The men worked some more on the basement. They are trying to get fixed up so we can put some of our classes down there. We keep increasing and so many kids in one room makes it hard to concentrate. I have Danny's group and have anywhere from six to ten. We had forty-seven at Sunday school today and several more come in to church. So we are pretty proud of us. I don't guess any church at Ninilchik has ever had that many before. Tom's teacher comes and brings five. The oldest is second grade, one in first, and three just babies. Boy does she have a time. The kids all seem to like going there just fine.

Well you can tell things are simmering down here some; I started embroidery. I'm fixing a pair of pillowcases for Bill and Danny. I am putting anchors and rope on them in bright red and blue. Also have a pattern for a big sailing ship they would like to have on curtains. They have only one small window so it would need just two panels so I may get it done. I even fixed a pot holder a piece for Amy and Peggy to work on. They have lots of time and Peggy wants to have a school all day and all night too. Their embroidery so far has been pretty messy but they have to learn I guess.

It's not too easy to get colors of embroidery floss here. Only blue, green, and brown, but the store at Ninilchik has those big 600 yard balls of bedspread crochet cotton for .39. I thought that was pretty good. They have four colors in it. Also she has lots of color of yarn. I don't know how high it is, but here prices on most dry goods (what she has) are really reasonable. I have some comfort tops I want to knot over some old quilts, and I think I can get outing flannel here at Ninilchik for them. I really don't need them now but may before spring.

I guess this is about all. Not much news but we are all fine. Peggy had a little head cold, but it cleared up and she's fine now. So I'll close for now. We didn't hear from you Thursday so will probably tomorrow.

Love,
Briar

November 13, 1958

Dear Folks,
Thursday night just finished supper. We sort of slipped this week, didn't write any letters for today's mail. So I'll start one now and answer your questions while I can still remember them. The flues you asked about, we have two. It's just stove pipe from the stove to the roof into what they call a roof jack, Then two joints of stove pipe above the roof. I put guy wires on it so it won't blow down. The roof jack is a square of galvanized metal with a stove pipe in it. That is the chimney of Alaska. We have never walled our cellar. I'll do that with slabs, "any day now." Yes we are really slowed down now. I cut a little wood and do a little dab of work on the house everyday. I have the gable end of the west end of the house about finished, work some of two days. I need about three more 1x4 strips nailed on the cracks and then three short ones above the window. Then I'll move the scaffold to the other end of the house.

Today I stripped the cracks in the doors, Briar said I'd get the house so tight that we could not breath in it. I told her she could always go outside to breath. It was 6 degrees above here this morning. At the village it was 20 below zero just 6 ½ miles away. It is always that much colder as it is right in the shore and no windbreak. It sure makes a difference out in the woods. We never told you about the turnips did we? Bells gave us some. Today, we finished one we already had three messes off of. It wasn't a very good one she threw a lot of it away. Two of them filled a milk bucket.

About the trees we cut. I cut all the trees clear around the cabin, but the rest I cut all over the thirty acres. The ones we sawed in three sides had to be pretty straight and not less than eight and a half inches at the top. The logs for lumber I cut all over the place just where they grew. The timber here is not big at all, nor is all of it good when you cut it down. The biggest trees I cut were not over twenty-one inches at the butt. We made roads with the tractor all around the place. Some places I'd cut several trees in a bunch. To the east of the cabin and the on the north we have a pretty good patch cleaned except for trees good only for firewood. I am cutting up down stuff we cut last summer now as long as it isn't buried under snow. We still have about six inches, it's dry and crusty. The weather is clear and cold and still. It don't bother as long as you keep your hands and feet dry.

I am getting caught up in my "sitting" now. No rush now. I have all my lumber either in the attic or under a tarp. The cabin is warm enough so we won't freeze 'til we get the other end covered. It's not too bad as it is, but there is quite a few big cracks in the boards. The first course I used the poorest ones I had, some had bark on the edges, a layer of tar paper then more boards makes it pretty tight.

We didn't go visit the people Briar told you about. We all worked on the church. They are finishing the basement for classrooms. I think we will go out there Sunday a week from this. Will continue this later.

Sunday night, Everyone else bedded down for the night. Last night we had a big snow about a foot. It sure was a beautiful sight this morning. The trees were just loaded and the sun came out about ten, and it was really beautiful. The roof has a foot of snow on it, and it hangs over the edge about a foot. Tonight there is about a foot of icicles hanging down. I had to break them off over the front door to go out and get wood. I haven't been cold out all today. I shoveled the paths out to the toilet and woodpiles and so on this morning, and it was warm enough I didn't need a coat.

Well, Friday I finished the gable on the west end of the house and move the scaffold to the other. Saturday, Tom and I worked on it, put all the wide boards on, now we've only the cracks to strip. It started snowing Saturday afternoon and the scaffold got too slick to work on so we didn't try to strip it. Got in a little wood and called it a day.

Today Tom and the other kids went to church, but Briar and I stayed home. She has had the flu and it has treated her pretty rough. The kids got dinner and I got supper and did all the dishes. I got my hands clean once anyway.

Guess that's all the latest so will sign off and go to bed.

By for now,

Chet and family

PS It comes daylight about 7:30 now of mornings and gets dark about 4:30.

Most of the day-to-day chores on a homestead were physically demanding, the rest were just plain hard work. The government didn't give people free land; they just didn't make them pay cash for it. It may well be that the end of homesteading for some folks was when they came against that inexorable fact and didn't like it. Any decent homestead was and is salty with sweat equity.

Folks like us, in their first year on the land, had to find time for collecting enough fuel in the fall to last a winter or they would end up scrounging for wood all winter. Dad thought he had plenty of scrap and slab left over from milling and building, but we went through that faster than we did moose meat. Firewood was a major undertaking in a northern home when the stoves were not efficient and the homes might be tight but not well insulated. That meant cord after cord of wood had to be sawed, hauled, stacked, and split. Even in our tight small cabin I bet we were going through a cord a month. That's a cord every month, October through April. Wood was plentiful but the real stickler was finding dry wood, and there were only a certain number of dead trees standing around waiting to be harvested. Most firewood was cut from green trees and left to cure for a year or more. During the first year in a new cabin, the woodcutter would scrounge what dead trees could be found and then make do with slow burning green wood that would foul the chimney and generally disappoint.

Coming as we were from the land east of the Mississippi, we were used to clean-burning hardwoods with a lot of heat in them. An armload of oak or maple will go a lot farther toward keeping a cabin warm than an armload of spruce. I'm sure that it took Dad a while to figure out the ins and outs of his boreal forest woodlot. He had three major trees to choose from for fuel: cottonwood, birch, and spruce. Cottonwood is slow to dry because it carries a lot of water, and it doesn't have much heat in it when it finally does. Birch was the best fuel but there is not as much of it, as there are few standing dead trees worth burning. Dead birch trees rot quickly, and even a standing dead birch is apt to be punky and useless under its healthy-looking bark. Birch bark is waterproof and holds the moisture in the deadwood so it rots quickly, leaving what appears to be a solid tree standing in the forest when actually it's a bark tube filled with rotten wood.

Spruce, on the other hand, is user-friendly and plentiful. Every stand of spruce will have a few dead trees that are as dry as the proverbial popcorn fart and ready to warm a cabin. Spruce contains a lot of creosote, so it makes a hot fast fire that burns down quickly since it is not very dense, while birch will burn long and slow. Even green birch will burn nicely if laid on a bed of hot spruce coals. The two woods work together well to heat cabins with the inefficient wood heaters we were using.

Mornings were cold in that cabin, but many other cabins were a lot colder. Dad built it tight, so there wasn't a lot of air moving through the house to cool it off. However, there was little or no insulation and no vapor barrier like the houses built within the last fifty years. Even this cabin with what Mom called "the warmest floors we have ever had" would be losing heat through the attic, where only an inch of lumber and a few layers of tar paper lay between the hot cabin and the Alaska winter.

No matter how warm the house was at bedtime, even coal or a birch log would burn out long before morning, and we woke to a cold cabin. I can remember listening some mornings from under my wool quilt as Dad got out of bed and built a fire in the cookstove and the box stove, trotted out back to take a leak, and then hopped back into bed until the place warmed up. From the sound of the bedsprings, he didn't always go back to sleep. The coffee pot was readied on the stove the night before and soon was perking us all awake, although we stayed deep in our beds as long as possible. With two stoves going, the temperature would rise from "colder than hell" to "open a door" in next to no time. By the time breakfast was cooked and eaten, the place was toasty as an oven.

The old saying goes "wood heats you twice." But whoever said that didn't have much firewood experience. It actually heats you four or five times. We never had enough time to build up a big heap of dry split wood for the winter, so Dad would spend a good part of each week, if not each day, gathering or splitting firewood, with some of it still green.

November 20, 1958

>*Dear Pop and Mom,*
>
>*Thursday morning clear and cool, All in pretty good shape. Briar's flu is better. Danny is a little cross and ouchy so momma's trying to keep him in bed today. He's laying there singing now, hope it lasts. It must be around zero this morning as the snow is dry and squeaky.*
>
>*We had quite an evening last night. The Bells came down and brought their projector and slides and showed us all they had. They are all colored and really beautiful. They have three hundred or more. They are all of around here except some they took when they took a trip back to the states a couple of years ago. We all had nice visit. Stayed up 'till eleven o'clock. It gets dark now about 4 pm and daylight about 7:30. The sun sets so low that it shines mostly in the tree tops.*
>
>*I walked, or rather waded, out in the woods back of the house yesterday and the snow is over knee deep most places. I cut a little wood every day and tinker around a little. We are really taking it easy. Monday I made a batch of bread and some doughnuts. They ate them just the same as if they were real good.*
>
>*You asked about the Cavanaughs, we are not sure if they are still around Homer or not. Stoddard went back to the states and is still there. He isn't too popular here. People didn't like some of the things he wrote about them. He still has his name on a mailbox down there though. There are lots of homesteads that people have left and went back to the states, things are just setting there. That's the way with his place.*
>
>*The country has developed quite a bit since he wrote about it. Some of the people are still here though. The road is lots better and the contracts have been let to black top it. They are working on it some now. Well that's all for now, be good and write. As ever, Chet and family*

Cavanaugh and Stoddard wrote the books about homesteading that Dad and Mom recommended to their folks. Curious, I dropped by the local library and gave each a quick read. I say a quick read because neither was the kind of book that aged well. The stilted language and quasi-folksy style was hard to stay with page after page.

Ethel Cavanaugh's book, *Wilderness Homesteaders*, recounts the experiences of a woman and her grown daughter as they explore, select, and prove-up on a homestead in the Fox River Valley at the head of Kachemak Bay in the forties. These women worked on their place part time over a period of several years, while they worked around the state to build a bankroll. This was an expensive endeavor. Everything brought to their homestead site had to be barged to the head of Kachemak Bay, up a glacial river, and then hauled several miles overland. The Cavanaughs eventually had a few good years in the cabin they built, but like so many of the remote homesteaders, they were relying heavily on luck, generosity, and money to establish their foothold in the wilderness.

The Cavanaughs seemed to approach homesteading as a great adventure to move on from like climbing a mountain or hiking the Appalachian Trail, and that's what the Cavanaughs did. Building an Alaska homestead near the road system was challenging, but going truly remote as these women did was a whole different mountain to climb. As a guide to potential pioneers, *Wilderness Homesteaders* reads like a cautionary tale of the trials, risks, expense, and challenges of carving a home from the Alaska wild. They were physically and technically out of their element without the critical skills needed to live and travel in the wilderness.

Gordon Stoddard wrote *Go North Young Man* and homesteaded in the late forties just a few miles south of us on the Sterling Highway. He was a bachelor and tried to make a go of it with horticulture and the greenhouse business, something with which he had some experience. Like the Cavanaugh book, Stoddard's writing leans heavily on hyperbole, exaggerations, and maybe a bit of fiction. I do tire of those who write about Alaska as if life here is one great survival experience after another. According to Stoddard, most of the winter was spent at twenty to thirty below. Ten miles up the road and ten years later my dad was cutting wood in his shirtsleeves in the winter. Yes, the Kenai Peninsula can get cold in the winter, but it's not Fairbanks where twenty and thirty below are common for extended periods of time.

I can see why people on the Kenai didn't receive Stoddard well. He brags that his is the nicest house in the area and denigrates his neighbors, particularly the women. He hints that his neighbors are not quite worthy of him, while these same people are helping him at every turn. It was, however, interesting to hear about the development of the southern peninsula and to begin to understand the homestead mystique. Stoddard describes cabin building, transportation issues, and the art and science of poaching moose.

The Cavanaughs and Stoddard along with the Walkers and so many others came and sweated out homesteads on the Kenai and for reasons as diverse as the people themselves left after a few years. Some wore out like the Cavanaughs, some lost interest and moved on like Stoddard, and some, like the Walkers, were forced out by life's misfortune.

A view of the cabin from the backyard. This is the last photo of the homestead cabin before it was destroyed by fire.

Twenty-Four

Berm pile: A raised row of dirt, gravel, or debris such as stumps, usually used as a barrier or to define a border; can be an attraction to wandering boys.

A bookshelf separated the kitchen and living room in our new home, and the bottom shelf was reserved for the new *Compton's Encyclopedia*, my version of the internet. It was through this set of twenty volumes that I visited the world. Archaic today, the encyclopedia of the fifties was packed with pictures, maps, and diagrams that transported me to the world of knowledge beyond our cabin in the woods. There was the full-page color picture of the bull moose I compared to my own observations. I peeled back the layers of acetate to expose the parts of the human body on a full color, multilayered diagram showing the muscles, bones, and inner organs.

The lack of a kindergarten program in Ninilchik didn't hold back my education, not with my parents, my siblings, and *Compton's Encyclopedia*. I spent many afternoons at my mom's feet as she sewed or knitted, and I practiced my writing or counting. Sometimes I paged through the encyclopedia, asking, I'm sure, more questions than would seem bearable. There was also the thread box to organize, dozens of spools of thread, through which I learned colors and sorting and counting. Yarn waited to be wound into balls from their tangled skeins. There were more counting and sorting puzzles when I played card games or jacks with my sister. I listened to stories my brother read me from books and the encyclopedia. There was the woodlot to survey with Dad, and tracks to find in the snow. I learned domestic skills like folding laundry, ironing handkerchiefs, and setting the table for dinner.

Kids in large families get so little one-on-one time with their parents that just being there was special. Each day, though, I was eager for the hubbub and wrangle of the other kids coming in from school with their salutes and sorrows, winnings and whinings of the day. I'm sure that on all but the ugliest of days, we were handed a cookie and kicked out the door to do chores or play, and through our play, we claimed our own piece of the homestead. My toy trucks built roads and my tractor plowed fields, and those same fields became battlefields when we warred with swords of pushki and spears of fireweed. We ranged through the clearing and into the trees to make trails and forts and hideaways that would become a part of the home as much as the table and chairs and Mom's fine cookstove.

At first our clearing with the cabin and outhouse was just a little opening in the virgin forest. Beyond this small footprint, the forest was untouched and the wild was at once attractive and intimidating to me. Dad had pushed rough logging roads into the woods a few hundred feet so that he could get to the trees for building, but it was a year before the site for the house was cleared of stumps and the brush piled and burned. In 1959, when the Caterpillar tractor came in and made the five-acre clearing, my world expanded with it. When the Cat removed the stumps from trees Dad had harvested, and they were piled in a long windrow around the perimeter of the clearing, the forest I feared was pushed back. This interlacing of stump, root, log, and sod created outlaw hideouts, ancient animals, pirate caves, and fairy nests for our imagining. As I grew older, I took to exploring more, and I found a nook in the berm pile, a nest really, a small bowl lined with grass and moss into which I could nestle on a warm day and watch the clouds or dream stories of adventure and exploration.

Beyond the berm piles was the woods, and there I was less confident, more the stranger, intimidated by the dark, tall, thickened forest. The imagination that helped me play safely around the house let me imagine the unseen danger of meeting bears, getting lost, or simply being engulfed by the wildness in the woods. Each year my confidence grew, and the places in the woods I would venture to alone expanded. Meanwhile I'd go anywhere with one of the older kids. Amy was fearless and seemed never to be turned back by the mysteries of the shadowed woods. And my brothers, of course, were old enough that they moved through the wild woods with élan, as if they were a part of the place already. I could see that someday I would be the same. But until then I stayed behind the log walls, imagining great dangers beyond them, confident that I was safe there at my mother's feet as I prowled through the magic encyclopedia.

Today in a thrift store or garage sale, when I see a weathered matched set of *Compton's Encyclopedia*, I am saddened that they have passed out of vogue along with the typewriter and phone booth. When my grandson paws through the pages of picture books studying dramatic illustrations of dinosaurs and earthmoving equipment, I think perhaps he wouldn't mind having a twenty-six-volume illustrated set of encyclopedias to explore, especially when the world outside seems a little too big.

November 23, 1958

Dear Folks,

Sunday evening again and not much news. I have been pretty completely bitten by the flu bug and not feeling so good but guess now I'll live. I have been doing a little embroidery to kill time. Finished a pair of pillowcases for Bill and Danny. I put a bright red anchor with blue rope on each. They think they are wonderful. We traced off a picture of a racing sloop (boat) they want on curtains. I guess I'll do them next.

Going to start sewing for Christmas pretty soon. Won't be much this year but I'm going to make us a round of shirts and dresses. Have quite a bit of material I brought along. The magazines will surely be welcome, even Peggy now reads everything that comes in the house.

Danny has found a page in the encyclopedia that has the subtraction and addition facts in it. He found it himself and recognized what Amy had been studying and the little dickens all by himself has learned about half of them. He went to school with Amy one day and when the teacher passed around the Arithmetic drills she gave him one to scribble on. Boy did she get a shock when he worked about 70 percent of them and every answer he put down was right. Not much use to keep him home from school. He looks at those encyclopedia all day. He always has something he wonders about picked out for Tom or Bill to read to him when they get home. Mike won't read to him unless forced. I read to him from his Bible storybook and Peggy reads that to him every evening, so he knows the bible nearly as well as the big ones.

He is sure going to give some teacher a rough time. He has been writing his ABC's a long time but has finally learned to start at the left of the page and has quit making backwards and he can count as far as I can. Don't you think he'll be a sweet nut by cracking time. They push them faster here than in Ohio though. Amy had to learn three or four things in arithmetic that they had here in the third grade, but she didn't have them last year. She got them ok though. She had a calamity today though for the first time this year she missed a word in spelling, it was awful.

Peggy too, had to catch up some but she is ahead now and doing ok. But I don't think she'll be as good a student as Amy. I may be wrong though. They have English and grammar here in the second grade and geography in the third. Amy had some catching up to do there all right.

Bill didn't seem to be behind any but there are no other good students in his class so he has it pretty easy. He has a man from Mississippi teaching him. He has Bill bluffed but at the same time he cuts up with them all so Bill likes him real well and that is a help. You know how he hated that Mrs. Griffith the last two years at the Ridge. Mr. Castle (Bill's teacher) has Mike and Kenny Kwasnikoff to write a play and Bill's class to give it for the assembly Wednesday. We have heard it 'til it runs out our ears so it ought to be a dandy with Bill in it and Mike directing it.

Mike must give them a rough time at school. They have got him busy at some such business all the time. He has reports to make out for history nearly every night. He gets extra credit on his grade for them. Also he does extra work in Algebra and gets extra credit. And Mr. Auten makes him put a full period a day with penmanship book. It sure is hard on his dignity, but it has improved his writing a little, and it surely did need it.

Tom has really changed in his schoolwork. To begin with, he had to, because this correspondence school is tougher and different from ordinary schoolwork. Then he got this bee in his bonnet that he wants to go to the university at Fairbanks. We are still reeling from the shock of that. The first papers he got back weren't so good, but he got really favorable comments on the last ones. He is typing his lesson now and that is supposed to add to his grade. He is nearly through his government book.

Mike is all hopped up about commercial clam digging. He's trying to get on with an outfit here. Several of the boys are. They leave the first of April and get back the last of June. They take them by boat to Swishak beach (pronounced just how it looks) on Chugiak Island. They pay for their own grub and are paid by the Blazo box full. The Blazo box is the homesteader's best friend. It holds two five-gallon cans of Blazo and homesteaders use them for chairs, cupboards, dressers, flour bins, sugar bins, potato bins, and also clam diggers measure their clams in them. $5.00 per box full. If they have a decent year and if they are reasonably good they make from $500 to $700 in the three months. But Mike is just a Cheechako (greenhorn) however, just look at the experience they have.

Tom hopes to get on with the Bureau of Public Roads. They have a program where they hire young men out of high school who are interested in engineering and keep them on during the summer. Then they keep their seniority even though they quit to go to college during the winter. It's a real good deal if he can get on. We have a neighbor who is pulling some strings for him.

We didn't go to church today. We were ready to go and the car warming when Glen Veator came over with the news that Al Sanborn had a moose down and wanted Tom to help butcher, so Chet went to take Tom over there and on the way the car quit. He hitched a ride back and got a spare distributor cap he had on hand. Jack Bell drove him back to the car on the tractor in case he had to tow it, but he made the switch and it took right off but too late for church. However, the Baptist church comes by here to pick up Bell's kids so our six went along with them tonight.

Anyhow, when Chet went after Tom, Al Sanborn said, "We'll have moose meat for Thanksgiving!" The Bells and Al are coming here for Thanksgiving dinner. He took great pains to let Chet know we'll have fresh meat. Al and Glen Veator have been coming over regularly to see if we are warm enough. Glen even brought us some coal "to keep the fire all night in the range during the cold snap." One day it was thirteen degrees below. But they needn't worry, we are plenty warm.

I hang clothes in the attic and they really dry in a hurry. If we had ash or locust or oak to burn we'd have to open the doors. I told Chet he would keep on until it got so tight we couldn't breathe. I'm used to a house with cracks here and there you can throw a cat through. These people ought to have to put in a winter in that house on the farm or that one over on the Ridge. But up here they build these log houses and plug them up so tight a ghost couldn't get in.

But we really have good neighbors. Some are a little or more "queer" but if they weren't queer they wouldn't be up here, us included. There is a couple at Anchor Point, Bob and Edna Williams from Durango, Colorado where Delbert Kier just moved from. They have been here five years. And they say the winters are not nearly so bad as there in Colorado.

Oh yes, today we were to go to some folks for dinner but didn't get to go (again) because of the car trouble. We may make it yet. I'm still anxious to see their place and all. I'll write you about it if I can ever get there.

Guess Chet told you I got a tablecloth with my birthday money. Oh yes, Tom took some pictures of the cabin etc. Soon as we get them back we'll send you some. We have to send them to Sears or Wards and it takes a while.

I guess Chet must know more about carpentry than I figured or else no one else around here knows anything. Everyone is sure bragging up the job he did on our cabin. And the whole entire deal cost less than $200. When we get a little money to pretty it up inside it'll really be nice. Most cabins here aren't much for beauty or style. Well, I'm about run down so will close this edition of the Happy Valley News. We didn't get a letter from you Thursday, so we'll probably get two tomorrow. We heard from the Butlers and they are still in Oregon and everything about as usual, I guess. Oh yes, I got elected Vice-President of the W.S.C.S. (Women's Society for Christian Service I think) just call me Rosie.

By now and be good,
Jeannette and all

PS Wish we could sell your eggs here. Fresh local eggs are $1.00 a dozen. We buy shipped in ones for $.70.

I'll just say hi. I read this mess and sure won't try to add anything. Chet

Twenty-Five

Paper birch (*Betula neoalaskana*): A deciduous tree with leaves broadly oval with long, pointed tips; bark red-brown on young trunks that lightens with age, thin and paper like; often in mixed forests with black and white spruce; excellent heating fuel; the bark makes fine fire starter.

Nov 30, 1958

Dear Folks,
Sunday Morning and the kids gone to Sunday school with the Bells. They send a "bus" out from Ninilchik Baptist Church and pick them up. It gives them something to do. We will go to the Methodist this afternoon.

We had Thanksgiving here, us, Bells and Al Sanborn. Al is a grass widower who lives over near where we first lived. He is a pretty good old boy. We are eating a moose he killed last Sunday. He kept a hind quarter and let us and Glen Veator divide the rest. We had to pack it a mile on snowshoes with a piece of meat tied on a backboard on our back. Now that was my first experience with snowshoes. The pack board is not much different from an Army pack so it wasn't bad. I did all right I guess in that I got the job done. It made me sore but that gets well quick. We (Veators and us) are going to can it and divide the can but I expect we will keep quite a bit to eat fresh. It will keep indefinitely as cold as it is. We hunted for the past two days on snowshoes but never got a shot. The snow is crusty and they can hear you walking a mile away.

The weather has been nice except for a little rain in the middle of the week. Tuesday night and Wednesday night enough to take the snow off the eaves of the roof. It melts off all but the overhang and it builds up and freezes all around there. That fell off with quite a crash.

For Thanksgiving dinner we had a big roast of moose meat, mashed potatoes, gravy, sweet potatoes, peas, cranberries, macaroni and cheese, dressing, baked beans, pumpkin pie, chocolate cake, and Jello salad, hot rolls jam jelly etc. Guess that was the menu. Everyone enjoyed it and ate too much.

We get the papers about two weeks late. And they are quite welcome. Well guess that about it for now. Must get my evening wood ready as we won't get back from church till after dark.

Bye now,
Chet and Family

Holidays have never been dramatic events in our family. Usually we celebrated with a hearty meal and time off from chores, except for cooking and cleanup, and even that was made simpler by skipping dinner and going right to supper. All day long the house smelled of fresh rolls, savory roasts, and sweet bubbling pie. After the long stretch between breakfast and supper, we ate like starved dogs. If just the Walkers and a couple guests were eating, we crowded around the dining room table with Blazo boxes for the extra chair or two we might need. Often, though, there was a crowd, so we filled the table with food and ate picnic style, sitting about the living room on chairs and stools with the floor or our laps for tables. The house was usually overheated by the time we'd get around to eating, so often the front door was standing open to cool things.

Our Thanksgiving decorations would be paper projects we kids brought from school or church, and speechifying was limited to a longer than normal prayer. Nobody in the family was musical, so we avoided any family concerts or sing-alongs; we relied more on stories, clever banter, and argument for our entertainment.

My mother always had a sense of history and drama that surely would have led her to comment on how significant this Thanksgiving was to us. Had we not just crossed the continent into the teeth of the unknown, placing our fate in the hands of God, good judgment, and our own hard work? Were we not warm, secure, and well fed in our own place ready for the dark heart of winter? This year, like no other before it, the Walkers would truly have given thanks for the great fortune we found in this new home in a new land. Surely someone said, "Hey, this is like the celebration the Pilgrims had so long ago in Massachusetts!" If they didn't, they should have. The intent of Thanksgiving is to celebrate good fortune, and this has been true since the first celebrants gathered in the American colonies and took stock of their good harvest. And like that day centuries ago, our feast was from the richness of the new land and dependent on the generosity of those who were already here to welcome us.

Dad, I imagine, was feeling most thankful and a bit smug at what had been done in six fast months. I would be. Except for the moose that he had yet to bag, my dad had done just about everything he set out to do. He brought his family from the bosom of his extended family in safe, tame southern Ohio to the edge of the earth without loss of life or limb or even any significant discomfort. He opened the forest and made from it a home of logs, straight, square, and tight. His eldest son was moving into manhood, and we others seemed to be showing promise. His well was dug, his larder full, and the love of his life was pregnant once again, though he gives no clue in his writings whether he knows this or not.

December 6, 1958

Dear Pop and Mom,

Saturday night 10 pm. The kids just now all in bed. Peggy and Danny went at least an hour and a half ago. The boys just now. Amy stayed or rather went home with the school bus drivers last night from church. We all went to Family night at the Baptist Church, had a real nice time and a good supper. One of the old timers had a birthday and a big cake. Most of the meat dishes were moose meat and one salmon loaf. There was a dish of baked beans with weiners in it but the rest was moose with spaghetti, moose steak, roast moose, and even a plate of moose liver and onions. After the meal they had talent night and it was real good. Our kids sang with some of the others. Also they had a couple of movies so it was a very pleasant evening and we got home around 10 pm.

We received our first copy of Popular Mechanics this week. That really pleases the boys and me too. We all enjoy it. Will let you know as the others come. We are going to send you some pictures pretty soon now. Also Tom has his graduation pictures and he is going to send you one of them.

I never got my moose, but I've not given up hopes. We finished grinding the "hamburger" off the one I helped pack out, today. We canned thirty-some quarts the other day and still have a piece of hind leg froze in a snow drift. We froze thirteen pounds of hamburger today.

The weather is real nice, it's been between 4 above and 20 and not any more snow for over a week now. We had a beautiful display of northern lights one night this week. The sky was red then pink then white in long fingers of light that seemed to move like a real slow beacon. The days are getting shorter. Light from 8 am 'til 2:30 pm now.

Briar wrote that we went visiting. We sure had a fried chicken supper and good old country milk and cream. They have chickens and cows. They came in by boat before there was a road here and he fishes during the season for salmon. They have a log cabin built with the logs stood on end. It's a strange thing here that furniture is so modest. Homemade tables and shelves, cupboards and benches. Old car seats and boxes and beds of all vintage, quite a few use army surplus bunks and lots of just board frames and mattresses.

I made one for Bill last week, we have them all downstairs now. We moved things around. So no one sleeps in the living room now. It was too hot early to get them to sleep. I put a three cornered desk in the corner of the living room between the two big windows in the front right hand corner. It's real nice to write on. Have all the windows double now but one in our bedroom. Have not did too much of anything this past week. Hunted some and cut wood. We are burning some birch now, it is better than spruce as it makes some coals but we have trouble getting the place too warm.

It sounds like you had a real nice time Thanksgiving and plenty to eat. We did too. Guess that's the story for now. This leaves us all "as usual."

By now,
Chet and family

With the Kenai Peninsula in the full heart of winter, we were all sleeping in two ten-by-ten bedrooms. As the youngest, I was in with Mom and Dad or shared Bill's bed in the loft until Dad built a bed for Bill in the second bedroom; then I moved in with Peggy and Amy. That would make for crowded bedrooms, but we didn't have much to store like clothes, toys, books, and games. According to Amy, she, Peg, and I shared a bed in Mom and Dad's room until that spring when he built the addition onto the back of the cabin that added the "boars' den," where we four boys slept on two sets of army surplus metal bunk beds. Not much heat made it back to that part of the house, and I can still feel the weight of the wool quilt pressing me down into the soft mattress and keeping out the cold of a winter night.

A picture from August 1959 shows the addition framed in, so Dad must have gotten to work on that as soon as the snow was off the ground in the spring. By June of 1959 when David was born, Dad was off doodlebuggin', and he hardly ever got home. In my thinking, Dad found out

Briar presents newborn David to his brothers and sisters. Mike is out of the picture playing photographer.

another kid was on the way and made two fast decisions: the Walkers needed more space, and he needed a job as soon as he could get one. As soon as the snow was off the ground, he would have to build a foundation of some sort, although it wouldn't be as good as the one under the main cabin. This addition could be framed up in a week of evenings. Then he could pick away at the details those few times he was home from work. But for now, with Christmas on the way, we were making do in this cozy log nest where we somehow found room for a Christmas tree.

December 6, 1958

I'll try to tell you all little more of the folks we visited. The house is log and like all "old" log houses, has cured out inside so it looks varnished but isn't. It amazes me how people can make and spend so much money and still live like they hadn't thirty cents to their name. Though they do have electric. Which means a radio, record player, washer, an old one about like Catherine's first one. Also they have two freezers larger than yours, full of chicken, wild geese, wild ducks, mountain goat, mountain sheep, homegrown beef, moose, fish, clams, bread (homemade) cottage cheese, rhubarb, blueberries and God only knows what else.

She told me it costs $1.50 per chicken two years ago to raise her fryers but that was her highest year. This year was much less because feed is so much cheaper. She keeps her hens one winter. When her pullets begin to lay she puts the old ones in the freezer. She uses no heat at all during the winter on them but she didn't say about lights and I forgot to ask. She says they lay very well all winter. I didn't get into the cow question very far but I want to when I go back. We want to go in the daytime so we can see her hen house etc. She cooks on a bottle gas range but has been here ten years and no sink and you can buy good used sinks here for $6.50 and in Anchorage for $1.00 and up. I don't figure it.

They heat their house with a stove just exactly like the one Uncle Leslie had. But so far at least this Alaska winter has been a big joke. We keep expecting it to freeze us to death but nothing happens. I'm sure glad we didn't buy a lot of extra heavy clothes. We don't even wear the sweaters we wore in Ohio last year. And at least half the time the house is way too hot. No telling what will come but so far so good.

I did buy Tom and Mike a cap apiece with ear flaps, but all they are doing is getting dusty on the shelf and only Peg, Amy, and I wear gloves at all. Tom is still wearing that lightweight gabardine jacket. Has worn his heavy coat maybe three or four times. Bill has to wear his mackinaw it's all he's got. Mike wears his about half and half.

Gail Veator, a neighbor, brought over some shaker sets to send you for Christmas. You have a set similar to one but not exactly and the others are Eskimos. I'll try to send them out Monday. She wanted you to have them from an "old Alaskan homesteader," she's twenty-three. And she has been in Alaska five years and on a homestead one. I told her you would be tickled to get them.

Well, I better sign off for now. Be good and write often.
Love,
Briar

Homesteaders are by nature independent folks, and the farther they are from the center of civilization the happier and more independent they seem to be. Part of this independence is reflected in their differing priorities. While someone down the road would have electricity and no kitchen sink, we had no electricity but did have running water, at hand right on the kitchen counter. The well was under the house and with it a tidy root cellar. There were shelves carved out of the dirt wall that served as our refrigerator, deep shelves stocked with canning jars full of Alaska's bounty, and by the second year bins full of potatoes, turnips, and cabbage. No one that we knew of had a well or a root cellar like ours.

Mom had written, "we really have good neighbors. Some are a little or more 'queer' but if they weren't queer they wouldn't be up here, us included." And that pretty well defines so many of the people found on this frontier or any other. These people are the wanderers of their families, the restless ones descended from the first generations of restless ones who left other settled places and came to America. Their descendants set off from the settled eastern United States to find wild places to the West and North. Perhaps the rambling is a genetic trait passed on to make more ramblers, and since most everyone in America came for somewhere else, like as not there is an American predilection for heading over the hill to find the next valley.

The independent character of our country owes a great deal to the fact that seekers created it, people who were by nature unsettled. As the frontier of American expansion moved west, it was pushed not by industry but by the pressure of people ready to move beyond the wall of civilization. It was an irresistible force that overwhelmed the indigenous people and the natural barriers that stood in the way, a restless wave of humanity reaching for the frontier.

Some would suggest that it was free land that got people packing up and headed down the trail to the next wild place, but it wasn't that simple. Most Alaska homesteaders were the type of people who would pick up and go for about any excuse: fur, land, or gold. Some people picked up and moved when there was someone to follow over the far horizon. The case of Homer's "barefoot boys" was one example of how people from all over the country followed a counterfeit Messiah to literally the end of the road. Others came to build something from scratch on their own in a new place. Out of this mix of temperament and motive came settlements and enterprises that made the countryside start to look like a community.

A few people came for the farming and made it work, but not many. For the most part, these were not farmers at all, for farmers are steady tillers of the soil with roots seeking ground in rich loam. In fact people survived on Alaska homesteads by doing anything but farming. They were trapping, fishing, logging, selling their labor in the infant oil patch, or working some craft. The homesteaders came to Alaska because it was there, because it was remote, because it was wild. And it was *away*.

A complex set of possibilities existed for people who found their way to a place like the Kenai Peninsula during the homestead boom. Some harvested those possibilities, became successful, and built communities that thrive today. They found their place on the new frontier and set down roots to build homes and families and towns. Others settled like a boat grounded on a sandbar during the highest tide of the year. They were high and dry for so long that "their get up and go got up and went," as my folks would say.

Dad and Mom shared a dream to start fresh in a new place, to build a life for their family. That's what made them head for Alaska. Their dream was driven with enough of the wanderlust to get them going, but not so much that they couldn't stop once the right place to make a home appeared. While Alaska attracted many of the world's misfits, and still does, they often move on and leave behind the people like my folks who found what they sought and then made it better.

I remember reading a book in fourth grade called *Back of Beyond* about a boy who runs off to travel the American West in search of the adventurous life of the mountain man. I reveled in such stories as a boy and wished I had been born in that time when I could roam the wilderness and make my way in it. The title of that book stays clear in my memory because it spoke to me of a frontier that was not only faraway and wild but also fraught with mystery, a remote and unfamiliar place. I didn't realize at the time that I was already there.

Twenty-Six

Cabin fever: Depression caused by loneliness and isolation for an extended period, often related to the long dark winters in the northern wilds; often cited as the cause for divorces and severed partnerships.

Once I recognized that these letters would not provide me a personality profile of my father or open some metaphysical, séance-like conversation with him, some clarity arrived and with it the realization that this journey of rediscovery is primarily one of introspection, an opportunity to examine who I am and was. Whether one is an adopted child seeking his birth parents or a son poring over a dead dad's letters, the seeker wants to know himself better. It's as if to know oneself gives a person some powerful secret of life.

As I age, the mirror reflects bits of my father but even more of his father. My face is a throwback to the long head and prominent nose of Clarence Walker. In my son, and I hope in myself, I see the generosity and love of children that my father had. On the wider plane, the Walker homestead experience obviously and inexorably defined my character. It may well be that our homestead time was so definitive because of my age, but the why of that matters little for the outcome is what it is. Within the incubator of that forest cabin I became the loner, the reader, the woodsman, the gardener that I am, and I remain in a place where a forest provides fuel and shelter, shelf and furniture, solace and sustenance, and I am comforted by the wildness around me.

Until I built my own home in 1982, Happy Valley was my home longer than any other place I ever lived. From there I would move to an apartment, then a two-bedroom bungalow in an urban neighborhood and back to an apartment, then dorm rooms and rentals and squatter's shacks all while I waited to build my own place and grow roots once more in a forest clearing.

When I finally put down those roots and built my own place, it was not in the clearing in Happy Valley. I could have easily moved a pregnant wife and child to that lonesome cabin and made it comfortable until I added on or constructed another dwelling on that same site. As it was so dear to me, I now ask why not? That question I cannot answer. It was a choice, perhaps unconscious, that depended more on the place of the homestead in the heart and memory than in the circumstances of my life at the time. It was a nest from which I was thrown like the unlucky robin chick tumbled from its cradle by the wind.

When I was an indecisive teenager, I returned to the neglected cabin during the spring after my first semester of college. I wasn't sure what came next in my life. I camped there living on bread and peanut butter, cutting wood to stay warm, and reading. A month previous I was working a full-time job, taking a full load at Anchorage Community College, and partying full bore like every week was Mardi Gras. That was an unsustainable juggling act, and my reaction was to drop it all and walk away, as we said back then, to "get my head together." I could say that like Thoreau, I went to the forest to live deliberately, but in reality I had nowhere else to go, and it was a place of refuge while I figured out what the hell to do with myself. I was completely unaware that any plan for life was a counterfeit treasure map that the desperate foist on themselves. Life has no map. Roads open as we drive, and we turn or don't turn by choice or chance, so the route we pick defines the road we follow, not the opposite. We make those choices one at a time, and if there is anything I learned from Chet and Briar Walker, it is that success usually follows smart hard work and even that needs a little luck.

Dec 10, 1958

We got our hockey rink ready for skating at school. Boy you ought to have seen me trying to skate. I went _____ over appetite innumerable times. And you talk about cold, boy that old North wind blew right through that peacoat. Once I unbuttoned it and held the sides out and boy I moved right along with no effort at all (one way). I haven't got as cold yet this winter as I did that day at your place. I don't think I have ever been that cold before or since.

We are having a Christmas dance at the American Legion Hall Friday night for all the teenagers in the area. I made four dozen cookies to take, and Mike's "mother-in-law" is making a big pot of chili out of ingredients that the other kids bring. We ought to have a ball.

Mom is keeping Veator's spoiled brat while they are in Seward at the dentist and boy is he a pistol. Bawl, my gosh, I saw the like. All you have to do to shut him up is to pick him up.

I say, I am doing OK in school but Mom and Dad say different. I am getting C's in Government, That's all I'm working on right now. I have to go wash the dishes now so will close. With love,

Tom

Dec 14, 1958

Dear Folks,

Sunday night and a little snow has been added. It started after dinner and snowed about a half an inch or so. Enough to make everything pretty and clean again. Also very slick. The roads were pure ice now. The loose snow on top makes it real slick. People here would rather drive on ice than gravel. It's not so rough and they don't tear up the tires like the stones do in summer.

The kids are all excited about Xmas as usual. The money you sent was most welcome. We got each a pretty nice gift with it. Tom a belt, Mike and Bill card games, Amy and Peggy toy jewelry, coloring books and crayons, Danny hammer and nails and a toy car. It sure was appreciated and will be more so Xmas. Briar is making shirts and dresses around. The kids are in programs at church and school too. They get out Xmas eve 'til January 5.

I am counting on getting the basement cribbed up while they are here to haul me boards and so on. We cut wood Saturday and made the clearing bigger. Starting cutting the ones I left standing that wouldn't make a log. We burned the brush as we trimmed them up made a good showing in a little while. Not doing much else but cut wood. Went to Anchor Point one day. Visited some people down there and shopped a little. Went up the lane to Bells Thursday and spent *most of the day. Helped him cut wood and fixed his saw so it would cut straight. It was filed wrong but I got it going after filing it three times. Mine has been doing fine. I've not even had the spark plug out since I got it over a year ago. Guess I'm pretty lucky as several around here are having trouble with theirs.*

The weather has been mild only a little below freezing not too much wind so we keep very comfortable. I cut wood in a shirtsleeves and stay good and warm. Tom has worn his heavy peacoat three or four days to school, the rest of the time only a light jacket. Only a hat when it's forced on him. The days are real short now not daylight until 8:30 and dark by 3:30. If we didn't have so many big windows we have to have a light most of the day. We know some people over where we first lived who live in a Quonset hut. It's an army surplus job that has only one window in it. They need a light nearly all the time. We don't get as much sun here as we would out in the open but we would sure get a lot more wind.

Tom and Mike went to a party Friday night and a dance given for the teenagers by the American Legion. Bill stayed the week end with the Coopers in the "village." Peggy went home with the school bus driver's girl for the weekend, and Amy brought a sister to the one Peggy went home with home with her so we had a change of noise. Tom and Mike were pretty well burned out Saturday but cut wood anyway, under protest of course, but they did real well. Guess that's about the story for now.

Bye for now,
Chet and Family

The Kenai Peninsula is about 450 miles south of the Arctic Circle, the land of the true midnight sun and the endless night. We are far north enough that the winter days are short and the low-hanging sun offers little heat. By Halloween the dark comes by dinnertime, and rather than pumpkins and cornstalks, our world is full of the white and gray of the winter season, which will continue until May. April usually acts like March in the southern latitudes—in like a lion, out like a lamb. Even then, the lamb is often more like a thick-necked ram that butts the warm weather far into May. By Easter, the days are long and bright, but we usually look for colored eggs in snowbanks stacked high on roadsides and yards. As I write this on May 15, the temperature is thirty-five degrees with snow falling on the Kenai Peninsula. Anyone here who doesn't embrace winter is in for a long haul.

It has often been said that it's not the cold and snow that wear cheechakos down but the darkness and the sheer length of winter. When I look at the failed homesteads along the Sterling Highway, I can't help but think that winter had a lot to do with some of them leaving, those who only stayed long enough to put together a cabin and open up a clearing in the forest with a garden and a woodshed or a greenhouse. They would tell each other that this was the place, this would be their home, forever. Then winter came in like an unwelcome relative, arriving sooner than expected and staying far too long. By the time the woodpile was depleted and the family was craving something on the menu besides canned moose or salmon and root cellar potatoes, the dark lid of winter had smothered their hope and optimism and left a plague of cabin fever, a fever so strong that even doses of pinochle, homebrew, and cribbage couldn't cure. If they made it through winter, then spring would crush their hopes for warm days without sweaters, and they'd up and move again, leaving their mark on the land and probably some of their rubbish and broken-down equipment too.

This trauma of winter has a modern name: seasonal affective disorder, or SAD. Experts say people who suffer from this malady, or malaise, are particularly sensitive to the lack of light, and as a result the dark, short days breed depression. Today you can buy lights that help treat this condition we called cabin fever. This malaise has been blamed for more than one "Alaska divorce," when one spouse kills the other. Usually people just left when things got to be too much. When a homestead experiment failed, another cabin stood empty in its fresh clearing with siding fading to gray, its tar paper flapping with no one nearby to tack it down. Just when a family thought they made it through winter, they found they couldn't last through spring.

Twenty-Seven

Winter solstice: The shortest and therefore darkest day of the year, which occurs when the sun reaches its lowest point on the horizon; traditionally the twenty-first day of December; a halt in the apparent descent of the sun over the earth's latitude. An excuse for a bonfire and a party in the northern country.

Dec 17, 1958 Happy Valley,

Dear Folks,
Wednesday evening, supper over and the girls and mama are dishwashing. Danny is writing Papaw a letter. You asked about our neighbors here. Bells are only about 5-600 feet back to the east of us. We built on their lane, between their house and the highway. Their lane goes across another man's homestead but his house is on the other side of the highway like so. So maybe you can figure it out. It's sort of confusing I know.

Maybe I'd better not say too much about the weather knowing how cold it has been there. The temperature has been just below freezing and above 20 degrees for past week or more. We had some wind but not enough to bother here in the woods. I know you can't believe it but we've been the warmest we have for years during the winter. We had both doors open last night to cool the place out. We've still some snow about a foot on the level but had only a wee bit in last three weeks. It rained snowed and sleeted yesterday but not enough to matter. I finally got around to finishing the gable on the east end yesterday, stripped the cracks and tore the scaffold down so that will be it on the outside for this winter.

No I didn't have to buy snowshoes. The fellow who helped pack the moose out loaned me an extra pair he had. Danny never tried them. Bill did and Tom has used them quite a bit. The days are really shorter now; had to light the lantern at three o'clock. Sunday is the shortest day of the year. Then soon they will be going the other way.

I've been doing some clearing so we can get a little more light. I've cut limbs off as high as I can reach in both directions from the house and have cut wood out of the back yard so we've really got a patch cut clear now. Danny told you I built a toboggan. I cut dead trees and birch on the back trail we dragged logs in on. It is too far to carry wood so I aim to haul it or try it. An ordinary sled is no good. The runners cut through the snow and it's deeper than a sled. This is flat on the bottom with the end turned up. Cut up old five gallon oil cans and covered the bottom. Will try it out tomorrow.

Don't hesitate to ask questions we will try to answer them. We sometimes don't have much to write only answers to questions. Tell Howard and Mary that the weather up here is much warmer than three below zero, and we've got used to the snow. Guess I've run down for now so will sign off.

Bye and Be good,
Chet and Family

Dear Folks,
Will just add a few lines instead of a book as usual. I'm sort of bushed from sewing but I'm all done but Chet's and if he stays out of the house tomorrow, I may finish it then. I made some dishtowels and potholders for Renee Bell and an apron for Donna. Their kids and ours are making little jimcracks back and forth. At least 75% of all gifts here are homemade. Renee is making a cute little Noah's Ark and about a dozen stuffed animals to go inside for Danny. I don't know what for the others but she is a whiz at things like that, and she just

loves to do it. She is really a wonderful person; they are a really nice family. Guess that's it for now. Here's wishing you all a merry, merry Christmas and a happy New Year.

 Lots of love always,
 Briar

In the darkest days of winter when the reality of the northern latitude takes hold, and the sun hangs low in the sky like a fading, foggy street lamp, some of us who grew up here look forward to these cozy, short days of December. We all move a little closer together, sleep a little longer, and walk through life at a slower pace. At solstice, on or about the twenty-first of December, the earth is tipped with the North Pole at its deepest angle away from the sun. This is the traditional first day of winter, but for us, winter had been in place for more than a month already.

 Many northern people treat solstice as a holiday, and we celebrate with outdoor parties. The traditional solstice party usually involves a bonfire, or at least a campfire, hot and cold snacks, beer, wine, and maybe peppermint Schnapps to cut the chill. We sit around on snowbanks or camp chairs in our insulated coveralls or snow pants and parkas, telling stories and evoking long-abandoned gods to bring back the sun for one more year.

 A few years ago, I spent some time in Grand Junction, Colorado, and when winter solstice came around, I was determined to have a solstice party as we would in Alaska. For my party, I had to settle for a chiminea instead of a campfire, and our few guests were a little confused that we would want to sit outside after dark when the temperature was hovering near freezing. We ate smoked salmon and sharp cheese, toasted with beer and wine, and by 7:30 p.m. everyone was gone. On his way out the door, the fellow from across the street said, "Solstice huh? You know we don't celebrate that here."

 He was right. My mission was misguided. In a place where daylight changes little from season to season it makes no sense to pay attention. But in the northern climates, we feel the full effect of the change and the little pagan that lives in all of us revels in the chance to howl at the moon and petition the powers above not to let us fall into endless winter. We bribe the gods with fire, food, and liquor to bring back the sun one more year.

December 22, 1958

Dear Folks —
Monday am. Clear and cool, maybe as cold as 20 degrees above. Had a little rain, a little snow and some mixed but no cold weather. I guess you are still getting winter. This leaves us about as usual the kids are off to school. It's two more days after today, then no more until Jan 5. They had their Christmas pageant at the Methodist church last night and it was very nice. The kids all did well. Tues night they are going caroling. Wed night the Baptist church has their program.

I guess we are about ready for Christmas. The boys have some work to do yet on the girls doll beds and high chair. I am going to make Danny a barn for his horses and little things. Briar has her sewing done. Will put the tree up today or tomorrow. It will dry out awful fast in here.

Mrs. Veator is cooking or at least planning Christmas dinner for us. Them and Al Sanborn, Bells were invited but they would rather stay home. We had planned it that way too but Mrs. Veator invited themselves and they don't have room for company. They live in a Quonset hut about 15 x 20 so they are crowded just three of them and a dog.

It's nine o'clock and almost daylight. It's dark by 3 o'clock but the days go to getting longer now and so it will soon be enough difference that we can notice it. I've got to rustle up some dry wood for kindling and Briar going to take a walk. So I guess I better get at it or it will be dark again.

Catherine's last letter accused Alaska of the cold weather you've been having, it's not so cause it's not cold up here. I quit wearing long johns and cut wood in my shirtsleeves. Be good and write.
Bye now,
Chet and Family

When the Walkers arrived in Happy Valley, they were strangers among strangers, for most of the people arrived just as we did, a family or two traveling alone to a place as foreign as another country.

Rarely did people arrive in large groups of a common background or religion. The communities that formed were a collective of disparate homesteading strangers, families rich in their diversity. They came from Minnesota and Maryland, Kentucky and Kansas, New York and New Mexico. Some probably on their second or third move, others like us uprooted from a community of relatives and friends. In these burgeoning homestead areas, communities tended to form among the people who lived near each other, without attention to social order, family, or church denomination. Without the big group of relatives or friends like they had left back home, people had to make do with whomever was around, and in the heart of winter these islands of people gathered and formed a continent of humanity, a community that embraced each other. By the next year, my family was tightly woven into the fabric of this place. We had become a part of the continuous celebration of life in the heart of winter.

On a typical Saturday night the community gathered at the Legion Hall for a movie, perhaps prefaced by a cartoon or newsreel, and we ate popcorn and drank soda pop to the clatter of the reel-to-reel projector. After the movie we moved back chairs and the dancing commenced. I would sometimes be Dad's aide after he became American Legion commander and had to open the hall on Saturday night. We entered the dark, cold building, groping to find the light switch, and I would shiver in the dimness as Dad lit the furnace and released the first blast of heat to start warming the old army barracks that seemed to cradle the chill of winter like it was an armory for cold. Organizing the folding chairs in rows was warming work, but we left our mittens on when we handled the icy metal chairs. We filled the popcorn machine (ten cents a bag) and started coffee. Soon the coats and mittens were off, and people began to help the furnace heat the winter night in the community hall.

Square dancing was big as were the polka, schottische, and the two-step stomp, all rowdy energetic dances that pounded the wood floor like a drum and cranked up the heat until the doors stood open on the coldest of nights. We learned the jitterbug and popular teen dances too. We were dancers of all ages and ability with no one too young or too old take a place among the swirling skirts and shuffling shoepacks. By midnight, we little ones were asleep on piles of coats and then swaddled like infants and toted out to idling station wagons for the ride home.

The Christmas holidays brought more community gatherings, and many folks would attend Christmas programs at all three churches, and then show up at the school concerts and plays. Once the community part of Christmas was done, we would gather by our tree and have Christmas the way we chose, including self-invited dinner guests.

December 24, 1958 Happy Valley

Dear Folks,

I drew you a sort of map of our location, maybe you can make head or tail of it. I'll now draw our forty. The cabin sits on the southwest corner. Next to the lane on the right coming in is a gas drum, then the Dynamo [generator]. It has a hood covering the whole outfit with side panels that come off. We have two heavy extension cords that plug in that run into the house. The driveway comes about 30 feet towards the road from the house and we have the tent just about straight in and midway off the west end of the house. We have odds and ends in there. West of the tent is the slab pile. Like so.

The toilet is about 50 feet from the house. There is only one tree left between the toilet and house.

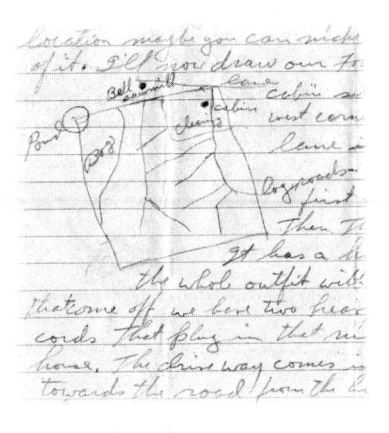

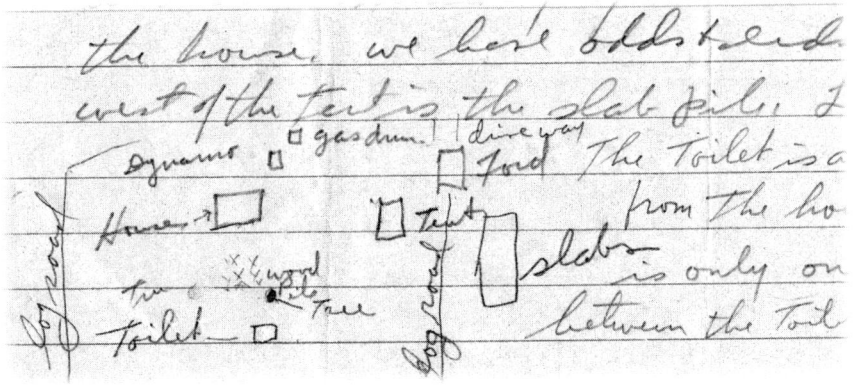

At the left or east side it's all clear to the log road about 100 ft and back about 50 ft behind the house. There isn't many good trees left right close and I've been cutting some for wood. Today I cut up a short log. I cut off the butt of a big log where the end was bad and the middle about 18 inches across. I split it up and put some in both stoves, yes we opened the doors and cooled the place out.

It's snowing again, has snowed about an inch since 3 o'clock but it's not much below freezing. This was the coldest day we had for awhile might have been as low as 20 at one time. I don't think as a whole we've had as much cold weather as you have. No we don't have telephone now since we moved. The Blossoms live about 16 mi. north of us. They came to Alaska by barge and unloaded their stuff on the beach. That was before they had a road down here.

Glad you got the films, hope some were good. The kids got their first Highlights today. They sure love it. We get Popular Mechanics, Saturday Evening Post and Highlights. We had a letter from Mom Wood and they are sending us Redbook, Reader's Digest and Jack and Jill, so we are set up pretty good for reading now.

Danny got his letter today and was he ever tickled. He sure likes Highlights too. Have been getting lots of cards but we never sent any this year. There is no stopping place and we didn't think we could afford it so we didn't do it. Thought I would answer your letter tonight then I'd remember the question you asked. Yes, the Christmas programs are much the same as we had back there.

The rabbit sounded good. I've not even seen a track up here. We acquired another hindquarter of moose last week so we are pretty well fed up on steak and stew. I can still eat a huge steak and like it. We had Mulligan stew tonight and cornbread. Made out of moose, potatoes, onion, rutabaga, peas, tomatoes, sure good.

What you know? It's Christmas Eve and clear and cold not lower than around 20 though. We went to the schoolhouse this morning for a school program and going tonight to a church program. The kids all did fine and the program was really good. Will sign off and put this in the mailbox, it may go out tomorrow.

Bye and be good,
Chet and Family

Where do I begin when describing that first Alaska Christmas on that homestead in Happy Valley? Shall I begin with the anticipation that we kids all brimmed with as we kept secrets from each other and sneaked around making gifts? Should I describe the strung popcorn on the tree, or the handmade gifts we gave? Should I begin with the things from that Christmas that became expectations for all Christmases to come?

Most holidays are just that, a day. But Christmas is a week or even a whole month of celebration, preparation, and anticipation that culminates, perhaps, with Christmas dinner and doesn't really end until the black-eyed peas of New Year's Day. Our first Alaska Christmas season progressed through programs at school, church, and the community hall. There were Christmas concerts, Christmas plays, and a Christmas movie; even Santa brought bags of fruit and candy for all the kids. The home part of the holiday was about baking and making, with paper snowflakes and store-bought icicles on the tree. For me, our Christmas would be one that defined the cliché, and perhaps created it.

Even today I can't eat a Mandarin orange without thinking how they tasted on a homestead Christmas. Every Christmas I can remember, we had a wooden box of Mandarin oranges. Inside the box, they were packed in tissue and sometimes, but only sometimes, some of them came out green with mold, a gift like coal for bad kids. And there was crinkle candy and bags of assorted nuts. These were all mystical, rare, and wonderful things that didn't exist at any other time of the year. From far-off lands they were brought to this place, this Christmas place, just for this special day.

Christmas is powerful in the north country, more powerful than in the lower latitudes, and this is no coincidence. Anyone who thinks that it's just coincidence that winter solstice, New Year's Day, and Christmas are celebrated so close to one another is not paying attention. These are the days in the high latitudes when the world seems to have fallen into a dark hole. The days are short, and the nights are long and cold. We know about solstice scientifically, and we understand the why, how, and when of the cold season. But in the emotional engine of our soul, the heart of winter is really the heart of darkness. And the birth of the light is to be celebrated the same as we celebrate the light of the world at Christmas and the dawn of a new year that soon follows. This is one big festival of life and renewal, optimism and hope, all of which begins and ends with family.

In a forest of Christmas trees, the perfect tree was easy to find. And it was decorated with paper chains, popcorn, and a sprinkle of store-bought tinsel. The family gifts were homemade in secret or with a bit of misdirection like the toy barn that Dad said he was making for Dicky Bell.

He was, but he also made one for me. There were hand-knit mittens and homemade shirts and blouses. The mailman brought boxes from mail-order catalogs and Ohio relatives who didn't forget us. But Santa Claus never visited the Walkers. We grew up knowing where Christmas came from, and it wasn't from some dwarf in red coming down the chimney. We opened our presents on Christmas Eve and slept through the hubbub most families experienced Christmas morning. In 1958 this all happened in a snapshot of Christmas card imagery with the lantern light haloing the spruce Christmas tree with its handmade ornaments and the moon reflecting off the snow and icicles hanging outside the window of our log cabin in the north woods where solstice by all its names really matters.

Twenty-Eight

Wolverine (*Gulo luscus* or *Gulo gulo*): This reclusive member of the weasel family can survive in the harshest of weather by eating carrion and has a special molar that helps tear frozen meat. Also called glutton, carcojou, or skunk bear; reputed to be vicious and hard to kill; mascot of Ninilchik School; distant relative of the Alaska homesteader.

As the north country enters the heart of winter, it is easy to imagine people hunkered in their cabins close about their heaters and waiting for spring. Such images fail miserably to show the real winter life. While the short days and the potential for bitter cold might have us rising later in the morning and heading home earlier come evening, the winter day is not wasted. The firewood trails that stretched out far from the back door of our cabin and the snowshoe tracks of the hunters who ranged for miles through the woods showed the ways of active people.

Yes, pulling stumps and clearing ground had come to a stop, and cabin building in the community had slowed. Only the crab fisherman were out on the water. There was more time for people to venture out on the snowy highway, sometimes dodging moose, frost heaves, and ice sheets to gather for meetings. My father and mother joined other adults at meetings of the American Legion, PTA, and the fair board, where they quickly became ones that others relied on to get things done. As we grew into and with the community, Mom got busy helping to create a library in Ninilchik, substitute teaching at the school, and organizing Sunday school or potlucks at church. Building a community out of a bunch of strangers seems to begin in two places. First, the community structures that are common throughout America, like churches, the American Legion, and the public school brought people together under one roof. The other way we bonded was through sharing moose kills and coal hauling, trading labor for horsepower, sharing our work and woe, harvest and heartache—the sharing that is so well documented in my parents letters.

In such a community of coincidence there were those who rose, or were lifted, among their peers and held with high regard by others. My father was such a man, and I think he was like the legend—this man-myth that I have lived with all these years is not some figment of collective family delusion. Dad was a jovial, kind man who was good to his word, hardworking, and strong; he was a man who went his own way but was a help and a leader for his neighbors. He was man you wanted on the other end of a load, and he was fine company after work too.

And while his résumé wasn't full of blue ribbon successes, he was in Happy Valley by choice, not desperation, and he made it a better place for everyone. I have always remembered my father this way, the ideal pioneer, and nothing I read tells me different.

December 28, 1958

Dear Folks —

Happy anniversary to us. Seventeen years have slid by, how time flies. We are all well and having a "quiet" Sunday afternoon at home. We went to Anchor Point to church this morning and really feel like we had been to church. We don't think we will go to the Methodist church here anymore. We just don't go along with their way of doing, so we are just very quietly changing. No use in causing a great big commotion about it you know.

The Veators and Al Sanborn were here for dinner and we all had a nice time. I went hunting the next day with Denny Bell. We snowshoed from 10am until 4pm, killed six ptarmigan. I killed three with the rifle. They are about the size of a pigeon, snow white with a few black feathers in their tails. Denny killed a wolverine Christmas day. A wolverine is of the weasel family. Looks somewhat like a bear but weighs about 25-30 lbs. They steal out of traps and live off anything they can get to eat. Its considered one of the fiercest animals for its size. He had quite a time killing it with a shotgun. Shot it nine times. Didn't have a heavy gun with him.

The weather is about the same, stays around twenty or a little less. Had just a little new snow but not over an inch—is trying to snow today but not doing much good at it.

We have had lots of Christmas cards back there and they all tell of the cold weather and all say they know its colder up here. They wouldn't believe Christmas night we went to the neighbors with light jackets on, I didn't even have on socks. Had only my "Sunday" slippers. Briar was bareheaded and had on a little sweater. The little new snow keeps everything fresh and clean looking. Yesterday the boys and I cut wood from ten till one then we dug the well about a foot and a half deeper. It almost went dry the Monday before Christmas but we dug down deeper and have plenty of water now. We are down about fourteen to fifteen feet now. We may have to dig it out more yet but it's not much of a job. Sure beats carrying water all the time. We all say thanks again for what you did for us for Christmas and we wish you a Happy New Year.

As Ever,
Chet and Family

Monday, P.M.

Dear Gramma,
We have received 4 copies of Popular Mechanics so far, October through January. While splitting wood Saturday I also took time to split my toe. We just got our school pictures today and one of each of us enclosed.

Also for Christmas I received a ping pong set from Louis (for us boys), a belt from Shirley, a pack of Pinochle cards and three pocket books westerns from Mom and Dad. At school I received a necktie, a handkerchief, and a watch that gains 5-6 hours a day.

We had a sledding party at a place near Clam Gulch some 25 miles away. We had coffee made in a 5 gallon can over a brush fire then went to Mrs. Jackinsky's, my algebra I teacher, for supper.

We have been going to church at Anchor Point for two weeks now.
Your Grandson, Mike

PS thanks for the Magazines

If my father was model homesteader, the quintessential pioneer, my older brothers were the typical frontier sons, a bit like the old man but bound from their first steps to manhood to exemplify the frontier man in their own distinct ways. Tom, as we've seen much of in these letters, was the golden boy coming of age on the northern frontier with brother Mike in the background, shadowlike, less in the front and less in the favor of our writers. Tom was able to adapt and quickly immerse himself in the fishing and hunting, logging and building with school pushed to the horizon. He was tall with a raw-boned frame, nearly a man who got a taste of adulthood that year he turned sixteen. Mike was not only younger, he was smaller, and the boots of a man would not yet fit him. He was less willing to fall in line anyway and more prone to wrestle with the world than he was to join it.

Tom was modeling himself after Dad, everyman's man, and Mike was not. Mike was independent and bullheaded, the frontiersman in the true sense of the word, one of the restless ones eulogized in Robert Service's poem "The Men Who Don't Fit In." He was smart and capable but more inclined to talk than act unless it was on his terms. He was unabashed by people's disapproval yet free with his own judgements and recommendations for others.

Mike was a bookworm, a math whiz, and bit of a know-it-all who did know an awful lot, but he wasn't interested in studying or in classes, which he passed only because they were easy, not because he tried. His calculator mind could figure out where the cards were in a pinochle game by how people played, and he was ruthless in his play without sympathy for age, inexperience, or mood. He seemed unable to tell when his words hurt someone's feelings, or perhaps didn't care. He was content to sit among the hubbub reading a western novel, unless there was a point of fact to interject or an argument to join.

Mike was at home in the Alaska frontier and lost in it. He was more connected to the past than the present and saw himself as an anachronism trapped in the twentieth century. At the same time, as if he were a character in one of his western novels, the sedentary homestead life was not for him. As a teenager, he went to work in road construction as a soils man and then a surveyor where he could use his mathematical mind and be outdoors all day. The height of his glory was when he led the point survey crew on the George Parks Highway project. This highway cut north from Anchorage to Denali National Park and Fairbanks as it crossed hundreds of miles of uncut wilderness, just the place for a misplaced mountain man. Those were his glory days, marching north each day with his chainsaw, ax, and siting glass, opening the last wilderness to the pioneers that followed. I wonder how life would have been for him if we had stayed in Ohio. Would he have found room there himself or would he have struck out for the frontier on his own?

January 1, 1959

> *Dear Folks —*
> *Will answer the letter we received today and mail them out at Homer tomorrow. I am going down to put in an application for a job. We are all able and had a Merry Christmas and started the new year right. We got too sleepy to stay up for New Years but I got up this morning to build fires and of course I started out back and I heard a moose eating birch brush just beyond the back of the house so I went back in and waited for enough daylight to see to shoot and kept looking out the kitchen window. It was light enough to see but not light enough to see the gunsights but it stayed there and ate a while, and I just drank coffee and watched. Finally it started to move out, and I opened the door and fired Old Betsy—it went about twenty feet and stopped, and I shot it again, and it went down, and I walked up and shot it again in the head.*
> *After I struck it and went in to get a coat and boots on, I went back out, I thought for a minute it was up walking around but it was another one, a big young bull calf, a yearling I assume. The one I killed was a dry cow and that no doubt was her calf but it was nearly as big as her. Then while the boys and I skinned her Briar saw another, a bull, back the log road straight behind the house. Tom said we were forty minutes completely butchering it out and disposing of the hide and guts. We buried them where we have had a brush fire for a month. Then cut more trees and burned the brush on top. It was a big cow. I'd say it dressed out 500 pounds of meat I'd guess. So you can bet we don't get meat hungry real soon. We still had part of a hindquarter Veator gave us. It's froze hard as a rock of course.*

I buried the meat in a snowdrift to cool it out. We didn't save the liver or heart as both bullets went through the ribs and tore the heart and liver up pretty bad so we didn't care for some. Anyway I'm real proud of a pile of fresh meat.

It's been around zero now most of the week but the house stays warm and is easy to heat. Our bedrooms are the warmest we've ever had.

as ever,
Chet and family

A couple of black-and-white photographs from a roll of film taken in 1958 made their way back into our hands with the letters along with some color snapshots, one with a note on the back: "Chester Walker's home in Ninilchik, Alaska, Aug 1959." The photos show the cabin and the new addition on the back all shaded by spruce trees. Most of the black-and-white photos are from the winter. In one creased and wrinkled print, I pose as a ghostly shadow at the front door, standing so that my head is even with the doorknob as if I am measuring myself against the structure. In the shots from 1958 the trees crowd the back of cabin, but by August of 1959, the trees stand well back. These are pictures I have never seen before, the oldest ones taken of the homestead. They make me want more.

What I'd give to have a photograph of Dad with that moose, or Mom canning salmon, a snapshot of our house packed full of us Walkers. But there are none, just this smoky shot of a little homestead boy standing against the door of a log cabin that he helped his pappy build. Later in the sixties, there would be more photos. Snapshots of the gardens, school pictures, Mom and Dad posing in their finest Sunday go-to-meeting clothes. But of this early homestead time we must make do with what we have.

The box of letters is nearly spent. The conversation with Chet and Briar across the years will end on January 11, 1959, and, of course I wonder why. But I ask without expecting an answer. History, especially family history, is an endless parchment that keeps unrolling. One would think that the past would be finite, fixed in context and volume, but it seems instead that the illogical, incongruous opposite is true. The more we find, the more we seek, and the more we know, the more we want to know. Answers lead to more questions, and from the letters, I turn to photographs, then to more photographs and other letters. By the time one gets down to who and what, the how and why start a whole new train of thought.

January 5, 1959

Dear Pop & Mom,
Received a letter from you today. The one where you asked about the clearing. Yes, I'm cutting all clean as I go now. I left two big trees in the back yard though. You asked about the McCalls. Yes, we got the first copy New Years Day. You can be sure the magazines are very much appreciated.

We had a quiet Sunday yesterday, went to church in the morning and then lazed around in the afternoon. Saturday, we cut wood and got it close to back door, had more snow about three inches over the weekend so everything is clean and white again. Briar washed today, and I briggled around splitting wood. Today was a beautiful day, temperature about 15 degrees above, still, and the sun shone about six hours, and it didn't get dark 'till four o'clock. We have some Icicles three feet long on the eaves where snow melted off the roof and froze.

Mike got reckless and split his big toe open with the axe Saturday while splitting wood, got back in the nail a little bit. It a wee bit sore you can bet but don't look bad considering.

The boys went to a coasting party Friday from ten in the morning until ten that night. They had a big time, of course, even if it did snow all evening.

We haven't tried any of our fresh meat except some "hamburger." I cut the flanks off when I cut it up. We ground that up Friday and it sure made good "burgers." The rest is still buried in a snow drift. We've had a "pet" around nearly every day. It's a nearly full grown young bull. You see they like birch twigs, the tip's ends, to eat and I've cut several for wood and left the brush lay so they would hang around. Danny sure likes to watch it eat. It's big as a Jersey cow and longer legged.

Aunt Mabel tells us Pop you are getting to be quite a rabbit hunter. I've not seen a rabbit yet, but I've seen some tracks about three miles from here. I'm going over there one of these days and see if I can get some. They are snowshoe rabbits. People say they are bigger than cottontails.

By now,
Chet and Family

We lasted seven years in that cabin in Happy Valley. Dad added a two-car garage with a breezeway that tied it to the rest of the house, and we got electricity. Tom, Mike, and Bill all graduated from Ninilchik High School, spending their teenage years repairing and souping up sedans in the garage, then wrecking them on the Sterling Highway.

David Kenai Walker was born in the spring of 1959, the one true native Alaskan in the family. He was the hundredth baby born in the Homer Hospital, and, since I was born six years before and the folks had me figured for the last, Dad called him "the afterthought." Oh well, there he was with the rest of us at his beck and call.

We grew up with the community. Every year more people came, the highway was paved, and the school got bigger. More tourists came from Anchorage on summer weekends. The American Legion, the Boy Scouts, and Independence Day with a parade and a rodeo united us with the rest of America until the Kenai Peninsula started to look more like rural America and less like the Alaska frontier.

On the homestead in Happy Valley, I first rode a bike and learned to read under a white gas lantern. It was there I made my first biscuits, and there that I first confronted the realities of life and death. Along the lane, I found a place to watch for my dad to come home. The root wad of a spruce trees was tipped on its side and with its dark moss and roots it appeared at first look to be a moose or a bear. Then I decided it looked more like a buffalo, but I used it as a horse. Riding on its back, I started waving when Dad turned into the lane and continue waving as he drove slowly up the dirt track that led past our house. Finally, I either outgrew the lookout horse or there was no longer anyone to wait for. I'm not sure which happened first.

Not far into the woods, my brothers built a tree house that stood seven feet above the ground. They found three trees nicely positioned to anchor three corners and added a post to support the other. Using slab and cast-off boards, they made an elevated little cabin with a roof and furnished it with an old car seat. As is typical with tree houses, about the time they finished it, they outgrew it, except as a place to hide from the folks and smoke cigarettes. Later my sisters and I took it over. When Homer Electric put in new powerline, the tree house was in the right-of-way and it passed into history.

Dad worked away from home for weeks at a time in those early years, so much so that David was six weeks old before Dad saw him for the first time. "Doodlebuggin'" is what Dad called his job with Western Geophysical. He worked on a crew that drove around the wilds of Alaska drilling holes in the ground and dropping explosive charges down them to explore for oil. He and Mom hated being apart, and he made lousy money, but he got to see places in Alaska like the ghost town of Katalla and far out in the Caribou Hills. The adventure of seeing the wild corners of the Alaska was no trade-off for a family man. It ate at him something fierce to not be at his son's birth, to be away during the bad days and the good.

Amy remembers one of Dad's returns clearly. She tells of him coming into sight walking up the lane and Mom seeing him out the kitchen window. She screams, drops what she was doing, and runs out the door and down the lane to rush into his arms. We have a notebook full of love letters from those months Dad and Mom spent apart. We always think of our parents as old and past romance, so it took math and a clear head to realize that in 1959, my mom was only thirty-five, a young woman, a young woman away from her man too long, a young woman destined to be a widow at forty-one.

At my father's grave beside the Holy Transfiguration of Our Lord Chapel, a Russian Orthodox Church in Ninilchik. My mother, three brothers, and one sister are also interred here.

Twenty-Nine

Doodlebuggin': Exploring for oil by drilling holes in the earth, setting explosive charges, and using seismic measuring equipment to locate potential petroleum sources. A variation on "doodlebug," another word for a dowsing rod used in water witching.

Happy Valley, Jan 11, 1959

Dear Pop and Mom,
Winter has really leveled off at around zero. Eleven below one night. The past six nights have been zero or below. We have been very comfortable though and are more pleased with our house every cold day or night. We seem bothered less by the cold weather than the old timers.
It takes lots of wood to keep warm due to the fact that spruce is a lot like pine or willow. When it's green it burns slow until it gets started then gets hot as _____ but don't last and you'd better get more in before it gets too low or it will go out. It's just wonderful dead and dry but burns awful fast. A little piece of paper will start it real good. It has never froze in the house of a night even when fires went clear out before morning. We've kept eggs in the bedroom window and they're not frozen either.
Had a very quiet Sunday. Went to church this morning and Mrs Bell came down and we played cards this afternoon. Now we are all writing letters, reading etc. All very peaceful for a change. We had a little snow the first of the week, no great amount. Then we had heap much wind but it didn't make the house shake or rattle nor did the floors get cold, so we are very happy with our house building.
We are still eating fresh meat like we hadn't had any all winter. We tried some seasoned like sausage. We ground hamburger: with lots of fat in it then

seasoned with salt, pepper and sage. Then fried it like sausage and it was just hard to tell that it wasn't made out of pork. The fat don't taste like beef suet when it's hot. You can use it for shortening like lard and it don't taste.

The days are getting longer now and it's still light when the kids get home from school and daylight when they leave of a morning. Our back yard is getting bigger all the time now. Everytime we cut a tree it is a little farther to carry the wood. Most of the tops from logs are covered with snow but some we can get to and work up as we come to it. We burn the brush as we go too. They start real easy and burn fast. There is a gum like rosin in it that really does burn. You know how cedar branches burn, that's the way spruce branches go. I've been cutting some nearly every day and Danny goes out and briggles around until he freezes out. About the difference between the way I dress to work up here is I have to wear mittens to cut wood or my hands freeze. Gloves just won't do the job.

Tomorrow is wash day, mail day, and I'll cut wood as usual. I sure have had good luck with my chainsaw, just goes right along everyday. Haven't even had the spark plug out of it since I got it last fall along in October some time.

Briar wants to know how you figure she'd have any sourdough batter left over when it takes a gallon of batter to feed this bunch. Twenty-five pounds of flour won't last a week to give you an idea. We buy flour in fifty pound white bags, "Gold Medal."

Tom just stepped on Mike's sore toe so we had some music. He played Lizzie Van Pelt with his toe and it is a little tender. He only split it back into the nail a little piece. The ax wasn't sharp or he'd cut it clear off, I guess. Well, be good and write.

Will sign off for now.
Chet and Family

And so the homestead letters end, at least the ones that still exist. We know that cut toes heal, the backyard became a giant garden, and the Walkers kept church shopping. We know that a man named Chet Walker never lived to see his youngest start school or his third son march off to war. We know that the boy "briggling" around in the outdoors on cold winter days still enjoys being out in it all. Letter writing continued and the envelopes traveled back and forth to Ohio, but they are in another shoebox, in another closet, or lost forever. We have what we have and no more.

These letters are stored carefully in a white three-ring binder, each letter in its own plastic slipcover, laid up by my sister-in-law in an archive-like manner. As I near the end of the pages, I sense a certain pressure from within, for although the ore is rich, I want more, and I find myself anxious that I will read the last of the letters and be disappointed. Perhaps I asked too much of this sixty-year-old paper and ink.

When we first found them, I was pleased that a piece of family history had been found, but only pleased, nothing more. As I began to read the letters and savor the density of them, my emotions thickened to true elation that such a rich vein of my bloodline had been uncovered. My father had come back from the dead to speak to me across the decades. But this is not some novel, rich with old wounds to be healed, no self-actualizing memoir, where all the issues of childhood find closure. My father is gone and has been for a very long time, and even letters as rich as these are not trans-temporal.

As innocent as the shoebox they were found in, the letters naively tell of one family's choice to make a new life in a new place and how that all came about. I can hear my father's words and see his daily labor and morning laughter and evening worry as he told it across the years and miles, but there is no discovery to be made, no cathartic actualization for a bruised psyche. I am not a prisoner of my childhood, so no rescue is needed, no therapeutic epiphany. Maybe that is the nugget I carry home when I lift my head from reading and look inward. Regardless of the regret at the time, the loss of my father made me who I am as much as the seven years of homestead living. I have no ax to grind with the fates, and the letters offer no evidence that I should.

Perhaps what these letters offer more profoundly is a chance to revisit with a certain honest clarity some of the richest time of my life that shaped me to become the man that I am, and as a part of that, to visit with Dad for a time. While I was surely bludgeoned by his passing, I wasn't broken. I still miss him and regret that I didn't have the teenage and adult years with him that I had with my own son. In the richness of my imagination, I did get to sit with him over coffee and a Camel cigarette on a January morning as he waited for enough light to shoot his first moose outside the back door of the cabin he built near Happy Valley.

There are more letters from Happy Valley, but those are from us kids written to Dad in the hospital. In the winter of 1964, he was knocked down with a heart attack, and the man who made a home from the wilderness, the man who could fix anything that had an engine could not heal himself. The man who everyone loved went to a place I couldn't go, struck down by a weakness he didn't know he had.

November 22, 1964

Dear Dad,
We are at home now, we been looking at some of Tom's stuff. He seems to be glad to get home. Seldovia played a game of basketball with Ninilchik at Ninilchik, Friday. They beat us 57 to 31, and they won 37 to 23 on Saturday.
Mitchell's got two moose today. Tom got me a Boy Scout pocket knife in Anchorage. I didn't write too much but by for know.
By for know, Dan W.

All that love, want, and need brought him home—and we had him back in a weak and broken and angry way of being back. The doctors had taken his cigarettes and most of his coffee. His only sinful pleasure was a shot of whiskey before bed, and he was not pleased.

As I write now, years older than my father lived to be, I can feel that anger, the restless, frustrated, wounded bear kind of anger from a man who could see the wealth of his life and know that he would never spend it. I feel it stronger than I did then, the man having more empathy than the boy. He had to know that his days were numbered and that he was dying. And he was dying just when he had it all to live for. His hardscrabble days as a tenant farmer and sharecropper were past, the great Alaska adventure had paid off, and the lean, hard years of homesteading had passed. His job with the State Road Commission was a good one and perhaps for the first years ever, we weren't living hand-to-mouth.

For a few short months, Dad would come home at night to the home he'd built and swat his wife on the ass and tease his kids as he watched them grow. His youngest children would listen enraptured as he read from *Robinson Crusoe* or *Tarzan of the Apes*. There were fish to catch and moose in the woods, movies and square dances at the American Legion Hall, and pinochle games on winter nights. He was a family man and a pillar of the community. This would slip away now, too soon. There must have been times when he roared at the moon with rage to leave the party early, to leave us.

It was February 1, 1965, the day before his forty-fifth birthday when we woke to Mom's terrified screams, and we knew from her panic that it was another heart attack. Away they sped in the station wagon, Mom in the backseat cradling Dad like an infant and Mike behind the wheel of a car he sent careening wildly down the winter ice for forty miles to Soldotna and the inevitable. This time Dad never made it to the specialist in Anchorage. A minister came to the school that day and quietly collected us kids to go back home to our mom and that log cabin in the woods that would never be the same again for any of us.

I didn't cry that day. I just ached with a desolate sadness that deepened when I looked at my mother, old and broken in the easy chair of our front room. I slipped away to my bunk in the boar's den. I thought how lost and helpless I felt that last day when the car left the driveway. I remembered the dream I'd had one night months before, that both my parents were dead and it was so real that I woke up crying. Now when my father was really dead, I couldn't cry at all. When the funeral came, again I couldn't cry, so besides the ache, I felt giant guilt for one thing I knew even at eleven years of age: people cry when they are sad and heartbroken. I thought people would think that I wasn't, sitting there dry-eyed in the front row of the Methodist Church. And later, during the wake in the church basement when people were laughing and telling stories about my father, I was confused by the joining of laughter and sadness. Papaw wasn't laughing and telling stories. He was just holding me, and I him, trying to stem the hurt.

After six years of dinners at the homemade table; six years of Jacks, Go Fish, and Chinese checkers on the floor by the woodstove; six years without knowing it wouldn't last, the Walkers had to leave. The homestead would become another abandoned cabin along the Sterling Highway waiting for weeds to drag it down.

I have always known, or believed, that we left the homestead after Dad died because Mom couldn't make a living there. Looking back now as an adult and having read these letters, I have a different view. It's more like we left the homestead because Mom couldn't be there without Dad. It wasn't about money; it was about love. Dad's heart failed, and Mom's heart broke, and she just couldn't be in that cabin they had made together. It was *their* place not *her* place, and too much a symbol of their great love for her to bear alone.

As I look back now at my mother, I realize what an incredible transition she made at the age of forty-one when she removed her apron and entered the hospitality workforce at the Anchorage Westward Hotel, starting at the bottom of the professional ladder. Ten years after that, she was building the ladder for others.

The lane is now Sunshine Drive, and if you turn east off the pavement of the Sterling Highway, you'll see a swaybacked shell of a two-car garage and a slab-sided chicken house still standing among the weeds. The clearing is now a dense stand of spruce, rising green and lush in the center of the scarred remains of a forest gutted by spruce bark beetles. This plague killed nearly all the mature trees in the area, and we and our neighbor sold off the dead trees between our place and the highway. Now the land is open and savanna like, nearly devoid of large spruces. In the true irony of the circle of life, the forest has become a clearing and the clearing has become a forest.

The cabin is gone, victim of two kids playing with fire. The volunteer fire department rushed to the scene, but a log cabin is nothing but tinder and fuel, so they stood vigil and consoled my sister. When Amy called me to tell me the place had burned, we were both in tears, and one would have thought we had lost a member of the family. I guess we kind of did. We had lost the carton of our memories, a monument to a time in a place when it was the best a time could be. We can now see, once the ache had healed, that we still have the important part. After years of loss and change, the memories are still alive, and like the letters, we'll keep those and let go of the ashes. In the shoebox of life's memorabilia, we find pictures, letters, sounds, smells, and recollections that elicit emotions that are rich and savory like skillet gravy. These memories are the sum of what was, is, and eventually will be, and that has to be enough.